ISSUES IN BIOMEDICAL ETHICS

# Moral Status

# ISSUES IN BIOMEDICAL ETHICS

*General Editors*
John Harris and Søren Holm

*Consulting Editors*
Ranaan Gillon and Bonnie Steinbock

The late twentieth century has witnessed dramatic technological developments in biomedical science and the delivery of health care, and these developments have brought with them important social changes. All too often ethical analysis has lagged behind these changes. The purpose of this series is to provide lively, up-to-date, and authoritative studies for the increasingly large and diverse readership concerned with issues in biomedical ethics—not just healthcare trainees and professionals, but also philosophers, social scientists, lawyers, social workers, and legislators. The series wll feature both single-author and multi-author books, short and accessible enough to be widely read, each of them focused on an issue of outstanding current importance and interest. Philosophers, doctors, and lawyers from a number of countries feature among the authors lined up for the series.

# *Moral Status*

*Obligations to Persons and
Other Living Things*

MARY ANNE WARREN

CLARENDON PRESS · OXFORD
1997

Oxford University Press, Great Clarendon Street, Oxford OX2 6DP
Oxford New York
Athens Auckland Bangkok Bogota Bombay
Buenos Aires Calcutta Cape Town Dar es Salaam
Delhi Florence Hong Kong Istanbul Karachi
Kuala Lumpur Madras Madrid Melbourne
Mexico City Nairobi Paris Singapore
Taipei Tokyo Toronto
and associated companies in
Berlin Ibadan

Oxford is a trade mark of Oxford University Press

Published in the United States by
Oxford University Press Inc., New York

British Library Cataloguing in Publication Data
Data available

Library of Congress Cataloging in Publication Data
Warren, Mary Anne
Moral status / Mary Anne Warren.
(Issues in biomedical ethics)
Includes bibliographical references.
1. Euthanasia—Moral and ethical aspects. 2. Abortion—Moral and ethical aspects.
3. Animal rights. 4. Duty. I. Title. II. Series.
R725.5.W37 1997 179.7—dc21 97–7803
ISBN 0–19–823668–9

1 3 5 7 9 10 8 6 4 2

Typeset by Invisible Ink
Printed in Great Britain
on acid-free paper by
Biddles Ltd., Guildford and King's Lynn

# Acknowledgements

My thanks go, first, to my spouse, Michael Scriven, who has provided moral support and valuable critical responses. Next, to the students and colleagues at San Francisco State University who have shared with me their thoughts about the ethical issues addressed here. Dianne Romain, Laura Purdy, Rita Manning, and other friends in the Society for Women in Philosophy have supported and encouraged me for many years.

I owe special philosophical debts to Michael Tooley, Peter Singer, Mary Midgley, and J. Baird Callicott, whose moral philosophies taught me much, even while inspiring disagreement on some points. Professor Tooley was head of the Philosophy Department at the University of Western Australia when Michael and I went there in 1982, and I benefited from the opportunity to compare our approaches to the problem of moral status. In 1986, I spent some time at the Centre for Human Bioethics at Monash University, which Professor Singer directed, and where some of the ideas for this book were hatched and tested. Professor Midgley was also a great source of inspiration. In 1990, she came to San Francisco State to speak at the conference on animal rights that I helped to organize; our conversations revealed similarities in our viewpoints that helped to persuade me that I was on the right track. Professor Callicott has been kind enough to give critical attention to my past work, which has helped me to clarify my views.

Finally, I am grateful to the two anonymous readers at Oxford University Press, whose comments substantially improved the book; and to my editors, John Harris, Peter Momtchiloff, and Angela Blackburn, for their assistance and support.

# Contents

# PART I

## *An Account of Moral Status*

# 1

## *The Concept of Moral Status*

This is a philosophical exploration of the concept of moral status. To have moral status is to be morally considerable, or to have moral standing. It is to be an entity towards which moral agents have, or can have, moral obligations. If an entity has moral status, then we may not treat it in just any way we please; we are morally obliged to give weight in our deliberations to its needs, interests, or well-being. Furthermore, we are morally obliged to do this not merely because protecting it may benefit ourselves or other persons, but because its needs have moral importance in their own right.

The questions addressed here involve the criteria that ought to be used in ascribing moral status to entities of diverse kinds. These questions are of more than academic interest, since our answers to them influence our positions on issues that are among the most pressing of our time, and show every sign of remaining so into the next century. These include the morality of euthanasia, under various circumstances; whether women have a moral right of access to safe and legal abortion; whether human beings are entitled to utilize other animals for food, biomedical research, and other purposes; and whether we have moral obligations towards natural plant or animal species, populations, and ecosystems, that are threatened by human activities.

In this introductory chapter, I comment on moral status as an intuitive or common-sense concept, and on two widespread—though not universal—beliefs about which things have moral status and which do not. Then I elaborate somewhat upon the concept of moral status, and consider why we need such a concept in order to make sense of our moral obligations towards human beings and the rest of the natural world. Next, I review some of the major positions on current issues that relate to moral status, outline the book's chapters, and preview some of its conclusions. The chapter closes with two responses to what is probably the most common objection to the type of account that I defend.

## 1.1. *Moral Status as an Intuitive Concept*

Is it morally wrong to take a stone and grind it into powder, merely for one's own amusement? Most people would say that it is not—unless there are special circumstances. Perhaps the stone belongs to someone for whom it carries precious personal memories. Perhaps it contains fossilized dinosaur bones from which important scientific knowledge could be gleaned, or valuable gems which could be sold to feed starving people. In these cases, we might say that it would be wrong to destroy the stone for no good reason. But most of us would regard it as wrong only in so far as it causes harm to human beings, or deprives them of important benefits. The stone itself does not seem be the kind of thing towards which we can have moral obligations.

In defence of this common-sense view it might be pointed out that, to the best of our knowledge, stones are both inanimate and insentient. That is, they are neither alive nor capable of feeling pleasure or pain. They have no desires or preferences which we might thwart by treating them in one way rather than another. As far as we can tell, a stone does not care whether it persists in an unaltered state for a billion years, or is immediately smashed into bits. It has no needs, interests, well-being, or good of its own, which we could or should take into account in our moral deliberations.

Is it wrong to kill a helpless human child, merely for one's own amusement? Most people would say that it is, and be taken aback that the question was even asked. A child is normally presumed to have not just some moral status, but a very strong moral status, fully equal to that of older human beings. (About human embryos and foetuses there is, of course, much less agreement.)

This widespread belief in the full and equal moral status of human beings may be defended in various ways, depending upon one's ethical or religious commitments. A theist who derives moral claims from the will of a deity may maintain that this being has endowed each of us with equal moral rights, dignity, value, or worth. A Kantian deontologist may say that all moral agents have an obligation to respect the autonomy of all other moral agents, treating them as ends in themselves and never merely as means. A classical utilitarian may say that moral agents are obliged to give equal consideration to the potential pleasures and pains of each human being who will be affected by their actions.[1] Some utilitarians go further, arguing that all beings that are sentient (that is, capable of experiencing pleasure and pain) are entitled to equal moral consideration, regardless of their biological species; but few utilitarians would deny that all sentient human beings are so entitled.

There is, then, substantial consensus about the moral status of those entities which appear to occupy the extreme ends of the spectrum. At the one extreme, stones and other inanimate objects are usually presumed to have no moral status at all, even though they may legitimately be valued and protected for other reasons. At the opposite extreme, human beings are usually held to have a moral status which is at least as strong as that enjoyed by any other entity—or at least any that is part of the natural world. Some people may believe that there are supernatural beings that possess a stronger moral status; but about the existence of such beings there is no general consensus.

## 1.2. Disagreements about 'Clear' Cases

Yet even when we confine our attention to the extreme ends of the spectrum of moral status, the consensus is not complete. Some philosophers reject the concept of moral status entirely, taking a sceptical view of all attempts to use that concept to work towards the solution of moral problems. Some argue, for instance, that the concept of moral status is inherently anthropocentric (human-centred) and elitist.[2] On this view, even the most basic presumptions about moral status that most of us share—for example, that human

---

[1] Classical utilitarianism is the view that morally right actions are those that produce the most pleasure and the least pain or suffering, with the pleasures and pains of each individual counting the same as those of each other. John Stuart Mill's *Utilitarianism* is the definitive statement of this theory: *Utilitarianism: With Critical Essays*, ed. Samuel Gorovitz (New York: Bobbs-Merrill, 1971), 11–57.

[2] See Thomas H. Birch, 'Moral Considerability and Universal Consideration', *Environmental Ethics*, 15, No. 4 (Winter 1993), 313–32.

beings have full moral status, while inanimate objects normally have none—are a reflection of overweening human pride.

Ethical egoists reject the presumption that all human beings have moral status for a different reason. In their view, each moral agent has obligations only to itself; each is, from its own perspective, the only thing in the universe that has moral status. Moral nihilists reject this presumption because they reject all moral principles, including those that are definitive of moral status. Cultural ethical relativists deny that any moral claim can have general or cross-cultural validity, because they believe that moral truth is entirely determined by the prevailing beliefs within a particular cultural group. On this view, there is no such thing as the moral status that an entity has, or ought to have, for all moral agents. Nothing has moral status except in the context of a culture wherein it is accorded moral status by a majority of persons; and the moral status that it has within each such culture is merely that which the majority of persons within the culture currently believe it to have. Finally, moral subjectivists hold that all moral claims, including claims about moral status, are strictly a matter of individual opinion. On this view, there can never be any rationally defensible basis for endorsing one opinion about moral status rather than another.

I hope in the chapters that follow to provide good reasons for rejecting these sceptical challenges to the concept of moral status. For the moment, however, I want to focus upon the views of those who do not reject the concept of moral status, yet who appear to reject one or both of these common presumptions about moral status.

Some people seem to ascribe strong moral status to things that are entirely inanimate. For instance, some philosophers in the Jain tradition hold that we have moral obligations to such things as earth, air, fire, and water. However, they do not in fact hold that wholly lifeless things have moral status. On the contrary, they urge the gentle treatment of earth, air, fire, and water precisely because they believe that these things are inhabited by many small beings. These beings are not only alive, but sentient; moreover, they can easily be killed or made to suffer by careless human actions.[3]

In some cultures, stones in general are not granted a strong moral

---

[3] Padmanab S. Jaini, *The Jaina Path of Purification* (Berkeley: University of California Press, 1979), 109: and S. Radhakrishnan, *Indian Philosophy*, vol. i (New York: Macmillan, 1929), 297.

status, but certain stones are regarded as sacred. Uluru, a red sand-stone monolith near Alice Springs, Australia, has been sacred to aboriginal peoples for millennia, as have many other places and features of the Australian landscape. Aboriginal Australians are not unique in ascribing sacredness to natural places and objects; there are sacred sites in every part of the world where animistic beliefs are extant. Thus, if sacredness is a form of moral status, then it is one that is often ascribed to what seem to be inanimate objects. Usually, however, the belief in the sacredness of a particular place or object is accompanied by the belief that it is, or contains, a living and sentient being (or beings), such as a deity of some sort, or the spirit of a human ancestor. Here too, we find that people rarely ascribe moral status to entities that they regard as entirely inanimate.

There are also people who deny that all human beings have full moral status. Racists deny the equal moral status of groups of human beings whose appearance and ancestry is, or is thought to be, different from their own. Sexists deny that female (or, occasionally, male) human beings have a moral status equal to that of the favoured sex. Prior to this century, the most illustrious philosophers in the Western tradition have all but unanimously relegated female human beings to a markedly inferior moral status. Philosophical luminaries as diverse as Aristotle, Augustine, Thomas Aquinas, David Hume, Immanuel Kant, Georg Wilhelm Friedrich Hegel, Arthur Schopenhauer, and Friedrich Nietzsche have maintained that women cannot be permitted the same autonomy as men, because they are naturally less capable of rational thought and action, and thus incapable of genuine moral agency.[4]

In our own time, philosophers are less likely to claim that women

[4] Aristotle, *Politics* (London: Heinemann, 1932), 63–5; Augustine, *Of the Work of Monks* (Grand Rapids, Mich.: Eerdmans, 1956), 40; Thomas Aquinas, *Summa Theologica* (New York: Benzinger Brothers, 1947), 466–7; David Hume, *Essays, Moral, Political and Literary* (London: Longman, Green & Co., 1987), 193; Immanuel Kant, *Observations on the Feeling of the Beautiful and the Sublime*, trans. John T. Goldwaite (Berkeley and Los Angeles: University of California Press, 1960), 78; Georg Wilhelm Friedrich Hegel, *Philosophy of the Right* (Oxford: Oxford University Press, 1966), 263–4; Arthur Schopenhauer, *Studies in Pessimism: A Series of Essays* (St. Clair Shores, Mich.: Scholarly Press, 1970), 106; and Friedrich Nietzsche, *Beyond Good and Evil* (Chicago: Henry Regnery, 1935), 166. The views of these and other philosophers respecting natural mental differences between women and men are explored in my 1980 book, *The Nature of Woman* (Inverness, Calif.: Edgepress).

and members of minority ethnic groups should not have full moral status. Yet we seem continually to discover new forms of bigotry, and new groups of persons whose moral status has been unjustly diminished. In addition to sexism, racism, and ethnic and religious bigotry, we are now aware of homophobia or heterosexism (the denial of full moral status to lesbians, homosexual men, and bisexual persons); ageism (the denial of full status to some persons because of their age); and ableism (the denial of full status to human beings with physical or mental disabilities). Worse, it is not always clear that these forms of bigotry represent minority opinions. For instance, many politicians in the United States still find it expedient to oppose legislation designed to protect homosexual persons from invidious discrimination; and many religious leaders support them.

And yet, the very fact that we now have specific pejorative labels for these anti-egalitarian views suggests that they are much more widely condemned than in the past. Certainly they are more often condemned within the academic world—sometimes with a vigour that leads to protests against 'political correctness'. This growing condemnation is not just a Western phenomenon. International agreements and the laws of many nations increasingly prohibit the use of racial, ethnic, religious, and sexual categories to detract from the moral or legal status of particular groups of people.[5]

In short, despite the many counterexamples, there is substantial agreement about the respective moral status of human beings and inanimate objects. This agreement does not in itself show that the views in question are true, or even that they will continue to be widely held in the future. It is conceivable—though unlikely—that the majority of people throughout the world will some day come to believe that there is no difference between the moral status of human beings and that of stones. They might, for instance, abandon the notion of moral obligation altogether, striving to construct a Skinnerian world in which human behaviour is scientifically manipulated, rather than shaped through the teaching of moral principles

---

[5] For instance, the United Nations Universal Declaration of Human Rights, the International Covenant on Civil and Political Rights, and the International Covenant on Economic, Social, and Cultural Rights. These are reprinted in James Nickel's *Making Sense of Human Rights: Philosophical Reflections on the Universal Declaration of Human Rights* (Berkeley and Los Angeles: University of California Press, 1987).

or concepts.[6] Nevertheless, these points of relative agreement provide a useful starting-point for an exploration of the concept of moral status. It is important that (1) most of us share a belief that there is such a thing as moral status; and (2) there is a substantial consensus about some of the things that have it, and some of the things that do not.

### 1.3. *What is Moral Status?*

Of course, moral status is not a thing, if by 'thing' we mean an object or phenomenon which we can observe in nature, e.g. through a microscope, or with the help of a CAT scanner. The concept of moral status is, rather, a means of specifying those entities towards which we believe ourselves to have moral obligations, as well as something of what we take those obligations to be.

A theory of moral status cannot be expected to answer all important questions about human moral obligations. Many of our obligations are based not only upon the moral status of those towards whom we are obliged, but also upon situational factors, such as a promise we have made, a personal relationship in which we are involved, a civil or criminal law that has been justly enacted, or a wrongful past action of our own that requires restitution or compensation.

Rather than delineating all of our moral obligations towards other individuals, ascriptions of moral status serve to represent very general claims about the ways in which moral agents ought to conduct themselves towards entities of particular sorts. For instance, if we say that all human beings have basic moral rights to life and liberty, then we are claiming for human beings a moral status that prohibits harming them in certain ways without exceptionally good reasons; and that on most interpretations also entails that should they be in need, those who are able to help—without excessive harm or risk to themselves—are morally obliged to do so. Thus, one important feature of the concept of moral status is its generality. Moral status is usually ascribed to members of a group, rather than merely to specific individuals. Moreover, it is usually ascribed on the

---

[6] B. F. Skinner, *Beyond Freedom and Dignity* (New York: Bantam Books, 1971).

basis of some property or properties that are thought to be possessed by all or most group members.

A second important feature of the concept of moral status is that the moral obligations that are implied by the ascription of moral status to an entity are obligations *to that entity*. To violate an obligation arising from A's moral status is to wrong A, and not merely some third party. For instance, if A's moral rights have been violated, then it is A that has in the first instance been wronged, and on whose behalf others may complain.

An example may help to clarify this distinction. Suppose that you go on vacation, leaving your house in the care of a friend, who then sells your kitchen appliances and absconds. A moral wrong has evidently been committed; but it is obviously a wrong against you and not against your stove and refrigerator, which do not have moral status. Had you, on the other hand, left your pet pig in the care of a friend, who then sold it to a meat packing plant, then it would have been less clear that a wrong had been committed only against you. And if you had left your baby with a friend, who then sold him or her to a black-market baby broker, almost no one would doubt that a wrong had been committed not only against you but also against the child. In each case, your friend wrongs you by selling something that ought not to have been sold under those circumstances; but only in the third case does that which is sold have a moral status that most people would agree precludes its being sold under any circumstances.

## 1.4. *Why Do We Need a Concept of Moral Status?*

There are many reasons why we might *want* a concept of moral status. In the worst case, we might want only to rationalize the power and privilege of our own group, *vis-à-vis* other people, non-human animals, or the rest of the non-human world. We have already noted some of the ways in which faulty standards of moral status can serve unjust partisan interests. But despite this danger, human beings badly need shared standards and principles of moral status, based upon arguments that most people can understand and accept. There are two obvious facts about human beings as a species that help to explain why we have this need, and why it is particularly acute at the present time.

The first obvious fact is that human beings are clever and opportunistic creatures who have recently come to possess an awesome capacity to do harm, both to one another and to the rest of the world. During most of the existence of *Homo* (the biological genus that includes our own species, and some that are now extinct) the human capacity to do harm was fairly modest, and exercised on a comparatively small scale. Early human populations are thought to have been surprisingly small.[7] Plant food was usually the largest part of the human diet, and the small-scale gathering activities of Lower Palaeolithic (early Stone Age) people probably had little negative impact upon the ecosystems in which they existed.

Of course, human beings have never been perfectly harmless. Lower Palaeolithic people probably fought and sometimes killed one another, and some of them probably killed animals from time to time to supplement their diets. (Chimpanzees, our nearest biological relatives, do both of these things.)[8] The development of projectile weapons made Upper Palaeolithic people more effective predators, and increased human predation may have contributed to the extinction of mammoths, and many other species of megafauna (large animals) in Eurasia, North and South America, and Australia some ten to twenty thousand years ago.[9] In addition, some early human groups may have contributed to the extinction of others. For instance, it seems likely that Cro-Magnon people contributed to the disappearance of Neanderthal people in Europe and Asia about thirty-three thousand years ago—although we can only speculate about whether they did so through violence, by spreading contagious diseases, or simply by competing more effectively for scarce re-

[7] Paul and Anne Ehrlich estimate that the global population at the start of the Neolithic era, about ten thousand years ago, was not over five million: *The Population Explosion* (New York: Simon & Schuster, 1990), 14.

[8] See Jane Goodall, *In the Shadow of Man* (Boston, Mass.: Houghton Mifflin, 1971), 197–208, and Adriaan Kortlandt, 'Spirits Dressed in Furs?', in Paola Cavalieri and Peter Singer (eds.), *The Great Ape Project: Equality Beyond Humanity* (New York: St. Martin's Press, 1993), 142.

[9] Controversy continues about whether hunting, climatic change, or some other factor was primarily responsible for the large number of megafaunal extinctions during the Pleistocene; but it seems likely that human predation played a contributory role in some cases. See P. S. Martin, 'The Discovery of America', *Science*, 179 (1973), 968–74. It has also been suggested that human migrations caused the extinctions by spreading pathogenic micro-organisms; see Carl Zimmer, 'Carriers of Extinction', *Discover*, 16, No. 7 (July 1995), 28–34.

sources.[10] Nevertheless, while human beings have probably never been entirely peaceful or benign, it seems clear that large-scale wars, and the decimation of major natural ecosystems, e.g. through unsustainable agricultural practices, have occurred primarily within the past ten thousand years.

Today our power to do harm is further magnified by our enormous population, and our ever-more-clever technologies. The history of the twentieth century abundantly demonstrates the human capacity to perpetrate horrors against one another on a scale which has no parallel in human history. Moreover, we are now damaging the global ecosystem far more seriously than we could have done even a century ago.

The second obvious fact about us is that we have a natural capacity to care about other living things, both human and non-human—and sometimes about things that are evidently lifeless, such as stones. Human beings who have not been psychologically or neurologically damaged are strongly inclined to care about many of the beings with which they interact, and to want to protect them. Most of us could not hear a child or a kitten crying from pain or fear, without wanting to help if we could. And our aesthetic, intellectual, and spiritual appreciation of even the non-sentient elements of the natural world—trees and rivers, for instance—impels us to oppose their wanton destruction.

David Hume argued—rightly in my view—that such 'moral feelings' constitute the essential and instinctive foundation of all human morality.[11] Upon this foundation we construct moral concepts, rules, principles, and theories. This task obviously requires thought and reason. But had our ancestors not been highly social animals, possessing a natural capacity to care for other members of the social group, they would never have become moral agents. Moral concepts cannot replace this natural capacity to care for and about others; but they can complement and strengthen it. And, as Hume argued, strengthening that natural capacity is very much in our own interest, both as individuals and as members of social communities.

---

[10] For a good discussion of the debate about why the Cro-Magnons prevailed over the Neanderthals, see Richard Leakey and Roger Lewin, *Origins Reconsidered: In Search of What Makes Us Human* (New York: Anchor Books, 1992), 232–5.

[11] David Hume, *Enquiries Concerning Human Understanding and Concerning the Principles of Morals*, ed. L. A. Selby-Bigge (Oxford: Oxford University Press, 1975).

Human beings are not the only terrestrial creatures with a capacity to care about other beings; but we appear to be the only ones who debate concepts of moral status. We can do this because we have certain intellectual, social, and linguistic capacities, such as the capacity to formulate and communicate moral ideas, and to evaluate them co-operatively by what we take to be appropriate criteria of adequacy. And we must do it, because our species' power to do harm is great and growing. If we fail to constrain our own destructive potential more effectively than we have done up to now, or fail to do it through agreements arrived at by peaceful means, then the next millennium will witness social and ecological catastrophes that will make the twentieth century look like the age of benevolence.

As reasoning beings who are highly social, we must have shared moral principles. To be useful, a moral principle must be based upon observations and arguments which are at least comprehensible to the majority of persons, whatever their cultural or religious background. It must also, as far as possible, be consistent with the strongly held moral convictions of well-informed and thoughtful persons. Both requirements arise from the need for moral standards upon which human beings can hope eventually to agree.

### 1.5. *Two Functions of the Concept of Moral Status*

The concept of moral status is one of the tools which we use to bring order to the welter of conflicting claims about what we ought and ought not to do. It is a somewhat blunt tool, in part because it can play more than one role in moral theory and human moral psychology. On the one hand, the concept of moral status can be used to specify minimum standards of acceptable behaviour towards entities of a given sort. Thus, the claim that all persons have full and equal moral status implies that we must not murder other persons, assault them, cheat them, torture them, imprison them unjustly, or fail to help them when help is needed and we have the means of providing it. Such minimum standards represent a floor below which we ought not to allow our actions, or those of other moral agents, to fall. When such standards of behaviour are violated, we are justified in protesting, objecting, and sometimes using force to prevent or deter further violations.

On the other hand, the concept of moral status may be used to establish moral ideals, such as the Christian ideal, to love one's neighbours as oneself; or the Jain ideal, never to kill or injure any living thing. Such ideals cannot fully be put into practice, except perhaps by a few unusual individuals. Yet they serve an important function by reminding us that, however scrupulous we may be in observing our obligations, we could be better people were we to do more than we are obliged to do. Moral ideals create a conceptual space for supererogation, encouraging individuals to move beyond conformity to minimum standards of acceptable behaviour, towards exceptional goodness, heroism, or saintliness.

Trouble can be expected, however, when pragmatically unattainable moral ideals are propounded as minimum standards of acceptable behaviour. People who are told that they must conform to moral standards which very few actually can meet are likely to conclude that morality is a set of hypocritical platitudes that only a fool would take seriously. (Think, for instance, of the reaction of most young people everywhere to the demand for lifelong celibacy, except within heterosexual marriage.) The opposite mistake can also have unfortunate consequences. When respect for minimum moral standards is treated as a moral ceiling—a cap above which we ought never to rise in aiding our fellow beings—the result is a mean-spirited morality.

The strategies that we use to resolve the tension between these two functions of the concept of moral status will influence our attitudes towards many practical moral issues. To the extent that we employ the concept of moral status to promulgate highly demanding moral ideals, we will be more likely to object to such practices as abortion, meat eating, and the use of animals in biomedical research. To the extent that we employ the concept of moral status to establish moral floors rather than moral ideals, we will be more likely to have a tolerant attitude towards such controversial practices, viewing them as possibly falling below the moral ideal, but as nevertheless often within the bounds of the morally permissible.

## 1.6. *Current Controversies about Moral Status*

In classical Greek thought, women, slaves, and barbarians occupied a moral twilight zone; their moral status was debated, but agreed by most learned men to be lower than that of free male citizens. Today foetuses, animals, biological species, and ecosystems occupy a similar twilight zone. Wildly diverse claims are made about their moral status. Each group has its partisans, who ascribe strong moral status to the entities in question, and often seek stronger legal protections for them. And each group of partisans has its critics, who maintain that the entities in question either have no moral status at all, or none that is strong enough to override the needs of (already-born) human beings. These critics point out that when we attempt to extend the moral community—the set of entities to which we ascribe full and equal moral status—too far, or in the wrong directions, we risk endangering the moral rights of human beings.

Such disputes are not unique to our time. Disagreements about the moral permissibility of killing non-human animals have been part of the Western philosophical tradition for at least three thousand years. Whether the non-human world has intrinsic or only instrumental value—whether nature is sacred or profane—is also an issue that dates at least as far back as the beginning of recorded human history.[12]

What may be distinctive of our postmodern era is the intensity, and often acrimony, with which we debate the moral status of both human and non-human entities. Of these debates, that on abortion is the most bitter—at least in North America—and the one on which the media endlessly dwell. Abortion opponents ascribe to human embryos and foetuses a moral status at least as strong as that of human beings who have already been born, and arguably somewhat stronger.[13] In their eyes, women who have abortions and physicians who perform them are guilty of premeditated murder, or something very like it. A few act upon this belief by shooting physicians who perform abortions, or persons who work in clinics where abortions are done.

In response, defenders of women's right to choose abortion argue that embryos and foetuses, especially during the early stages of their

---

[12] See Riane Eisler, *The Chalice and the Blade* (San Francisco, Calif.: Harper & Row, 1987).

[13] Frances Kamm argues persuasively that the rights that are ascribed to foetuses through the claim that they may never be aborted are stronger than those that law and common-sense morality ascribe to human beings that have already been born: *Creation and Abortion: A Study in Moral and Legal Philosophy*, Oxford University Press, 1992.

development, do not yet have full moral status. They contend, further, that women cannot be equal and responsible members of the human moral community if they are denied the right to terminate unwanted or abnormal pregnancies, for what they themselves believe to be sufficiently good reasons.[14]

Meanwhile, another movement to expand the moral community has been gaining strength. Animal advocates hold that some non-human animals have a moral status which is the same, or very nearly the same, as that of human beings. Some animal rights theorists would extend moral equality to only a small subset of sentient non-human animals, whose mental capacities seem most nearly to resemble our own.[15] Others would extend equal moral status to all sentient animals, that is, all those that can have experiences, including experiences of pleasure and pain.[16] The sentience criterion implies the moral equality of most vertebrate animals, and probably many invertebrate animals as well. Despite such disagreements, animal advocates agree that much of what is routinely done to animals, for instance in the production of food and in scientific research, is morally objectionable.

Both the anti-abortion and pro-animal movements are individualistic, in that their goal is to raise the moral status of certain individuals, and to strengthen the legal protections provided to them. In contrast, the environmentalist movement is holistic, in that its primary goal is the protection of certain *groups* of living things, i.e. natural biological species and populations, natural biotic systems, and ultimately the entire terrestrial biosphere.[17] From an ecological perspective, our obligation to protect stands of old-growth redwoods derives less from the properties of individual redwood trees than

[14] Not all feminists defend abortion in terms of women's rights. Adherents of the feminist ethics of care, for instance, sometimes reject the concept of a moral right as indicative of 'social atomism'. See Allison Jaggar, *Feminist Politics and Human Nature* (Totowa, NJ: Rowman & Allanheld, 1983), and Elizabeth Wolgast, *The Grammar of Justice* (Ithaca, NY: Cornell University Press, 1987).

[15] For instance, Tom Regan holds that only animals that are subjects-of-a-life have full moral status; his view is discussed in Chapter 4. (*The Case for Animal Rights*, Berkeley and Los Angeles: University of California Press, 1983.)

[16] See Peter Singer, *Animal Liberation: A New Ethic for Our Treatment of Animals* (New York: Avon Books, 1975).

[17] J. Baird Callicott calls attention to this difference, in 'Animal Liberation: A Triangular Affair', *In Defense of the Land Ethic: Essays in Environmental Philosophy* (Albany, NY: State University of New York Press, 1989).

from the role which their species plays within the ecosystems of which it is part. The death of the last snow leopard would be tragic, not primarily because individual leopards have properties that imply a strong moral status, but because if the last one dies there will never be any more, and the world will be permanently impoverished by the loss of a magnificent species.

Not all environmental ethicists seek the extension of moral status to non-human elements of the natural world. Some—so-called 'shallow' environmentalists—hold a strictly anthropocentric view of moral status. They maintain that, although only humans have moral status, a biologically diverse and healthy biosphere is of such great value to us and our posterity that it is in our own interest to protect it. They argue, for instance, that the remaining tropical rainforests ought to be preserved because, by removing carbon dioxide from the atmosphere and adding oxygen, they help to maintain the health of the planet (and our own); and because they contain numerous plant and animal species which may some day be found to have medicinal or commercial value. 'Deep' ecologists, in contrast, maintain that we have moral obligations to protect the natural world from our own destructive propensities, not just for our own sake and that of future human generations, but because plants, animals, and ecosystems have a moral status which is independent of their usefulness to us.

## 1.7. *Outline of the Book*

In Chapters 2–5, the major alternative theories of moral status are critically examined, with an eye to their practical consequences, and their consistency with the common-sense convictions that few of us would be willing to surrender. The theories considered in Chapters 2–4 are what I call *uni-criterial*. Each focuses upon a certain intrinsic property: life, sentience, and personhood, respectively. Each of these properties has been identified by some philosophers as the single necessary and sufficient condition for the possession of moral status. In each case, I argue that while the property in question is sufficient for a particular type of moral status, treating it as the sole criterion of moral status leads to consequences that are intuitively implausible and pragmatically unacceptable.

Chapter 2 examines the ethic of Reverence for Life developed by

Albert Schweitzer, and defended in modified form by some contemporary environmental ethicists. I argue that, although life is a plausible basis for according an entity a moral status that precludes killing it without good reason, it is not a sufficient condition for the full moral status that we want for ourselves and those we care about. Depending upon the definition of 'life' which we employ, it may not even be a necessary condition for full moral status. Should we some day meet or manufacture machines that were sentient and self-aware, we might or might not classify them as alive; but in either case we would probably be morally obliged to accord them a moral status as strong as that of naturally evolved organisms with comparable mental and behavioural capacities.

Chapter 3 examines the sentience criterion, which has been defended by such utilitarian theorists as Jeremy Bentham and Peter Singer. I argue that a being's capacity to experience pleasure and pain provides a sound reason for recognizing a moral obligation not to kill it, or inflict pain or suffering upon it, without good reason. Nevertheless, sentience is not a sufficient condition for full moral status. There are sound reasons for recognizing stronger obligations towards some sentient beings, such as those that are moral agents, those that are members of our social communities, and those that belong to ecologically important species that are endangered by human activities.

Chapter 4 examines two variants of the concept of a person, and considers the arguments for regarding personhood, in either of these two senses, as the sole criterion of moral status. While there is little agreement about exactly what 'person' means, most philosophical analyses of the concept of a person suggest that persons are beings that are not only sentient but also possessed of more sophisticated mental capacities, such as those that are often subsumed under the concepts of rationality and self-awareness. The first, and more exclusive, concept of personhood emphasizes the mental capacities that are essential for moral agency, such as the capacity to deliberate about moral questions, and voluntarily to conform to moral standards. The less exclusive 'subject-of-a-life' criterion proposed by Tom Regan emphasizes the capacity to have beliefs and desires, to remember the past, to anticipate the future, and to act intentionally.[18]

---

[18]   *The Case for Animal Rights*, 243.

I argue that personhood, in the full-blooded sense that requires the capacity for moral agency, is indeed a sufficient condition for full moral status. It is not, however, a necessary condition; infants and mentally disabled human beings ought to have the same basic moral rights as other sentient human beings, even though they may not be persons in this sense. In the weaker sense which does not require moral agency, personhood is sufficient for a moral status stronger than that of mentally simpler organisms such as worms or oysters, but it is not sufficient for full moral status. Genetic humanity, on the other hand, is at best an indicator, not an independently valid criterion, of moral status. Some genetically human entities (e.g. sperm and ova) may have little or no moral status, while some non-human entities may have full moral status.

Chapter 5 examines two theories of moral status which are based upon relational rather than intrinsic properties. Some deep ecologists, such as J. Baird Callicott, hold that the moral status of a member of a particular biological species depends entirely upon that species' role—positive or negative—within a social or biotic community. Feminist ethicists, such as Nel Noddings, have argued that the moral status of living things always depends upon our emotional connections to them.[19] I argue that both these theories contain insights that need to be incorporated into an adequate account of moral status; but that neither membership in a social or biological community nor emotional connectedness can serve as the sole criterion of moral status.

Chapter 6 proposes a new account of moral status, which gives weight both to such intrinsic properties as life, sentience, and personhood, and to social, emotional, and biosystemic relationships. (I shall say more about this presently.)

In Part II, this multi-criterial approach to moral status is applied to three contemporary moral issues. Chapter 7 reviews the principles proposed in Chapter 6, and previews the arguments of the next three chapters. Chapter 8 explores the moral permissibility of euthanasia, under various controversial circumstances. Chapter 9 deals with the ethics of abortion; and Chapter 10, with the moral status of non-human animals. Chapter 11 presents a few concluding remarks

---

[19] Nel Noddings, *Caring: A Feminine Approach to Ethics and Moral Education* (Berkeley and Los Angeles: University of California Press, 1984), 86–8.

about the goal of achieving a greater consensus in our judgements of moral status.

While no theory of moral status can yield incontrovertible conclusions on such contentious issues, I argue that a multi-criterial approach enables us to take better account of the full range of morally relevant considerations than is possible with any of the uni-criterial approaches. It enables us to see, for instance, that what we owe to human foetuses is often different from what we owe to human beings who have already been born, or to non-human animals; and that none of these obligations can be understood in isolation from the others, or from what we owe to natural plant and animal species, and to ecosystems.

## 1.8. *Moral Status as a Multi-Criterial Concept*

Christopher Stone aptly describes the uni-criterial approaches to moral status, as those which

propose . . . that there is a single key [property]: life, or the capacity to feel pain, or the powers of reason, or something else. Those things that possess the key property count morally—all equally and all in the same way. Those things that lack it are utterly irrelevant, except as resources for the benefit of those things that do count.[20]

Stone rejects this kind of moral monism. He refers to his own approach as 'moral pluralism'. Although my views are in some respects similar to his, and indebted to them, I do not follow him in this usage. In much contemporary philosophical discussion, the term 'moral pluralism' refers to the view that there is an irreducible plurality of moral theories, which are mutually incompatible and yet equally rationally defensible. On this view, we are doomed to live with many moral disagreements of the most basic sort, with no hope that the global human community can ever agree about even the most fundamental moral principles. While this may be true, it is not a view that I wish to defend.

My view is, rather, that any satisfactory account of moral status

---

[20] Christopher D. Stone, *Earth and Other Ethics: The Case for Moral Pluralism* (New York: Harper & Row, 1987), 13.

must be a multi-criterial one, comprising a number of distinct but related principles. I shall argue: (1) that there is more than one valid criterion of moral status; (2) that there is more than one type of moral status, with different types implying different obligations on the part of moral agents; and (3) that the criteria of moral status must include both certain intrinsic properties, including life, sentience, and personhood; and certain relational properties, which sometimes include being part of a particular social or biological community.[21]

To adopt such a multi-criterial view of moral status is to recognize that many moral problems are more complex than they appear from the perspective of the moral monist. Uni-criterial theorists seek to simplify the resolution of moral issues by reducing it to the consistent application of a single general principle. By so doing, they hope to enable all rational and informed persons to arrive at the same conclusions about controversial moral issues. Callicott is one proponent of this approach. He argues that multi-criterial theories are unacceptable, because

In moral philosophy, when competing moral claims cannot be articulated in the same terms, they cannot be decisively compared and resolved. Ethical eclecticism leads, it would seem inevitably, to moral incommensurability in hard cases. So we are compelled to go back to the drawing board.[22]

Since conceptual simplicity is an important virtue in a moral theory, this is potentially a serious objection to the approach that I advocate. But the arguments for rejecting each of the uni-criterial approaches are strong. These arguments will emerge as we study each of the major candidates for the role of the single necessary and sufficient condition for having moral status. However, two points may be made now in response to this objection.

The first point is that simplicity is not the only virtue that a moral theory needs. It may not even be the most important virtue. To be credible, a moral theory must be reasonably consistent with 'the common (and good) sense judgements that initially give rise to

---

[21] A thing's intrinsic properties are those which it is logically possible for it to have had were it the only thing in existence. Its relational properties are those that it would be logically impossible for it to have had were it the only thing in existence.

[22] J. Baird Callicott, *In Defense of the Land Ethic: Essays in Environmental Philosophy* (Albany, NY: State University of New York Press, 1989), 50.

philosophical reflection on morals'.[23] A theorist may be justified in rejecting some of the elements of common-sense morality; but in that case the theorist bears the burden of demonstrating that these elements are based upon errors of one sort or another—e.g. poor reasoning, false empirical beliefs, or ignorance of relevant facts. If none of the uni-criterial theories is sufficiently consistent with the elements of common-sense morality that we cannot reasonably be expected to jettison, then the goal of theoretical simplicity must be compromised for the sake of the equally important goal of adequately representing the moral data.

The second response to Callicott's objection is that greater simplicity at the level of moral theory does not guarantee greater ease in the resolution of practical moral issues. For instance, utilitarianism (in any of its several forms) provides a conceptually simple criterion of moral right and wrong; yet applying that criterion in real-life cases is a notoriously difficult task—so much so that even well-informed utilitarians often disagree.

Consider, for instance, the relatively simple thesis that all and only human beings have moral status, and that all of them have it equally. Does the relative simplicity of this thesis really help us to decide, for instance, whether we should prohibit further logging of old-growth forests in the Pacific Northwest, or whether a highway should be built through one of the last remaining tracts of virgin rainforest in Queensland? It might seem to, since we are now free to ignore the well-being of the forests and their plant and animal communities, focusing solely upon human interests. But the appearance of simplicity is illusory; for the questions that environmentalists couch in terms of the needs of the ecosystem will return as questions about the needs and interests of present and future human beings. Weighing the interests of those human beings who would profit from the destructive exploitation of the forests against the interests of those who would derive more benefit from their preservation may be intellectually no easier, and no more productive of an eventual consensus, than a process that gives moral weight to the needs of birds and trees, as well as those of human beings.

In short, a simple theory, which ascribes moral status on the basis of a single principle or criterion, provides no real guarantee of ease

---

[23] Thomas E. Hill, Jr., 'Kantian Pluralism', *Ethics*, 10, No. 4 (July 1992), 346.

in the resolution of practical moral issues. An account which accommodates a greater diversity of ethical insights, drawn from a number of cultural and intellectual traditions, is likely to prove more useful in practice than one that pursues theoretical simplicity above all else. This, at least, is what I hope to show.

# 2

## *Reverence for Life*

Is life a valid criterion of moral status? On what I call the Life Only view, being a living organism is the *only* valid criterion of moral status. This is the view which Albert Schweitzer defended. On this view, organic life is both necessary and sufficient for full moral status. Thus, not only do all living organisms have moral status, but all of them have exactly the same moral status. Conversely, things that are not alive can have no moral status.

On what I call the Life Plus view, life is a valid criterion of moral status, but it is not the only valid criterion. On this view, life is sufficient for some moral status, but not for full moral status. Because there are other valid criteria of moral status, and because some of these (e.g. sentience and moral agency) entail a stronger moral status than does life alone, living things of different types often differ in moral status. Moreover, on the Life Plus view it is possible for non-living things to have moral status by virtue of satisfying other criteria. The Life Plus view is often defended by environmental ethicists, who ascribe moral status to all living organisms, while also arguing that we owe more in the way of assistance and protection to organisms that belong to endangered species, or that are especially important to the ecosystem. Some environmental ethicists also ascribe moral status to entities that are not (individual) biological organisms, including plant and animal species, natural ecosystems, and such non-living parts of the natural world as oceans, rivers, and mountains.

The chapter begins with comments on the meaning of 'life'. Next I consider Schweitzer's case for the Life Only view, and the major problems that this view faces. I examine two objections which Schweitzer and others have made to the view that living things differ in moral status: the objection from anthropocentrism, and the slippery slope objection. Finally, I consider a different argument for the claim that life is a sufficient condition for some moral status: the argument from teleological organization.

## 2.1. Defining 'Life'

When we speak of 'living things', we usually refer to *organisms*, rather than to their component cells, organs, or tissues—although these are also alive. And when we ascribe moral status to living things, it is usually to individual organisms or groups of organisms, rather than to parts of organisms. Occasionally it can be difficult to determine whether a particular biological entity (e.g. a sponge, or a termite colony) ought to be regarded as a single organism or as a community of organisms.[1] Most of the time, however, we have no difficulty distinguishing between organisms and their parts. There are biologists who believe that the entire Earth should be regarded as a single living organism.[2] And some cosmologists have suggested that the universe may be an organism, or very like one.[3] But, as interesting as these suggestions are, it is the ordinary concept of an organism which I shall employ.

What does it mean to say that something is alive, or a living organism? The ordinary concept of life has two primary elements, both of which appear in the standard dictionary definitions. For example, *Webster's Encyclopedic Unabridged Dictionary of the English Language* defines 'life' as 'the condition that distinguishes animals and plants from inorganic objects and dead organisms, being manifested by growth through metabolism, reproduction, and the power of adaptation to environment through changes originating internally'.

The first part of this definition presents a dual contrast: living things are neither inanimate (never alive), nor dead (no longer alive).

---

[1] An interesting case is that of the quaking aspen (*Populus tremuloides*). Groups of thousands of what appear to be individual trees have been found to share a single root system and genetic constitution, thus constituting a single organism—at least on the biologists' definition of 'single'. See Michael Grant, 'The Trembling Giant', *Discover* (Oct. 1993), 84–8.

[2] See James Lovelock, *The Ages of Gaia: A Biography of Our Living Earth* (New York: Bantam Books, 1990).

[3] John Gribbon, 'Is the Universe Alive?', *New Scientist* (15 Jan. 1994), 38–40.

Although this part of the definition is circular, the circularity is not entirely vicious, since most of us can distinguish fairly reliably between living things and those that are dead or inanimate. In making those distinctions, we demonstrate a substantial grasp of the concept of life.

The second part of *Webster's* definition lists some of the fundamental capacities that are characteristic of terrestrial organisms. Living things are generally capable of ingesting food, metabolizing it to produce energy,[4] growing, reproducing their kind, and maintaining their internal states within limits compatible with survival.

These characteristic capacities of living organisms can serve as criteria of life. For instance, if we wanted to find out whether a strange stone-shaped object was alive, we might look for signs of ingestion, metabolism, growth, or reproduction. The more of the characteristic capacities of living things the object possessed, the more confident we would be that it was alive. Yet none of these characteristic capacities is a necessary condition for being alive. Not all organisms grow throughout their life spans, and many (the great majority in some species) are never capable of reproducing. An organism that will never again be able to ingest food or metabolize it may nevertheless still be alive. These capacities are not individually sufficient conditions for life, either. A crystal can grow, and give rise to more crystals of the same mineral; yet science and common opinion agree that it is inanimate.

It should not surprise us that there is no single (or multiple) necessary and sufficient condition for the proper application of the ordinary concept of life. Many concepts are like this, including—as I argue—the concept of moral status. Basic practical concepts, such as that of life, develop through many generations of experience. Consequently, such concepts often lack the clarity and simplicity that are desirable in, for instance, mathematical or scientific theories. New concepts can be arbitrarily and neatly defined in ways that serve the goals of theory building. But the complexity and the unclear boundaries of many of our ordinary concepts cannot readily be defined away, except at the cost of substituting a different concept for the original one.

---

[4] Temporary states of hibernation, sleep, or torpor do not constitute a loss of the capacity to ingest and metabolize food—only a suspension of the first and a slowing down of the second.

For example, most of us know quite well what lions are, and probably could list some of the characteristics that enable us to recognize lions when we see them, or (more often) photos of them. But very few of us could formulate a precise and substantive definition of 'lion' which would be sufficient to settle all conceivable questions about what should and should not count as a member of the species *Pantera leo*.[5] Fortunately, we do not need such a sharp-edged definition, since we are rarely confronted with animals that cannot readily be classified either as lions or as non-lions, on the basis of our ordinary criteria. If and when we encounter—or genetically engineer—such animals, then we may need to refine our criteria of 'lionhood' in order to decide what to call these animals, and how we ought to treat them. There is, however, no urgent need to undertake such conceptual reform in advance. An artificially sharpened definition might even prove harmful, for instance if it led to the inappropriate exclusion of some lion-like animals from the legal or moral protections extended to lions.

Similarly, our ordinary criteria of life serve us well enough for most practical purposes. Nevertheless, they carry no guarantee of an unambiguous answer regarding the aliveness of novel entities, or familiar entities in novel circumstances. For example, in the 1960s, when it had become possible to maintain human beings on mechanical life-support systems for a period of time after their brains had completely and permanently ceased to function, urgent questions arose regarding the status of these 'brain-dead' individuals. The 'whole-brain' definition of death classifies a person as dead when it has been ascertained through appropriate diagnostic techniques that his or her entire brain has permanently and irreparably ceased to function.[6] This definition has become the legal standard throughout most of the world; yet there is still some debate about whether

М

---

[5] As a rule, two groups of organisms can be assumed to belong to the same species if they can interbreed and produce fertile young. There are, however, counterexamples to this generalization, e.g. numerous cases of hybridization between related plant species. See Ernst Mayr, *Toward a New Philosophy of Biology: Observations of an Evolutionist* (Cambridge, Mass.: Harvard University Press, 1988), 319.

[6] The classic statement of the whole-brain definition of death is 'A Definition of Irreversible Coma', by the Ad Hoc Committee of the Harvard Medical School to Examine the Definition of Brain Death, *Journal of the American Medical Association*, 205, No. 6 (6 Aug. 1968), 337–40.

brain-dead persons should be classified as deceased for legal and moral purposes.[7]

This disagreement is due, at least in part, to the fact that our ordinary concept of life does not include criteria that are precise enough to resolve all possible disputes about life's boundaries. Brain-dead persons whose heartbeat and breathing are artificially maintained are evidently alive in some respects, but no longer alive in others: substantial parts of their bodies are still functioning, but their brains are not, and never will. The question, then, is not whether they are alive according to the ordinary concept of life; for to that question there can be no clear answer. Rather, the question is whether it is morally desirable to refine our concept of life so as to include these human beings among the living, or whether it is morally better to regard them as having already died.

Nevertheless, philosophers would like to have a clear and simple definition of 'life' that captures the intuitive core of the concept. It is now generally recognized as unsatisfactory to define 'life' in terms of the presence of some special vitalistic or spiritual entity or power. Such definitions rely upon empirical hypotheses which find no support from contemporary biology.

A more promising approach is to define living things in terms of their teleological (goal-directed) organization. Paul Taylor, for instance, defines an organism as

a teleological center of life, striving to preserve itself and realize its good . . . To say it is a teleological center of life is to say that its internal functioning as well as its external activities are all goal-oriented, having the constant tendency to maintain the organism's existence through time and to enable it successfully to perform those biological operations whereby it reproduces its kind and continually adapts to changing environmental events and conditions. It is the coherence and unity of these functions of an organism, all

---

[7] For a thoughtful critique of the whole-brain definition of death, see Hans Jonas, 'Against the Stream: Comments on the Definition and Redefinition of Death', in *Philosophical Essays—From Ancient Creed to Technological Man* (Englewood Cliffs, NJ: Prentice-Hall, 1974), 132–40. For a classic defence of that definition, see the President's Commission for the Study of Ethical Problems in Medicine and Biomedical and Behavioral Research, *Defining Death: Medical, Legal and Ethical Issues in the Determination of Death* (Washington, DC: US Government Printing Office, 1981). For an overview of the debate, see Charles M. Culver and Bernard Gert, 'The Definition and Criterion of Death', in Thomas A. Mappes and Jane S. Zembaty (eds.), *Biomedical Ethics* (New York: McGraw-Hill, 1991), 389–96.

directed toward the realization of its good, that make it one teleological center of activity.[8]

Teleological organization helps to explain why living things seem fundamentally different from things that are dead or inanimate. Yet teleological organization, at least as Taylor defines it, is not a necessary condition for life. Suicidal individuals, whose external activities are currently directed towards self-destruction rather than survival, reproduction, or adaptation to the environment, may nevertheless still be alive.

Teleological organization is not a sufficient condition for life either. The existence of human-made artefacts which pursue goals through complex feedback mechanisms shows that this form of organization is not unique to the entities that we are at present willing to call living organisms. Taylor's response to this objection is that teleologically organized machines are not alive, because

[t]he goal-oriented operations of machines are not inherent to them as the goal-oriented behavior of organisms is inherent to them . . . the goals of a machine are derivative, whereas the goals of a living thing are original. The ends and purposes of machines are built into them by their human creators.[9]

Unfortunately, this argument begs the question; for how are we to determine whether a teleologically organized system has goals of its own, rather than merely derivative goals, except by first determining whether or not it is alive? If we regard the goals of machines as not really their own because human beings built those goals into them, then what are we to say about a (thus far hypothetical) 'test-tube amoeba'—one 'built' by human beings, but otherwise indistinguishable from a naturally generated amoeba? Surely the test-tube amoeba's artificial origin would not disqualify it as a living thing. Moreover, it is not clear that the goals of organisms are any more their own than are those of machines. Individual organisms do not design and create themselves, any more than individual machines do. Their teleological organization is largely the result of the physiological structure and composition that they inherit from their progenitors. Even animals that have the capacity to learn, thereby

---

[8] Paul Taylor, *Respect for Nature: A Theory of Environmental Ethics* (Princeton, NJ: Princeton University Press, 1986), 121–2.
[9] Ibid. 124.

altering their own behavioural 'programs', do not as a rule choose their most fundamental goals—such as survival and reproduction—but only some of the routes to those goals.

Taylor admits that the distinction he draws between organisms and machines may not hold in the case of 'those complex electronic devices now being developed under the name of artificial intelligence'.[10] These, he says, may eventually come to be seen as having a *telos*, a good of their own, and thus as alive. But complex teleological organization alone would probably never induce us to regard mechanical artefacts as alive. The Macintosh computer on which I am working is a much more complexly organized machine than any in existence a century ago; but that does not much incline most of us to call it a living organism. If, on the other hand, we were to produce machines that had, in addition to complex teleological organization, such characteristic features of life as the capacities to feed, metabolize, grow, and reproduce their kind, then we would probably be more inclined to regard them as artificial life forms—even if their internal organization were considerably simpler than that of a Macintosh. If a machine were successfully programmed to be sentient and self-aware, that fact would also be relevant to the decision to regard it as alive. For although only some of the living things on this planet seem to have these particular capacities, we have yet to encounter any non-living things that have them.

I conclude, therefore, that teleological organization is not a necessary and sufficient condition for life. Rather than searching further for a sharp-edged definition, I think it best to stay with a definition similar to *Webster's*, i.e. one that lists characteristic features that can serve as criteria of life, but that does not attempt to resolve in advance all possible uncertainties about what ought to count as a living thing.

## 2.2. *Albert Schweitzer's Defence of the Life Only View*

Although Schweitzer's humanitarian achievements are widely known and admired, his moral philosophy has not received much attention from academic philosophers. This is probably due in part to

---

[10]   *Respect for Nature*, 124–5.

the strength of the mystical and religious elements of his thought, and in part to his tendency to present his conclusions rather cryptically, without giving the philosophical arguments for them in much detail. Nevertheless, I believe that it is possible to glean from Schweitzer's work a consistent theory of moral status. Even if my interpretation of his thought is not flawless, it can serve as a useful basis for reflecting upon the strengths and weaknesses of the Life Only view.

Schweitzer's theory of moral status is based upon what he calls 'the most immediate fact of man's consciousness', namely that 'I am life that wills to live, in the midst of life that wills to live'.[11] From this premiss, he draws the conclusion that 'Ethics . . . [consists in] responsibility without limit towards all that lives'.[12] He concludes, further, that all attempts to sort living things into groups whose members have different moral status are dangerous and misguided.[13]

Schweitzer admired Kant's rationalistic ethics and, like Kant, he believed that an adequate ethical theory must be both universally valid and evident to reason. He criticized Kant, however, for giving his ethics too little specific content, and for failing to give adequate weight to the duties of beneficence. He attributed these failings to Kant's failure to ground his moral theory in what Schweitzer called 'elemental' experience, that is, experience that is available to all human beings.[14] As a theologian, Schweitzer valued the thought of Jesus and St Paul—in particular, their call actively to care for other human beings. However, he found the Judaeo-Christian moral tradition remiss in that it focuses upon our obligations towards human beings, to the all but total neglect of our obligations towards the rest of the universe.[15] He was deeply attracted to the Jain and Buddhist doctrine of *ahimsa* (non-violence), which forbids all acts that harm

[11] Albert Schweitzer, *Out of My Life and Time: An Autobiography* (New York: Holt, Rinehart & Winston, 1933), 157.

[12] Albert Schweitzer, *Civilization and Ethics: The Philosophy of Civilization Part II* (London: A. & C. Black, 1929), 248.

[13] *Out of My Life and Time*, 233.

[14] *Civilization and Ethics*, 106–15.

[15] Schweitzer actually speaks of 'the relations of man to man' (*Out of My Life and Time*, 158), and of 'man to the universe' (*The Words of Albert Schweitzer*, ed. Norman Cousins, New York: Newmarket Press, 1984), 17. Since in his time few feminists objected to such androcentric (male-centred) language, it would be uncharitable to take him to task for this usage.

living things; but he rejected what he called the 'world-denying' elements of these religions, i.e. their tendency to counsel ascetic withdrawal rather than active engagement in the world.[16]

Schweitzer searched, therefore, for a fundamental moral principle which would be (1) accessible to both thought and experience; (2) relevant not only to relationships amongst humans, but to the relationship of humanity to the rest of the universe; and (3) world-affirming, in the sense of requiring active service rather than the mere avoidance of wrongdoing. In his autobiography he describes the moment when, while travelling by boat in what was then French Equatorial Africa, he finally arrived at the principle for which he had been searching:

Lost in thought I sat on the deck of the barge, struggling to find the elementary and universal conception of the ethical which I had not discovered in any philosophy . . . Late on the third day . . . when, at sunset, we were making our way through a herd of hippopotamuses, there flashed upon my mind . . . the phrase, 'Reverence for Life' . . . I had . . . found the idea in which affirmation of the world and ethics are contained side by side.[17]

'Reverence for Life' implies the extension of moral concern to all living things. It also entails the recognition of an obligation not to harm even the 'lowliest' organism. A person who reveres life, Schweitzer says,

tears no leaf from a tree, plucks no flower, and takes care to crush no insect. If in the summer he is working by lamplight, he prefers to keep the window shut and breathe a stuffy atmosphere rather than see one insect after another fall with singed wings upon his table.[18]

A person who reveres life will not only strive to avoid harming living things, but will also aid and succour life whenever possible. 'If I save an insect from a puddle, life has devoted itself to life . . .'[19]

At the same time, Schweitzer was intensely aware that it is often pragmatically impossible to avoid deliberately harming living things:

The necessity to destroy and to injure life is imposed upon me . . . In order to preserve my own existence, I must defend against the existence which injures it. I become the hunter of the mouse which inhabits my house, a mur-

---

[16] Albert Schweitzer, *The Teaching of Reverence for Life*, trans. Richard and Clara Winston (New York: Holt, Rinehart & Winston, 1965), 10.

[17] *Out of My Life and Time*, 156.

[18] *Civilization and Ethics*, 247.

[19] Ibid. 250.

derer of the insect which wants to have its nest there, a mass-murderer of the bacteria which may endanger my life. I get my food by destroying plants and animals.[20]

Thus, although he ascribes equal moral status to all living things, Schweitzer does not conclude that we ought to abandon such practices as killing insects or rodents that invade our homes, or pathogenic bacteria that infect our bodies. Nor does he condemn the killing of animals for food. Vegetarianism does not eliminate the need to kill *some* living things in order to eat; and Schweitzer permits no principled distinction between the moral status of plants and that of animals—or humans. 'The ethic of Reverence for Life establishes no dividing line between higher and lower, between more and less valuable life.'[21]

How, then, can we justify such ordinary assumptions as that whereas it is morally innocuous to pull up carrots and eat them, it is abominable to kill human beings and eat them? Schweitzer's answer is that we *cannot* justify such ordinary assumptions, except on the basis of our own arbitrary preferences. He opposes all attempts to work out a compromise between the ethical requirement to respect life and the practical requirement sometimes to take life. We must, he says, reject any 'relative' ethic, i.e. one that implies that while some killing is wrong, it is acceptable to kill certain sorts of organisms under certain circumstances.[22] In his view, *all* actions that harm living things are morally wrong. Since we cannot always avoid such actions, each of us is compelled 'to decide for himself in each case how far he can remain ethical and how far he must submit himself to the necessity for the destruction of and injury to life, and therewith incur guilt'.[23]

## 2.3. *Objections to the Life Only View*

Few philosophers share Schweitzer's belief that all living things have full and equal moral status.[24] Yet his theory repays careful consideration, because it has important virtues. Schweitzer's criterion of

---

[20] Ibid. 254–5.          [21] *Out of My Life and Time*, 233.
[22] *Civilization and Ethics*, 264.          [23] Ibid. 255.
[24] Paul Taylor is one exception; he argues that all living things have equal moral status: *Respect for Nature*, 129–34. His view is discussed below, p. 38.

moral status is relatively clear and simple. All disputes about the relative moral status of diverse life forms are swept aside in favour of a radical biological egalitarianism. The human capacity for empathy is extended to its apparent limit, and anthropocentrism is firmly rejected. Nevertheless, Schweitzer's theory faces powerful objections. The most serious of these involve (1) the weaknesses of the argument from the will to live; (2) the practical impossibility of consistently acting on the view that all living things have equal moral status; (3) the theory's failure to provide practical guidance; and (4) the excessive guilt which the theory requires us to bear.

## The Weakness of the Argument from the Will to Live

Schweitzer's case for the Life Only view is based upon the claim that all (and only) living things *will* to live. But why should we believe that all living organisms will to live? Schweitzer seems to have been influenced by Arthur Schopenhauer's metaphysics, in which the ultimate reality is not matter, but will.[25] Schweitzer at times speaks of the universal will to live as a transcendent reality that lies 'behind all phenomena',[26] and of all living organisms as part of that universal will. 'Whenever my life devotes itself in any way to life,' he says, 'my finite will-to-live experiences its union with the infinite will in which all life is one . . .'[27] To adopt the ethic of Reverence for Life is to enter into a relationship with the universe that is spiritual, and 'independent of intellectual understanding'.[28] Mike Martin describes this view as 'somewhere near pantheism but . . . closer to *biotheism*—the view that God is manifested in and constituted by all life'.[29]

Unfortunately, those who do not share Schweitzer's biotheistic beliefs are unlikely to share his conviction that all living things have a will to live. The problem is that willing, as each of us experiences it in our own case, is (at least in part) a conscious mental activity, and thus unlikely to occur in plants, micro-organisms, and other life

[25] Arthur Schopenhauer, *The World as Will and Representation*, trans. E. F. J. Payne (New York; Dover, 1966).

[26] *The Philosophy of Civilization* (Buffalo, NY: Prometheus Books, 1987), 308.

[27] *Civilization and Ethics*, 250.

[28] *The Teaching of Reverence for Life*, 33.

[29] Michael W. Martin, 'Rethinking Reverence for Life', *Between the Species*, 9, No. 4 (Fall 1993), 205.

forms that evidently lack the neurophysiological equipment to engage in conscious mental activity. Schweitzer says that we can *experience* the will to live that is in all life, in much the same way that we can experience our own individual will to live. But this experience, even for those who share it, is not persuasive evidence that plants, bacteria, or viruses consciously will to live; for it may equally well be a result of the natural human tendency sometimes to anthropomorphize—that is, to ascribe human-like minds and emotions to entities that are not mentally or emotionally similar to human beings. If prevailing scientific opinion is correct, the teleological organization of terrestrial organisms is the result of aeons of natural selection for physiological structures and processes that tend to contribute to survival and successful reproduction. It is not, therefore, evidence of a conscious will operating within each bacterium, any more than it is evidence of a conscious intelligence guiding the evolutionary process.[30]

One response to this objection to Schweitzer's argument from the will to live is to interpret the claim that all living things will to live in a way that does not presuppose that all living things are capable of conscious experience. However, Schweitzer himself does not do this. Rather, he suggests that all living things possess the capacity to experience pleasure and pain, as well as desire and fear. He says, for example, that

As in my own will-to-live there is a longing for wider life and for the mysterious exaltation of the will-to-live which we call pleasure, with the dread of annihilation which we call pain; so it is also in the will-to-live all around me, whether it can express itself before me, or remains dumb.[31]

If having a will to live means desiring pleasure and fearing pain, then it is unlikely that all organisms have a will to live. Pleasure and pain, like the desire for the one and the fear of the other, are experiences, and elements of sentience. Sentience and the grounds for ascribing it to particular organisms are topics to be explored in the next chapter. For the present, it is enough to note the absence of empirical evidence for the claim that all living things are capable of

---

[30] Two good books dealing with teleological explanations in biology are Larry Wright, *Teleological Explanations* (Berkeley and Los Angeles: University of California Press, 1976), and Michael Ruse, *The Philosophy of Biology* (London: Hutchinson, 1973).

[31] *Civilization and Ethics*, 246.

having conscious experiences. We each know from personal experience that it is possible to be alive and yet (at times) to experience nothing. Our own capacity for experience requires a functioning central nervous system. Particular sensory modalities, such as sight and hearing, depend additionally upon the presence and proper functioning of our sensory organs. Our capacity to feel pain depends upon the existence and functioning of the relevant receptor nerves, and the brain's capacity to process input from them. It is reasonable to believe that other vertebrate animals also have a capacity for sentience, since they too have sense organs and central nervous systems. Moreover, they often act as if they were sentient. For instance, they often seem to enjoy themselves, e.g. when eating or interacting with others of their kind; and when injured they often act as though in pain. Microbes and plants, in contrast, do not have central nervous systems; and they do not, on the whole, behave as if they were sentient.[32]

But how can we *know* that plants and microbes are not sentient? Might they not have pleasant or painful experiences of which we know nothing, but which are as vivid to them as ours are to us? Perhaps they even have a conscious will to live. How can we know that they do not, when we cannot experience their existence 'from inside', as we do our own?

If we begin by demanding that all knowledge be undergirded by an absolute guarantee of truth, then we will indeed be forced to admit that we do not know whether or not stones, plants, or even other human beings are sentient. Descartes made this demand of all the beliefs that he had previously held, and soon concluded that not even his belief in the existence of a world external to his own mind could be regarded as knowledge—except, so he argued, on the hypothesis that there is an omnipotent and morally good God, who would not deceive him about something so basic.[33]

But Descartes demands too much of ordinary human knowledge. It is unreasonable to insist upon security against even the most re-

---

[32] There are some interesting apparent exceptions, such as the Venus flytrap (*Dionaea muscipula*), a small carnivorous plant which closes the halves of its 'trap' when the trigger hairs are touched, e.g. by an insect or other small creature. Such examples of responsiveness to touch may seem to constitute proof of sentience, but are now thought to be explicable without that hypothesis.

[33] René Descartes, *Discourse on Method and the Meditations* (New York: Penguin Books, 1968), 133, 158.

mote possibility of error, particularly in an empirical field. In inquiring about the possible sentience of a bacterium, as in any other factual investigation, we have no practical alternative but to base our conclusions upon the best available evidence. On that basis, it is reasonable to conclude that terrestrial organisms which lack nervous systems are probably incapable of having conscious experiences. Of course, anyone is morally entitled to believe that they are as conscious as we are. Schweitzer's belief in the universal will to live deserves as much respect as any sincere and thoughtful religious conviction. But we cannot afford to base our moral theories upon unsupported empirical hypotheses, since we cannot reasonably expect other people to make the same leaps of faith that we do.

## *The Impracticality of Radical Biological Egalitarianism*

If we take the Life Only view seriously, we find that it has very strange consequences. It implies, for instance, that many ordinary and essential human activities—such as cooking, cleaning, bathing, brushing one's teeth, and using antibiotics or disinfectants to treat or prevent microbial infections—are the moral equivalents of mass homicide. Schweitzer, indeed, describes himself as 'a mass-murderer of . . . bacteria'.[34] Moreover, his insistence that we cannot justify the belief that our lives are more valuable than those of bacteria shows that this language cannot be dismissed as mere hyperbole.

But is this an ethic by which we can agree to live? The answer is clear. Any human society which treated ordinary acts of food preparation, personal hygiene, and medical care as the moral equivalents of mass homicide would jeopardize its own survival. For if, on the one hand, members of the society adopted the view that the destruction of micro-organisms is as serious a crime as we consider homicide to be, and consistently sought to prevent such destruction, then the health of the human population would suffer severely. And if, on the other hand, they came to see homicide as no more serious a wrong than we consider the destruction of micro-organisms to be, then the society's survival would be threatened by uncontrolled intra-human violence.

It might be argued that the Life Only view need not lead to such

---

[34] *Civilization and Ethics*, 255.

absurd conclusions. Perhaps the killing of micro-organisms in the course of necessary routine activities can be justified as a form of self-defence, even if all living things have equal moral status. This is the approach taken by Paul Taylor. Taylor, like Schweitzer, is a radical biological egalitarian. In his view, 'every entity that has a good of its own [should be regarded as] possessing inherent worth—the same inherent worth, since none is superior to another.'[35] But unlike Schweitzer, Taylor holds that we are sometimes morally justified in killing living things. He proposes a set of principles for resolving conflicts between human and non-human interests which, he says, do not presuppose that humans have a stronger moral status than other organisms. These include the principle of self-defence, i.e. 'that it is permissible for moral agents to protect themselves against dangerous or harmful organisms by destroying them'.[36]

Taylor's self-defence principle seems to permit us to kill harmful micro-organisms. But on closer inspection, that it does becomes less clear. Because he accepts the Life Only view, Taylor cannot accept any justification for killing a microbe that would not be equally acceptable as justification for killing a human being. Lethal self-defence against other human beings is usually held to be permissible only when necessary to protect the agent from a serious and unjustified threat. Indeed, Taylor's self-defence principle is even more stringent than this: it permits killing only when 'absolutely required for maintaining the very existence of moral agents'.[37] This principle would therefore excuse microbe killing in relatively few cases, namely those in which the microbes pose a severe and immediate threat to the survival of a moral agent. Were a human being to threaten me with a harm no more serious than that which I would incur by failing to brush my teeth tonight, I could not on this principle justifiably kill that human being in self-defence. Thus, the principle of self-defence provides no escape from the impractical consequences of the Life Only view.

## Lack of Guidance

As we have seen, Schweitzer opposes the formulation of conditions under which we are morally justified in killing living things. His view

---

[35] *Respect for Nature*, 155.        [36] Ibid. 264–5.
[37] Ibid.

is that harming life is always wrong, even though often necessary for human survival and well-being. That being the case, he concludes, each moral agent must decide individually when it is necessary to harm living things. 'In ethical conflicts', he says, 'man can only arrive at subjective decisions. No one can lay down for him at what point, on each occasion, lies the extreme limit of possibility for his persistence in the preservation and promotion of life.'[38]

There is some truth in this reflection. If the life in question is that of a common microbe or a mosquito, then it is largely a subjective and personal question just how much risk or inconvenience justifies taking that life. But it cannot be *entirely* up to each of us individually to decide when it is morally right to harm living things. Not everyone's conscience can be counted upon to yield results as exemplary as Schweitzer's. A moral code backed by praise, blame, and occasional acts of overt coercion has been an indispensable part of the culture of every known and successful human society. To do its job, a moral code must include, at least implicitly, a theory of moral status. It must, among other things, provide guidance about when it is morally permissible to harm living things, and when it is right for third parties to intervene in order to prevent that harm, either coercively or through moral suasion. Should we, for instance, intervene legally or through civil protest in order to prevent biomedical researchers from experimenting on mice or monkeys? Should abortion be treated as a crime? Which animals, if any, should it be legal to hunt for food or for sport? Should some plants and animals be protected more strictly than others, because their species are rare and endangered? The ethic of Reverence for Life can give us little practical guidance regarding such questions, because answering them requires us to make distinctions which this ethic precludes.

## Excess Guilt

Schweitzer is critical of common-sense morality for its compromises with practicality. It is better, he believes, to make no excuses and offer no justifications for the harms that we do to living things. In his view, it is a tragic fact that in a world in which life feeds upon life no one can always do what is morally right. At the same time, no one

---

[38] *Civilization and Ethics*, 255–6.

can escape moral guilt for failing to do what is right. To harm life—
however great the necessity—is to act wrongly, and thereby to incur
guilt.

This heroic attitude towards the acceptance of guilt runs contrary
to a principle that has been accepted as a truism by many moral
philosophers, namely the principle that 'Ought implies can'. On this
principle, it cannot be morally obligatory for a person to perform an
act unless it is *possible* for that person to perform that act. Of course,
a person can sometimes be blamed for bringing about conditions
that prevent their fulfilling all of their moral obligations; for instance, for making two promises when they ought to have known
that they could not keep both of them. But if the circumstances
which make it impossible for a person to fulfil an apparent moral
obligation are entirely beyond their control then, on this principle,
the apparent obligation is not morally binding. Thus it would be inappropriate for others to blame that person, or for that person to
feel guilt. On this view, if we cannot live, or live reasonably well,
without frequently causing the deaths of microbes, then causing the
deaths of microbes is not always morally wrong, and we need not always feel guilty about it.

But is it true that 'Ought implies can'? Some philosophers argue
that there are situations in which we cannot fulfil all of our moral
obligations, and yet none of these obligations cease to be binding.
Ruth Barcan Marcus holds that such moral dilemmas are common-
place. She says that one may through no fault of one's own be placed
in a situation in which one is morally obliged to do $x$ and also to do
$y$, and yet it is impossible to do both $x$ and $y$. In such circumstances,
she says, blame and guilt are sometimes appropriate.[39] She argues
that it is important to recognize 'the reality of dilemmas and the
appropriateness of the attendant feelings', since the guilt that we
experience because of unfulfillable obligations may motivate us
'to arrange our lives and institutions so as to minimize or avoid
dilemmas'.[40]

This is a sound point, provided that the moral dilemmas in question *can* be avoided by rearranging our lives or institutions. If, however, we cannot avoid a particular type of action—such as killing

---

[39] Ruth Barcan Marcus, 'Moral Dilemmas and Consistency', *Journal of Philosophy*, 77, No. 3 (Mar. 1980), 121–36.
[40] Ibid. 131.

microbes—by any feasible alteration of the way in which we live, then it is inappropriate to feel guilt over that action. Guilt feelings are useless if they cannot motivate better behaviour. Useless feelings of guilt may even motivate worse behaviour, by creating cynicism about a morality that judges all of us blameworthy, regardless of how diligently we seek to do what is right.

The problem here is not just that it is generally inappropriate to feel any appreciable guilt over the destruction of microbes. It is also that the magnitude of the guilt which Schweitzer's theory requires us to bear is wildly out of proportion. If the moral status of microbes were identical to that of human beings, then it would be insufficient to feel just a little guilt over the killing of billions of viruses or bacteria; it would be more appropriate to feel a stupendous and overwhelming guilt. For, although the magnitude of a wrong is not always directly proportionate to the number of victims, the enormous numbers here must add substantially to that magnitude—if microbes are our moral equals.

## 2.4. *Two Objections to the Life Plus View*

These points illustrate the unpalatable consequences of the view that life is the only valid criterion of moral status. As we have seen, Schweitzer was aware of these consequences. Why, then, did he reject the Life Plus view? This view, like his, implies that we should not knowingly harm living things without good reason; but it does not require us to regard all living things as our moral equals. Schweitzer presents two objections to the view that living things differ in moral status: the objection from anthropocentrism, and the slippery slope objection. These objections may initially seem compelling, but neither stands up to critical scrutiny.

### The Objection from Anthropocentrism

Schweitzer says that we should not 'undertake to lay down universally valid distinctions of value between different kinds of life', because if we do, then we

will end in judging them by the greater or lesser distance at which they seem to stand from us as human beings—as we ourselves judge. But that is a purely subjective criterion. Who among us knows what significance any other kind of life has in itself, and as a part of the universe?[41]

Many people find this argument persuasive. We do, it seems, often assign moral status to non-human organisms largely on the basis of their phylogenetic distance from *Homo sapiens*. Chimpanzees—our closest non-human relatives—tend to attract more sympathy than gophers, and gophers more than clams and mussels; and very few people sympathize at all with bacteria. What is this but rampant human chauvinism?

The answer depends upon how good our reasons are for making the distinctions that we commonly do. We cannot assume at the onset that all possible reasons for distinguishing between the moral status of human beings and that of bacteria are unsound. Nor are we necessarily refuted by the fact that we have placed ourselves on the favoured side. If that argument were sound, we would be equally unable to justify any distinction between the moral status of living things and that of inanimate objects, since (living) humans fall on the favoured side of that line too.

There are many bad reasons for holding that the moral status of human beings is different from that of microbes. It is implausible, for instance, to claim that membership in the species *Homo sapiens* is in itself a sufficient condition for the possession of a higher moral status than that held by the members of any other species. It is an accident of evolution and history that all of the beings to whom we customarily accord full moral status belong to our own biological species. Had things gone differently, there might have been dozens of terrestrial species whose members had the intelligence, power, and communication skills to persuade us to recognize them as moral equals. Furthermore, there are non-human terrestrial species whose members arguably *ought* to be recognized as moral equals, even though most of us have been slow to arrive at that conclusion.[42]

There may, however, be better grounds than rampant human chauvinism for the claim that we owe more to other human beings than to bacteria. As will be argued in Chapter 3, the fact that some

[41] *Out of My Life and Time*, 233.

[42] See Cavalieri and Singer (eds.), *The Great Ape Project: Beyond Human Equality*. The contributors include philosophers, biologists, and ethologists, who argue that chimpanzees, orang-utans, and gorillas should be accorded basic 'human' rights.

organisms are sentient and others are not is a plausible basis for the claim that we owe more to some organisms than to others. And, as will be argued in Chapter 4, moral agency is a plausible basis for making further distinctions in moral status. Neither the sentience criterion nor the moral agency criterion is overtly anthropocentric, since neither permits us to give special preference to human beings simply because of their biological species.

But, it will be replied, these criteria are covertly anthropocentric. Are we not picking out properties that we value in ourselves, and assuming without justification that these properties must have some cosmic value or significance? The answer is that we are not. In making judgements about the moral status of living things, we are not (or should not be) seeking to estimate their value from the viewpoint of the gods, or that of the universe. We are not gods but human beings, reasoning about how *we* ought to think and act. Our moral theories can only be based upon what we know and what we care about, or ought to care about. If this makes our theories anthropocentric, then this much anthropocentrism is inevitable in any moral theory that is relevant to human actions. Such a minimal degree of anthropocentrism need not render our moral theories relevant *only* to human behaviour. If our moral concepts and principles are based upon a fairly sound understanding of the world, then well-meaning moral agents of other species—if and when we meet them—might find at least some of those concepts and principles comprehensible, and substantially consistent with their own.

However empathetic we are, we cannot extend our moral concern equally to all of the living things that exist in time and space. As William Grey points out, the extension of human moral concern 'is intelligible only as long as it relates to a scale which is recognizably human, and to that extent, anthropomorphic'.[43] On a cosmic or even a planetary scale, very little that we humans do is likely to matter much. Why, Grey asks, should we strive to protect the Great Barrier Reef, when in a few million years the continent of Australia will have moved to a new location, and an entirely new reef system will have formed? Even if we were to destroy most of the biological species on the planet, he says,

---

[43] William Grey, 'On Anthropomorphism and Deep Ecology', *Australasian Journal of Philosophy*, 71, No. 4 (Dec. 1993), 167.

For planet Earth that is just another incident in a four and one half billion year saga. Life will go on—in some guise or other. The arthropods, algae and the ubiquitous bacteria, at least, will almost certainly be around for a few billion years more.[44]

Thus, some human-centredness is inevitable in any human moral code. We need to reject fallacious forms of anthropocentrism; but not all forms of anthropocentrism are fallacious. It is not fallaciously anthropocentric to give priority in our moral deliberations to living things which are close enough to us in time and space to be affected by our actions, and close enough that their fate will affect us or future human generations. Nor is it illegitimate to recognize stronger moral obligations to those living things which resemble human beings in morally significant respects.

## The Slippery Slope Objection

Schweitzer's second objection to the Life Plus view is that, once we permit distinctions in moral status to be made, 'there comes next the view that there can be life which is worthless, injury or destruction of which does not matter. Then in the category of worthless life we come to include, according to circumstances, different kinds of insects, or primitive peoples.'[45]

This is a 'slippery slope' argument. Such arguments seek to discredit one idea—which may seem harmless in itself—on the grounds that it is apt to lead to other ideas, which are less acceptable. Slippery slope arguments are common in moral debate, and they are often unsound—so often that some critical thinking texts speak of 'the fallacy of the slippery slope'.[46] But not all slippery slope arguments are fallacious. Sometimes accepting one idea does lead, in one way or another, to accepting other ideas which are worse. Some slippery slope arguments warn of the *logical* consequences of an idea, i.e. consequences which are avoidable only at the cost of inconsistency. Other slippery slope arguments warn of the *psychological* consequences of an idea, that is, conclusions that are not logically

---

[44] 'On Anthropomorphism and Deep Ecology', 168.
[45] *Out of My Life and Time*, 233.
[46] See Howard Kahane, *Logic and Contemporary Rhetoric: The Use of Reason in Everyday Life* (Belmont, Calif.: Wadsworth, 1992), 46–7.

implied by it, but that many people may nevertheless be predisposed to draw from it.

It is not clear whether Schweitzer is making a logical or a psychological claim in the passage just quoted. However, it is clearly false that any distinction that we draw between the moral status of people and that of bacteria will have, as a *logical* consequence, that there are some people who have the moral status of bacteria. (For instance, both the sentience and moral agency criteria logically suffice to block that inference.) It is more likely, then, that Schweitzer is describing what he takes to be a psychological tendency—the tendency, having once established distinct categories of moral status, to place some persons in the lowest category.

Schweitzer's argument, thus construed, may appear plausible. It is true that many people habitually demean others by comparing them to forms of life that are considered especially unattractive, such as pond scum (algae). Perhaps if we saw algae as our moral equals, we would also be more inclined to see other people that way. There is, however, no persuasive evidence of the psychological slide that Schweitzer warns against. Persons who routinely kill algae and feel no guilt about it (aquarium keepers, for instance), do not seem to be especially likely to harm other persons, or seriously to equate their moral status with that of algae. The robust distinction that most of us make between the moral status of human beings and that of algae prevents us from making any inference from the permissibility of harming algae to the permissibility of harming human beings. Thus, the psychological slope is less slippery than Schweitzer would have us believe.

### 2.5. *The Argument from Teleological Organization*

Schweitzer has not presented a persuasive case for the Life Only view, i.e. that life is a necessary and sufficient condition for full moral status. Even the Life Plus view—that life is sufficient for some moral status, but not for full moral status—receives little support from his argument from the will to live. This argument presupposes that all living organisms are sentient, and this presupposition is not supported by the available evidence. It would be premature, however, to conclude that life is not a valid criterion of moral status.

There are arguments for the Life Plus view that do not require so great a leap of faith as Schweitzer's. Perhaps the most important of these are those which appeal to the ecosystemic relationships amongst terrestrial organisms. These arguments are explored in Chapter 5. At present, however, I want to focus upon an argument which appeals only to the intrinsic properties of living things.

Some environmental ethicists argue that living things have moral status because of their teleological nature, i.e. because of the ways in which they are internally organized to maintain (for a time) their own existence. Teleological organization is said to be sufficient for at least some moral status, because it demonstrates that the organism has a *telos*, or good of its own, and that it can therefore be harmed or benefited by human actions. This is the argument that Paul Taylor gives; and there are many environmentalists who accept this argument, even though they reject Taylor's further claim, that all living things have the same moral status.[47]

Although generally suspicious of efforts to draw sharp lines between what is and is not morally considerable, Val Plumwood nevertheless suggests that autonomous teleological organization may be a necessary condition—and perhaps a sufficient one—for meriting moral respect and consideration. She points out that

there needs to be something that can be turned aside or frustrated by our actions, so that the concept of respect or consideration can get a foothold, as it were . . . Wherever we can discern an autonomous . . . teleology the concepts of respect and moral consideration have a potential for application.[48]

Holmes Rolston III puts the point somewhat more strongly. He argues that the teleological nature of living things is a sufficient basis for some moral status, because it means that all organisms have intrinsic value. Organisms, he argues, are 'evaluative systems', i.e. sys-

---

[47] Examples include Holmes Rolston III, 'Environmental Ethics: Values in and Duties to the Natural World', in Earl R. Winkler and Jerrold R. Coombs (eds.), *Applied Ethics: A Reader* (Oxford: Basil Blackwell, 1993), 271–92; John Rodman, 'Four Forms of Ecological Consciousness Reconsidered', in Donald Scherer and Thomas Attig (eds.), *Ethics and the Environment* (Englewood Cliffs, NJ: Prentice-Hall, 1983), 90; Hans Jonas, *The Phenomenon of Life* (Chicago, Ill.: University of Chicago Press, 1966), 84–91; and Taylor, *Respect for Nature*, 124, 153.

[48] Val Plumwood, *Feminism and the Mastery of Nature* (London: Routledge, 1993), 210.

tems that demonstrate through their goal-oriented behaviour that they have values. Such systems, he says, are intrinsically valuable: 'the oak grows, reproduces, repairs its wounds, and resists death. The physical state that the organism seeks, idealized in its programmatic form is a valued state . . . the living individual . . . is *per se* an intrinsic value.'[49]

While I will argue that life is a valid criterion for some moral status, I am not convinced that this conclusion can be established merely by pointing to the teleological nature of living organisms. Organisms are not unique in being organized teleologically. The argument from teleological organization does not explain why living organisms should have a moral status different from that of other teleological systems, such as goal-oriented machines, or many of the *parts* of complex living organisms. Janna Thompson notes that

Once we come to appreciate how a kidney or some other internal organ develops . . ., how it functions and maintains itself, what makes it flourish and what harms it, then [as] surely as in the case of the butterfly . . . we have to recognize that it has a good of its own . . . For the same reason, it seems that we also ought to say that . . . a piece of skin, a body cell, or a DNA molecule has a good of its own.[50]

A defender of the argument from teleological organization might reply that a part of an organism is never teleologically organized in the way that the organism as a whole is. But this will be a difficult claim to prove. The internal teleological organization of, for instance, human mitochondria[51] is as evident as that of any free-living micro-organism. If mitochondria are held to lack (the right kind of) teleological organization because of their small size, or their relatively simple structure, then we must draw the same conclusion about all free-living microbes, such as many viruses and bacteria, which are no larger or more complex than mitochondria.

Alternatively, a defender of the argument from teleological organization might simply accept the implication that both organisms and their parts can have moral status. But ascribing moral status to

[49] Rolston, 'Environmental Ethics', 278.

[50] Janna Thompson, 'A Refutation of Environmental Ethics', *Environmental Ethics*, 12, No. 2 (Summer 1990), 152–3.

[51] Mitochondria are cell-like structures that exist within other human cells, and serve to process energy. Some biologists think that they are descended from one-celled organisms that originally lived independently.

parts of organisms is highly counterintuitive.[52] It is obvious that an act which damages part of an organism may be wrong because it harms the organism as a whole. But if removing an infected tonsil will improve a person's health, then few would argue that the surgeon might wrong the tonsil by removing it. The *person* might be wronged, for example if the surgery were done badly; but that is another matter. The point is not that the moral status of tonsils is eclipsed by the stronger moral status of persons, but rather that tonsils are normally presumed to have no independent moral status.

Perhaps this objection could be met through a more careful analysis of the type of teleological organization which is distinctive of whole organisms. However, the argument from teleological organization suffers from a more fundamental problem. The fact that organisms are goal-directed is insufficient to establish that they have moral status, because not all goals are sufficiently important to give rise to human moral obligations. While it may be the (unconscious) goal of each bacterium to survive and multiply, it is not self-evident that we ought to be concerned about the goals of individual bacteria. Bacteria do not experience pain, frustration, or grief if their goals are thwarted. They do not care whether or not they survive and multiply, any more than stones care whether or not they are smashed into bits. And if bacteria do not care about their own goals, then why should *we* care about those goals?

One answer is that it behoves us to care about the well-being of some micro-organisms because they are important to our own well-being. Without the appropriate microbes, we could not make wine or beer, bread would not rise, cheese would not ripen, our digestive systems would not work properly, and soils could not maintain the fertility necessary for plants to grow.[53] Bacteria serve as energy reprocessing plants, converting the remains and waste products of some organisms into nutrients for other organisms. They also fix nitrogen in the soil, making it possible for plants to grow. Were there suddenly no micro-organisms at all, the rest of the biosphere would

---

[52] One counterexample is that of conjoined twins who share a single lower body. When both are sentient, and it is unlikely that both could survive surgical separation, it may be appropriate to regard them as a single organism and yet as two human beings, who have separate and possibly competing moral rights.

[53] For an engrossing account of the roles played by micro-organisms in these and other processes, see Bernard Dixon, *Power Unseen: How Microbes Rule the World* (New York: W. H. Freeman, 1994).

quickly follow them into oblivion. These are sound reasons for paying attention to the effects of human actions upon certain microbial populations. They are not, however, reasons that directly imply that microbes have moral status. The undoubted instrumental value of some microbes does not in itself show that we ought to accept moral obligations towards them.

## 2.6. *Conclusions*

We have not discovered any intrinsic property that is common to all living organisms, and persuasively linked to the possession of moral status. Schweitzer's argument for the Life Only view fails because there is no good reason to believe that all living things have a will to live. The argument that all living things have moral status because of their internal teleological organization is not entirely persuasive either.

So long as we retain the view that the moral status of an entity must be based entirely upon its intrinsic properties, we will find it difficult to demonstrate that life is a sufficient condition for even a modest moral status. However—as I argue in Chapters 5 and 6— once we take into account the biosystemic relationships amongst living things, we may find good reasons for ascribing some moral status even to unicellular life forms.

Respect for life is a worthy ideal, provided that it is not conjoined with the unreasonable demand that we respect all life forms equally. We are not morally obliged to treat pathogenic microbes as our moral equals. The Life Plus view is more consistent with common sense than the Life Only view, and has many of its other virtues. It prohibits us from establishing any category of 'worthless life'—life that may be destroyed merely for human amusement, or for no reason at all. It rejects the assumption that we can have moral obligations only to members of our own species. It requires that no living organism be harmed without reason; but it does not require that we pursue Schweitzer's impossible goal of never harming any living thing—or never without experiencing feelings of guilt.

# 3

## Sentience and the Utilitarian Calculus

Sentience is a plausible criterion of moral status, because sentient beings are capable of experiencing pain, and we normally assume that it is wrong to inflict pain without good reason. The ordinary concept of cruelty applies to the needless infliction of pain, or any other form of suffering, upon human beings or other sentient animals. People often disagree about whether particular practices cause pain or suffering to animals or human beings, or whether those that clearly do are unjustified, and therefore cruel; but few seriously maintain that the gratuitous infliction of pain is morally innocuous.

Nevertheless, Western moral philosophers have often explained the wrongness of cruelty to non-human animals in ways that avoid ascribing moral status to them. Immanuel Kant holds that we can have duties only to rational moral agents, and that no non-human terrestrial animals are capable of rational moral agency. In his view, cruelty to animals is wrong, but not because we have obligations towards them. Instead, 'our duties towards animals are merely indirect duties to humanity'.[1] He says:

> If a man shoots his dog because the animal is no longer capable of service, he does not fail in his duty to the dog, for the dog cannot judge, but his act is inhuman and damages in himself that humanity which it is his duty to show towards mankind.[2]

This account of the wrongness of cruelty to animals is inadequate. No doubt some portion of our disapproval of such cruelty is due to the knowledge that people who cannot be trusted with animals often cannot be trusted with human beings either; a child

[1] Immanuel Kant, 'Duties to Animals and Spirits', *Lectures on Ethics*, trans. Louis Infield (New York: Harper & Row, 1963), 239.
[2] Ibid. 240.

who enjoys torturing small animals had better not be left alone with the baby. But that cannot be the whole story. For if needlessly harming animals were not morally objectionable in itself, then it would be difficult to explain why it should be either a cause or an indication of moral corruption.

In 'Ethics and the Beetle', A. M. MacIver says,

If I tread wantonly on a woodlouse, I do wrong. It is an evasion to pretend that the act is in itself morally indifferent and then say that it ought nevertheless to be condemned as gratification of an impulse which would have produced wrongdoing if gratified upon a human being. There would be nothing wrong about the impulse, as gratified in this case, unless this act were, in and by itself, wrong.[3]

MacIver is not suggesting that it is a *serious* moral wrong to tread wantonly on a woodlouse. Indeed, he goes on to say, 'it is only a very small wrong, and to exaggerate its wrongfulness is sentimentality'.[4] Nevertheless, if wantonly treading on a woodlouse is wrong simply because it needlessly harms the woodlouse, then it would seem that the woodlouse has moral status. It would seem, that is, that our moral obligation not to needlessly harm it is, at least in part, an obligation to it, and not merely to our fellow human beings.

But what sort of moral status might a woodlouse have? Some philosophers maintain that sentience is the sole valid criterion of moral status; this is what I call the Sentience Only view. On this view, sentience is (1) a necessary condition for having any moral status at all; and (2) a sufficient condition for having full and equal moral status. Thus, if the woodlouse is sentient, then on the Sentience Only view it has exactly the same moral status as we do. If, on the other hand, it is not sentient, then on the Sentience Only view it has no moral status at all, and we can have no moral obligations towards it.

On the Sentience Plus view, sentience is a valid criterion of moral status, but it is not the only valid criterion. If an entity is sentient, then we have moral obligations towards it. Some of the most important of these obligations are suggested by the common-sense objection to cruelty. However, on the Sentience Plus view, there may be valid reasons for ascribing moral status to some entities (e.g. biological species or ecosystems) that are not sentient. There may also

---

[3] A. M. MacIver, 'Ethics and the Beetle', *Analysis*, 8, No. 5 (Apr. 1948), 65.
[4] Ibid.

be valid reasons for ascribing stronger moral status to some sentient beings than to others. Thus, on the Sentience Plus view, sentience is not a necessary condition for any moral status. It is, however, a sufficient condition for some moral status—though not for full moral status.

In this chapter I first consider the meaning of the term 'sentience', and comment on two theories that deny that pleasure and pain are real processes that occur within sentient organisms. Then I consider the types of evidence that can lend support to the conclusion that a particular entity is sentient, and summarize some of the evidence regarding the probable distribution of sentience amongst terrestrial organisms. Next I explore the views of Peter Singer, a defender of the Sentience Only view, and present some pragmatic objections to Singer's sentience-based theory of moral status. Finally, I return to the Sentience Plus view and explore its comparative advantages.

### 3.1. *Defining 'Sentience'*

Sentience is the capacity to feel pleasure or pain. Feelings of pleasure or pain are experiences, but not all experiences are (or include) feelings of pleasure or pain. For instance, many of our ordinary perceptual experiences, such as those involved in seeing or hearing, are neither pleasurable nor painful, but affectively neutral. To understand the relevance of sentience to moral status, it is necessary first to consider the concept of conscious experience.

#### *Consciousness: Being a Being*

Experiences are conscious mental states or events. An entity that has experiences, however simple or primitive, is not just a thing, but a being, a centre of consciousness. If an organism has experiences then, in Tom Nagel's words, there is 'something it is like to *be* that organism—something it is like *for* the organism'.[5] When one tries to imagine what it would be like to be a stone, Nagel says, there is nothing to imagine—just a blank. But bats, for instance, are creatures

---

[5] Thomas Nagel, 'What Is It Like to Be A Bat?', *Philosophical Review*, 83, No. 4 (Oct. 1974), 436.

that have conscious experiences. It may be very difficult for us to imagine what a bat experiences as it flies about in the twilight using its 'sonar' to catch insects, or spends the day hanging upside down in a cave with many others of its kind. But if bats are conscious beings, then whether or not we can clearly imagine it, there is something that it is like to be a bat.

To say this is not to be committed to any particular metaphysical or ontological account of what conscious experiences are. Nagel argues that it is difficult (though perhaps not impossible) for a reductive materialist to give a plausible account of what experience is. But we do not need such a reductive account to be confident that experiences occur. We can agree that we have conscious experiences, such as experiences of pain, without agreeing about whether these experiences are best understood as purely physical processes within our central nervous systems, or as emergent phenomena that cannot fully be explained in terms of physical and biochemical events.

Not all philosophers agree that experiences are real events, physical or otherwise. Eliminative materialists argue that conscious experiences are elements of a discredited dualistic worldview, and that talk about experiences eventually will be replaced by more veridical ways of describing the world.[6] Logical behaviourists have claimed that statements about an organism's conscious experiences can be logically reduced to statements about the organism's behaviour and behavioural dispositions.[7] To respond in depth to these sceptical views would take us too far afield. Nevertheless, a few comments are in order.

Cognitive scientists disagree vigorously about the scientific legitimacy of the 'folk psychology' that underlies our ordinary concept of experience, as well as such concepts as thought, belief, and intention. Some maintain that if experiences and other mental phenomena cannot be identified with specific neurophysiological states and events, then we must grant them no ontological status—that is, we must regard them as unreal.[8] Others argue that the practical explanatory

---

[6] See Richard Rorty, 'Mind–Body Identity, Privacy, and Categories', in John O'Connor (ed.), *Modern Materialism: Readings on Mind–Body Identity* (New York: Harcourt, Brace, 1969), 145–74.

[7] See Rudolf Carnap, 'Psychology in Physical Language', in A. J. Ayer (ed.), *Logical Positivism* (New York: Free Press, 1969), 165–98.

[8] See Paul M. Churchland, 'Folk Psychology and the Explanation of Human Behavior', in John D. Greenwood (ed.), *The Future of Folk Psychology* (Cambridge:

value of our ordinary folk-psychological explanations of human behaviour is so great that no reductive theory is likely to replace them. In their view, our failure (thus far) fully to explain folk-psychological entities, such as pleasure and pain, in terms of purely physical states of our brains poses no credible threat to the common-sense belief that these phenomena are part of the universe.[9]

I believe that the defenders of folk psychology are right. Whatever the correct metaphysical account of conscious experience may be, it is clear enough that our talk about pains and other conscious experiences often refers to something that is real. Talking about pains is not like talking about ghosts, goblins, and demons, as Richard Rorty has suggested,[10] because pains are not hypothetical entities that might turn out not to exist. Our experiences of pain may not tell us much about what pain is, but they leave us in little doubt of its reality.

To say this is not to claim that pains are wholly private objects, which no one other than the being who experiences them can ever observe or detect. That view was effectively debunked by Ludwig Wittgenstein, who pointed out that if pain were a such a radically private phenomenon, then the term 'pain' could have no public meaning; it would not be possible for its meaning to be taught or learned, and we would have no way of knowing what people were talking about when they claimed to be in pain.[11] Observable behaviours are among the criteria by which we can know when others (and sometimes we ourselves) are in pain. Nevertheless, individual occurrences of pain are logically distinct from the externally observable behaviours by which they may be detected: a being may feel pain without displaying the usual behavioural indications, or vice versa.

Some philosophers, while not doubting that *they* have experiences, have doubted that other human beings do—or at least that there is any sound proof that they do. The well-known 'argument from analogy' provides one good reason for putting such doubts

Cambridge University Press, 1991), 51–69; and S. P. Stich, *From Folk Psychology to Cognitive Science: The Case Against Belief* (Cambridge, Mass.: MIT Press, 1983).

[9] See John D. Greenwood, 'Reasons to Believe', in Greenwoood (ed.), *The Future of Folk Psychology*, 51–69.

[10] Richard Rorty, 'Mind–Body Identity, Privacy, and Categories', 150.

[11] Ludwig Wittgenstein, *Philosophical Investigations*, trans. G. E. M. Anscombe (New York: Macmillan, 1959), 92–6.

aside. Each of us knows that the bodies, brains, and sensory organs of other human beings are very similar to our own; and this, together with their reporting of experiences similar to ours in basic ways, gives each of us excellent reason to believe that they really do have such experiences. To put the point in another way, none of us has any good reason to suppose that we are unique among all of humanity in having conscious experiences. To be justified in thinking oneself unique in this way, one would need some evidence that one's own brain is radically different from the brains of all other humans.[12]

## Consciousness vs. Sentience

We may be each confident, then, that we are conscious, and that many other human beings are conscious too. Sentience is the capacity to have, not just experiences of some sort or other, but experiences that are felt as pleasurable or painful. To be sentient is to be capable of at least some of the many forms of suffering and enjoyment—from simple feelings of pain or pleasure, to more complex emotions, moods, and passions.

Because not all conscious experiences are either pleasurable or painful, evidence of consciousness is not necessarily evidence of sentience. It seems likely, however, that most naturally evolved organisms that are capable of having conscious experiences are capable of experiencing (among other things) pain and pleasure. The capacity to feel pain and pleasure is invaluable to mobile animals that must use their perceptual abilities to find food and shelter, escape from danger, mate and rear young, and so on. The organization of experience along the pleasure/pain axis makes it possible for such creatures to learn from their mistakes, as well as from what they do right. Organisms that are incapable of locomotion generally have less need for sentience, since they cannot flee from approaching dangers, or pursue distant sources of satisfaction.[13]

---

[12] See Paul Ziff, 'The Simplicity of Other Minds', in Thomas O. Buford (ed.), *Essays on Other Minds* (Urbana, Ill.: University of Illinois Press, 1970), 197.

[13] I am not suggesting that mobility as such requires sentience. Dandelion seeds and lava flows move, but that is not evidence that they are sentient. What I am suggesting is that sentience is a normal concomitant of the type of perception-guided locomotion of which an antelope is capable, but a dandelion seed is not. Hans Jonas provides an insightful discussion of why locomotion, perception, and sentience are

But even though most organisms that are conscious are probably also sentient, consciousness is not a logically sufficient condition for sentience. One can imagine a being that has conscious experiences of many sorts, but that never experiences pleasure or pain, or any other positive or negative feeling, mood, or emotion. Such a being would be conscious, but it would not be sentient. Data, the brilliant and personable android of the television series *Star Trek: The Next Generation*, is described by himself and other characters as such a being. Although he is conscious, rational, morally responsible, and highly self-aware, his programming includes no capacity to experience pain, pleasure, or emotion. As I argue in Chapter 4, such a being would have strong moral status by virtue of its moral agency; but it could not have any moral status that is contingent upon sentience.

## Sentience as a Capacity

Sentience is the capacity to feel pleasure or pain. To say that a being is sentient is not to say that it is feeling something pleasant or painful at this very moment. The capacity to feel is an ability or power that need not be exercised continuously. Most sentient organisms are not continuously awake throughout their lives. Many have diurnal cycles of sleep and wakefulness, and some frequently hibernate for months or even years.[14] During some of these periods of time, they may have no experiences at all—not even dreams. Sentient beings can also suffer injury or illness that renders them temporarily comatose, i.e. incapable of being aroused to consciousness. None of these facts refute the claim that they are capable of sentience. So long as their nervous systems and other essential organs remain sufficiently intact to permit the eventual return of consciousness, they are still, in the relevant sense, sentient beings.

## Sentience vs. the Potential to Become Sentient

The capacity to feel must also be distinguished from the potential to develop the capacity to feel. The newly fertilized ova of species

likely to evolve together: *The Phenomenon of Life* (Chicago, Ill.: University of Chicago Press, 1966), 101–2.

[14] For instance, some desert-adapted frogs survive successive dry years by remaining buried in dried mud until rain arrives.

whose older members are sentient are not yet sentient, although they may become so later, when they develop functional sense organs and nervous systems. Some philosophers may wish to claim that the potential to develop the capacity for sentience is itself a valid criterion of moral status. However, the arguments for ascribing moral status to sentient beings that we will consider in this chapter do not apply in any straightforward way to non-sentient entities that have the potential to develop into sentient beings. (I discuss that case in Chapter 9, in connection with the ethics of abortion.)

### 3.2. *Drawing the Sentience Line*

Normal human beings, once past some early developmental stage, are sentient; but what about other animals? Descartes held that all non-human animals are automata, incapable of either thought or sensation. His primary argument for this is that animals do not use language, and that only language users can think or feel. He also argues that if animals could think or feel, then they would have immortal souls, which they do not.[15]

Peter Carruthers defends a contemporary version of Descartes's first argument. Carruthers believes that animals have experiences, but he holds that they are never *conscious* of their experiences. He suggests that 'what constitutes . . . [a] feeling as a conscious rather than a non-conscious state, is that it is available to be consciously thought about'.[16] In his view, beings that cannot use language cannot consciously think about their experiences, and therefore cannot be conscious of them. Human beings, he says, sometimes have experiences of which they are not conscious. For instance, while driving a car one may become so engrossed in thought that one ceases to be conscious of the road, and the act of driving; or, while experiencing a headache, one may be distracted, and cease to be aware of

---

[15] René Descartes, 'Animals Are Machines', in Tom Regan and Peter Singer (eds.), *Animal Rights and Human Obligations* (Englewood Cliffs, NJ: Prentice-Hall, 1976), 60–6. For a cogent rebuttal of these Cartesian arguments, see Denise and Michael Radner, *Animal Consciousness* (Buffalo, NY: Prometheus Books, 1989), 37–58.

[16] Peter Carruthers, *The Animals Issue: Moral Theory in Practice* (Cambridge: Cambridge University Press, 1992), 181.

the pain.[17] Animals, in his view, are always unconscious of their experiences; they never *feel* anything painful when they are in pain. If Carruthers is right, then Nagel is wrong to say that there is something which it is like to be a bat; bats are as incapable of having conscious experiences as stones.

The claim that thought and sensation require the possession of a human-style language will be considered in Chapter 4. For now, I want only to note the empirical implausibility of the claim that animals do not feel their pains. As Joseph Lynch points out, it is difficult to understand how the capacity to experience pain could have survival value for animals, if animals never felt their pains.[18] How could an animal react appropriately to pain, or learn to avoid pain-causing situations, if pain never impinged upon its consciousness? 'The process of conditioning is utterly mysterious unless it is presupposed that stimuli can be *felt*.'[19] Lynch points out that the cases which Carruthers cites as examples of non-conscious experience in humans are not persuasive evidence that all non-human experience may be non-conscious. These examples seem better described not as instances of wholly non-conscious experience, but rather as instances in which one is only dimly or peripherally conscious of some experiences, because one's attention is focused elsewhere. If a driver were *entirely* unconscious of the road, driving would be impossible; and if a headache were never felt at all, it would not be a headache.[20]

Language is one way of expressing feelings; but feelings can also be expressed through a variety of non-linguistic behaviours. As Darwin pointed out, the expressive behaviours of many animals are very similar to our own. These similarities, together with the similarities between their sense organs and nervous systems and ours, and the phylogenetic proximity of many animal species to our own, make it extremely unlikely that all non-human animals are non-sentient. In James Rachels's words,

The reason Descartes's view of animals is not possible today—the reason his view seems so *obviously* wrong to us—is that between him and us came Darwin. . . . Darwin stressed that, in an important sense, their nervous sys-

[17] *The Animals Issue*, 170.
[18] Joseph J. Lynch, 'Is Animal Pain Conscious?', *Between the Species*, 10, Nos. 2 and 3 (Winter–Spring 1994), 4.
[19] Ibid.                                                                    [20] Ibid. 5.

tems, their behaviours, their cries, *are* our nervous systems, our behaviours, and our cries, with only a little modification. They are our common property because we inherited them from the same ancestors. Not knowing this, Descartes was free to postulate far greater differences between humans and non-humans than is possible for us.[21]

## Mistakes about Simplicity and Subjectivity

Those who claim that non-human animals cannot feel pleasure and pain sometimes claim that this is a simpler hypothesis than its contrary, one that employs Occam's Razor to eliminate the unnecessary postulation of extra entities or events. But, as Donald Griffin points out, explanations of animal behaviour that avoid reference to animal experience are not necessarily more parsimonious. On the contrary, it is often impossible to say anything illuminating about what an animal is doing, without presupposing that it has conscious experiences. Griffin cites as an example the behaviour of some species of plovers, which appear deliberately to lead predators away from their nests by pretending to have a broken wing. He says:

it is often taken for granted that purely mechanical, reflex-like behaviour would be a more parsimonious explanation than even crude subjective feelings or conscious thoughts. But to account for predator-distraction by plovers, we must dream up complex tortuous chains of mechanical reflexes. Simple thoughts could guide a great deal of appropriate behaviour without nearly such complex mental gymnastics on the part of the ethologist or the animal.[22]

Simplicity is not the only perceived advantage of the claim that animals cannot have conscious experiences. This denial is often assumed to be more objective, more scientifically hard-headed, than the common-sense view that many animals do have feelings. Mary Midgley suggests that one reason for this assumption is

a fairly simple confusion about the status of subjectivity itself, an impression that to study subjective phenomena is the same thing as 'being subjective'—that is, being tossed about by one's own moods and feelings. This seems to be the same mistake as supposing that the study of folly must be a

---

[21] James Rachels, *Created from Animals: The Moral Implications of Darwinism* (New York: Oxford University Press, 1991), 131.

[22] Donald R. Griffin, *Animal Thinking* (Cambridge, Mass.: Harvard University Press, 1984), 94.

foolish study, or the study of evil conduct an evil one, or in general (as Dr. Johnson put it) that 'who drives fat oxen should himself be fat'.[23]

There is a more serious worry about the study of animal consciousness than the spurious fear of subjectivity. The difficulty of knowing, or even imagining, exactly what other animals experience—especially those whose sense organs and modes of life are very different from ours—must often deter a careful observer from speculating at any length about those experiences. But this pragmatic difficulty lends no credence to the conclusion that no non-human animal has conscious experiences. Given our own limitations as observers, it should not surprise us that the experiences of animals are often very difficult for us to comprehend.

## The Distribution of Sentience among Terrestrial Organisms

But how can we know which non-human organisms are sentient? (How, for that matter, can we know that stones and automobiles are not sentient?) There are at least four sorts of evidence that can lend support to the claim that a particular entity is capable of feeling pleasure or pain. First, we may ask whether it has a nervous system. If it does, we may inquire into the structural and functional similarities between its nervous system and our own. Second, we may observe its behaviour when it is injured or exposed to noxious stimuli. Does it cry, howl, weep, wince, writhe, convulse, shriek, whine, moan, or try vigorously to escape? A third type of evidence for sentience is the presence of sense organs and/or behaviour indicative of perceptual ability. For, although sensory perception is not a logically sufficient condition for sentience, it is apt to be accompanied by it.[24] A fourth form of evidence, and one that will probably become increasingly important to the study of non-human consciousness, is the presence of neurochemicals that in humans are related to the experiencing of pleasure, pain, or emotion.

None of these forms of evidence is individually sufficient to establish with certainty that an animal is conscious; indeed, all of them together are insufficient for absolute certainty. However, it is

[23] Mary Midgley, 'Are You an Animal?', in Gill Langley (ed.), *Animal Experimentation: The Consensus Changes* (New York: Chapman & Hall, 1989), 11.
[24] See Jonas, *The Phenomenon of Life*, 101–2.

just as difficult to obtain such absolute certainty in the case of other human beings as in the case of animals. In either case, the more of the usual indications of sentience are present, the more confident we may be about the attribution of sentience.

For readers who wish to investigate in greater depth the scientific evidence for the sentience of particular types of animals, there are several excellent studies. Among the most noteworthy are Donald R. Griffin's *The Question of Animal Awareness: Evolutionary Continuity of Animal Experience*; Denise and Michael Radner's *Animal Consciousness*; Rosemary Rodd's *Biology, Ethics and Animals*; and Bernard E. Rollin's *The Unheeded Cry: Animal Consciousness and Animal Pain*. What follows is an overview of some of that evidence.

The evidence for the sentience of mammals and birds is particularly compelling. These 'higher' vertebrate animals have sense organs and nervous systems that are very similar to our own; and many of their expressive behaviours are also very similar to ours. With respect to these animals, the argument from analogy is scarcely less compelling than it is with respect to other human beings. True, animals cannot report their experiences in any conventional language (or any that is comprehensible to us); but this fact no more refutes the claim that they are sentient than the fact that human infants do not speak refutes the claim that they are sentient. Given the strength of the behavioural and physiological similarities between human beings and these other vertebrate animals, the most plausible hypothesis is that these animals can experience pleasure and pain.

Because the neurophysiology and behaviour of fish, reptiles, and amphibians are somewhat less similar to our own than are those of mammals or birds, we cannot be quite as confident of the sentience of these 'lower' vertebrates. Nevertheless, the similarities between their behaviour and neurophysiology and our own are sufficient to place the burden of proof upon those who deny that these animals are sentient.

It is more difficult to be certain about the sentience of complex invertebrate animals. The neurophysiology and behaviour of, for instance, cephalopods (squids, cuttlefish, and octopuses) and arthropods (insects, crustaceans, millipedes, centipedes, mites, and spiders) are so different from ours that many people find it impossible to believe that these animals are sentient. Our natural ability to interpret the behaviour of humans and human-like animals in terms of their conscious psychological states does not extend easily to animals that are so radically unlike us. Yet many of these animals are highly mobile, and possessed of sophisticated sense organs and nervous systems; moreover, their behaviour when injured is often strongly suggestive of pain. Thus, I think it reasonable to conclude that many of these complex invertebrate animals are sentient.

What about less complex multicellular animals, such as worms? Darwin spent several years studying earthworms, which he regarded as sentient, and perhaps even capable of some form of reason.[25] The idea is not absurd; earthworms are mobile animals with sense organs and nervous systems. When injured, they often behave in ways that suggest sentience. Moreover, they have been reported to produce neurochemicals similar to those that in humans are associated with the experience of pain.[26]

Nevertheless, many invertebrate animals are probably non-sentient. Peter Singer remarks that 'somewhere between a shrimp and an oyster seems as good a place to draw the line as any, and better than most'.[27] This is a plausible suggestion. Some molluscs—e.g. squid and octopuses—appear to be not only sentient, but surprisingly intelligent. But oysters (at least as adults)[28] are sedentary creatures with very simple nervous systems, and behavioural repertoires that do not seem to demand sentience. (For instance, an oyster's capacity to close its shell in response to vibrations in the water could be a reflex that requires no conscious mediation.)

What about mobile unicellular animals, such as paramecia and amoebas? These organisms are generally assumed to be non-sentient, because they lack nervous systems—or nervous systems that we can recognize as such. Yet the eminent microbiologist H. S. Jennings wrote that, after an extensive study of amoebas, he was convinced

[25] Charles Darwin, *The Formation of Vegetable Mould, Through the Action of Worms* (London: John Murray, 1881), 2–3; cited in Rachels, *Created from Animals*, 134–6.

[26] Rollin reports that in 1979 four Swedish researchers found B-endorphins and encephalins in earthworms. These are chemicals that are similar in their structure and narcotic properties to opium, and that in humans may serve to moderate severe pain. Bernard E. Rollin, *Animal Rights and Human Morality* (Buffalo, NY: Prometheus Books), 31.

[27] Singer, *Animal Liberation*, 179.

[28] Like many bivalves, oysters begin their lives as free-swimming larvae, which appear to have greater capacities for perception and sentience than do the much more sedentary adults.

that if the amoeba were a large animal, so as to come within the everyday experience of human beings, its behavior would at once call forth the attribution to it of states of pleasure and pain, of hunger and desire, and the like, precisely on the same basis as we attribute these things to the dog.[29]

Some biologists believe that no one-celled organism can be sentient. Rosemary Rodd says that 'the association of many cells to form multicellular bodies . . . [is] essential for the possibility of sentience'.[30] Rodd may well be right. Nevertheless, the apparent perceptual abilities of some unicellular organisms suggest that we should at least consider the hypothesis that they possess some form of sentience.

In contrast, plants, bacteria, and viruses are almost certainly non-sentient. Popularly reported experiments which supposedly demonstrated the sentience—and even telepathic talent—of plants have not been persuasively replicated.[31] As far as we can tell, these organisms have neither sense organs nor nervous systems; and their behaviour rarely seems indicative of a capacity for pleasure or pain. Thus, while it is impossible to be absolutely certain that these organisms are not sentient, it is a good bet that they are not. This argument applies even more strongly to most inorganic objects, which exhibit neither physiology nor behaviour that is strongly indicative of sentience.

This completes our survey of the probable distribution of sentience amongst terrestrial organisms. We turn now to the moral significance of sentience. What difference, if any, does an organism's sentience make to its moral status?

## 3.3. *Peter Singer's Defence of the Sentience Only View*

Peter Singer is a moral theorist whose work has done much to reinvigorate the animal liberation movement. His criticisms of in-

---

[29] H. S. Jennings, *Behavior of Lower Organisms* (New York: Columbia University Press, 1906), 336; cited by Charles Birch and John B. Cobb, Jr., *The Liberation of Life* (Denton, Tex.: Environmental Ethics Books, 1990), 125.

[30] Rosemary Rodd, *Biology, Ethics, and Animals* (Oxford: Oxford University Press, 1990), 22.

[31] For instance, P. Tompkins and C. Bird, in *The Secret Life of Plants* (New York: Harper & Row, 1973), claim to demonstrate the sentience of plants. Their results have not been replicated by other researchers, despite many attempts.

humane practices in the production of meat have persuaded many people throughout the world to adopt a vegetarian or vegan diet;[32] and his descriptions of scientific experiments which inflict suffering and death upon sentient animals without evident necessity have inspired a renewed opposition to vivisection. Although Singer's 1975 book, *Animal Liberation*, is better known, his utilitarian theory of moral status is presented in greater depth in his 1979 book, *Practical Ethics*.[33]

Singer describes himself as a preference utilitarian. Preference utilitarianism is a modification of the classical utilitarian theory of Jeremy Bentham, Henry Sidgwick, and John Stuart Mill. Utilitarianism is a consequentialist moral theory, i.e. one that evaluates actions as morally right or wrong on the basis of their causal consequences. Utilitarians hold that we should always strive to act so as to maximize utility, or that which is intrinsically good. Classical utilitarians define utility as *happiness*, which in turn is defined as pleasure, and the absence of pain or suffering.[34] (For this reason, classical utilitarianism is sometimes called 'hedonistic' utilitarianism.) For the classical utilitarian, the fundamental moral principle is that 'actions are right in proportion as they tend to promote happiness, wrong as they tend to promote the reverse of happiness'.[35]

This classical utilitarian definition of utility is subject to the objection that pleasure and freedom from pain are not the only things that people value. Some people choose to spend time in ways that are evidently less pleasurable than some of the alternatives, but that they consider more worthwhile. John Stuart Mill sought to meet this objection by distinguishing between 'lower' pleasures (those of bodily sensation) and 'higher' pleasures (those of intellect and imagination), and arguing that persons who have experienced both types of pleasure will always prefer the higher type.[36] Unhappily for this argument, not all experienced persons prefer the 'higher' pleasures.

---

[32] A strict vegetarian diet does not include meat, but may include eggs or dairy products; a less strict vegetarian diet may exclude red meat but include fish, shellfish, or poultry. A vegan diet includes no meat, milk, cheese, or eggs; strict vegans also avoid using leather, or drugs or cosmetics that were tested on animals.

[33] Singer, *Animal Liberation: A New Ethic for the Treatment of Animals* (New York: Avon Books, 1975); *Practical Ethics* (Cambridge: Cambridge University Press, 1979).

[34] Mill, *Utilitarianism*, 18.      [35] Ibid.      [36] Ibid. 18–21.

Some prefer eating, drinking, and making love to sophisticated intellectual or creative endeavours, and it is tendentious to insist that these people are never as happy as those who have the opposite preference.

Preference utilitarians respond to this objection by defining happiness as the satisfaction of preferences. This amendment permits the good of individuals to be determined by their own values, rather than by an impersonal evaluation of the quantity and quality of their pleasures and pains. (Problems continue to arise, however, from the fact that some individuals may have preferences which are vicious, or which cannot be satisfied without violating the rights of other persons; these problems are considered in Section 3.5.)

Some utilitarians deny that we are obliged to include the happiness of animals in our calculations of utility.[37] In contrast, Jeremy Bentham and Henry Sidgwick maintained that the pleasures and pains of animals must be included in our moral calculations. In a frequently cited footnote, Bentham says that 'the question is not, Can they *reason*: nor, Can they *talk*? but, Can they *suffer*?'[38] Sidgwick makes the point as follows: 'It is . . . "happiness" or "pleasure", at which a Utilitarian considers it his duty to aim: and it seems arbitrary and unreasonable to exclude from the end, so conceived, any pleasure of any sentient being.'[39]

Singer's theory of moral status is inspired by that of Bentham and Sidgwick. In Singer's view, all valid moral claims can be derived from a single principle: the principle of equal consideration of interests. This principle requires that the comparable interests of all sentient beings be given equal weight in our moral deliberations.[40] In Singer's words,

The principle of equal consideration of interests acts like a pair of scales, weighing interests impartially. True scales favour the side where the interest is stronger or where several interests combine to outweigh a smaller number of similar interests; but they take no account of whose interests they are weighing.[41]

---

[37] See Jan Narveson, *Morality and Utility* (Baltimore, Md.: Johns Hopkins Press, 1967), 86. Narveson is no longer a utilitarian, but still holds that animals do not have moral status; see *Moral Matters* (Peterborough, Ont.: Broadview Press, 1993), 137.

[38] Jeremy Bentham, *An Introduction to the Principles of Morals and Legislation*, ed. J. H. Burns and H. L. A. Hart (London: University of London Press, 1970), 283.

[39] Henry Sidgwick, *The Methods of Ethics* (New York: Dover, 1966), 414.

[40] *Practical Ethics*, 19.        [41] Ibid.

Giving equal consideration to the comparable interests of all sentient beings does not mean treating them exactly alike, since animals of different species often have different needs and interests. For instance, normal adult human beings can benefit from the right to vote in political elections, but animals of other species cannot. Animals do, however, benefit from pleasure and freedom from pain. The principle of equal consideration means that the moral weight of a being's pains and pleasures does not depend upon its species: 'How bad a pain is depends on how intense it is and how long it lasts, but pains of the same intensity and duration are equally bad, whether felt by humans or animals.'[42]

## Sentience, Interests, and Moral Status

Singer argues that all and only sentient beings have moral status, because all and only sentient beings have interests. The principle of equal consideration applies only to the interests of sentient beings, for the simple reason that these are all of the interests that there are. The capacity to experience suffering and enjoyment is, he says,

*a prerequisite for having interests at all*, a condition that must be satisfied before we can speak of interests in a meaningful way . . . If a being suffers there can be no moral justification for refusing to take that suffering into consideration. . . . If a being is not capable of suffering, or of experiencing enjoyment or happiness, there is nothing to be taken into account.[43]

The term 'interest' is highly ambiguous. When we say that someone has an interest in something, we may mean that they *take* an interest in it, i.e. that they consciously desire and pursue it. Alternatively, we may mean that, whether or not they take an interest in it, having it would be *in their interest*, i.e. beneficial to them.[44] As a result of this ambiguity, there has been much philosophical debate about the sorts of entities that can really have interests. At the one extreme, R. G. Frey argues that only human beings have interests.[45]

---

[42] *Animal Liberation*, 18.　　　　　　　　　　　　　　　　[43] Ibid. 8–9.

[44] Meredith Wilson discusses the distinction between taking an interest and having an interest, in 'Rights, Interests, and Moral Equality', *Environmental Ethics*, 2, No. 2 (Summer 1980), 152–3; also see S. F. Sapontzis, *Morals, Reason, and Animals* (Philadelphia, Pa.: Temple University Press, 1987), 161–3.

[45] Frey argues that having interests requires beliefs and desires, and that beliefs and desires require the capacity to use language, which no non-human animal has:

At the opposite extreme, some environmental ethicists argue that all living things (and possibly some that are not living) have interests, because they are teleological systems which have a good of their own.[46]

What, then, is meant by the claim that all and only sentient beings have interests? Bernard Rollin explains as follows:

any animal, even man, is not explicitly conscious of all or probably even most of its needs. But what makes these needs interests is our ability to impute some 'mental life', however rudimentary, to the animal, wherein . . . it seems to care when certain needs are not fulfilled. Few of us humans can consciously articulate all of our needs, but we can certainly [sometimes] know when these needs are thwarted and met. Pain and pleasure are . . . the obvious ways these facts come to consciousness, but they are not the only ones. Frustration, anxiety, malaise, listlessness, boredom, [and] anger are among the multitude of indicators of unmet needs, needs that become interests in virtue of these states of consciousness.[47]

This is essentially the point that Singer is making when he says that only sentient beings can have interests. Sentient beings are, by definition, the only entities that can experience either suffering or enjoyment. Non-sentient organisms may have needs, and thus a good of their own, but this is not an experiential good; they experience nothing unpleasant when their needs are thwarted, nothing enjoyable when their needs are met. Consequently, they cannot 'mind' what happens to them, in the ways that sentient beings can.

## Why Speciesism is a Sin

Singer argues that the moral equality of all sentient beings follows from the general principle that 'ethical judgments must be made from a universal point of view'.[48] This does not mean that ethical judgements must be based upon exceptionless rules, e.g. that no one

R. G. Frey, *Interests and Rights: The Case Against Animals* (Oxford: Oxford University Press, 1980).

[46] See, for instance, Taylor, *Respect for Nature*, 63; John Rodman, 'The Liberation of Nature?', *Inquiry*, 20 (1977), 83–145; and Holmes Rolston III, *Environmental Ethics: Duties to and Value in the Natural World* (Philadelphia, Pa.: Temple University Press, 1988), 98–101.

[47] *Animal Rights and Human Morality*, 40–1.

[48] *Practical Ethics*, 12.

should ever tell a lie. It means, rather, something similar to the Golden Rule, which 'tells us to go beyond our personal interests and "do unto others as we would have them do unto us."'[49] For the preference utilitarian, the need to make moral judgements from a universal point of view implies that 'my own interests cannot, simply because they are *my* interests, count more than the interests of anyone else'.[50] Just as one's own interests cannot count more than those of other individuals, neither can the interests of one's own racial, ethnic, religious, or gender group count more than those of other groups of human beings. Those who ignore the interests of persons of races other than their own are racists; those who ignore the interests of (usually) women and girls are sexists; and those who ignore the interests of sentient non-human beings are guilty of speciesism.[51]

Most people who believe that sexism and racism are unjust forms of discrimination also believe that there are morally significant differences between human beings and other animals that justify treating human interests as more important. But Singer argues that, once we understand the philosophical basis of the principle that all human beings are morally equal, we will understand that the principle of equal consideration must apply to all sentient beings—not just to those that are human. He points out that the claim that human beings are morally equal does not presuppose that human beings are equal in intelligence, strength, moral virtue, or any other empirical characteristic. It is a claim about how human beings are to be treated, not about what they are like. Similarly, 'the fact that other animals are less intelligent than we does not mean that their interests may be disregarded'.[52] If it did, then we would be equally entitled to disregard the interests of less intelligent humans, such as infants and those who are mentally impaired:

If we use these characteristics to place a gulf between humans and other animals, we place these unfortunate humans on the other side of the gulf; and if the gulf is taken to mark a difference in moral status then these humans would have the moral status of animals rather than humans.[53]

---

[49] *Practical Ethics*, 10.                                                    [50] Ibid. 12.
[51] The term 'speciesism' was coined by Richard Ryder.
[52] *Practical Ethics*, 49.
[53] Ibid. 65.

## Sentience and the Value of Life

Singer's view is that, although sentient animals are entitled to equal consideration of their comparable interests, we need not always place an equal moral value upon their lives. He says that the lives of persons—sentient beings that are self-aware and capable of reason—are more valuable to them than are the lives of beings that are not persons. This is because only persons can conceptualize their own futures and consciously desire to go on living. While the great apes and some other non-human animals may be persons,[54] mice and other small-brained animals probably are not. Thus, it would not be speciesist to judge 'that the life of a normal adult member of our species is more valuable than the life of a normal adult mouse'.[55]

This does not mean that killing a mouse is never morally wrong; if it reduces the total amount of happiness in the universe, then it is to that extent morally undesirable. However, killing a person is inherently worse than killing a mouse, because it not only risks reducing the total amount of happiness in the universe, but also guarantees the frustration of whatever preferences the person may have had regarding their own future. As we shall see, Singer's defence of the Sentience Only view depends upon the questionable soundness of this argument.

## Practical Implications

From the principle of equal consideration, Singer concludes that most human beings ought to be vegetarians. The majority of people who eat meat can obtain nutritionally adequate substitutes; thus, he says, the preference for a non-vegetarian diet is largely a matter of taste. Liking the taste of meat does not constitute an interest strong enough to override the interests of animals in avoiding pain and suffering. While it may be morally permissible on Singer's theory to eat animals that have had reasonably good lives and have then been killed humanely, it is difficult for most people to obtain meat produced without the infliction of substantial pain and suffering.

---

[54] Singer says that the great apes are the best non-human candidates for personhood, but that cetaceans, cats, dogs, and pigs may also be persons: *Practical Ethics*, 98.      [55] Ibid. 89.

(Farmed or wild-caught fish might suffer little, but there are serious questions about the ecological impacts of large-scale fishing and fish farming.) Most of the meat that is available to consumers in industrialized nations comes from animals that have been reared, transported, and slaughtered under conditions that are likely to cause them considerable suffering. Chickens reared in tiny crowded cages, and veal calves confined throughout their lives to stalls too small to turn around in, are among the most dramatic examples.

A second moral argument that Singer gives for vegetarianism is that it is wasteful to grow grain and other plant crops to feed to animals which will then be consumed by humans. In his view, more people could be better fed if most people were vegetarians, and plant crops were grown primarily for human consumption. This argument does not preclude eating animals that have been grazed on land that is unsuitable for cultivation, or fed only products unfit for human consumption. However, most of the poultry, pigs, and cattle produced for the modern market are fed some grain. (I shall return to this argument in Chapter 10.)

Unlike the more radical proponents of animal rights, Singer does not maintain that it is *always* wrong for human beings to kill and eat animals. It is consistent with his approach to argue that persons who need meat or other animal products for their own survival have an interest in those products that is strong enough to outweigh the value of the lives of animals that are not persons. For example, human beings whose subsistence unavoidably depends upon hunting animals are probably not morally culpable on Singer's theory— provided, of course, that the methods they use do not cause needless pain or suffering.

Singer's condemnation of the use of animals in biomedical research is somewhat more sweeping. He says, 'If the experimenter would not be prepared to use a human infant then his readiness to use non-human animals reveals an unjustifiable form of discrimination on the basis of species . . .'[56] Unless attitudes towards infants undergo drastic change, such a test will preclude virtually all research on animals, apart from that which can do them no harm. Yet Singer does not think that absolutely all painful or lethal research should be banned—even with respect to unconsenting human sub-

---

[56] *Animal Liberation*, 75.

jects. 'If it really were possible', he says, 'to save many lives by an experiment that would take just one life, and there were *no other way* those lives could be saved, it might be right to do the experiment.'[57]

### 3.4. *Objections to the Sentience Only View*

The conclusions that Singer draws from the principle of equal consideration entail that many of us should change our daily behaviour, especially our diets. Yet these conclusions are more consistent with practical necessity than are some of the implications of the Life Only view. While no one can exist without causing the deaths of many living things, most people could lead satisfactory lives without consuming animal products that are produced in inhumane ways.[58] Some people gain important medical benefits from the continued use of animals in biomedical research; but equivalent expenditures on education, housing, and other social needs might produce as great an overall improvement in human welfare, with less non-human suffering.

Unfortunately, the Sentience Only view has implications which are more troubling than the ones that Singer emphasizes. There are four potentially fatal objections to the principle of equal consideration. Three of these—the environmentalist, Humean/feminist, and human rights objections—spotlight problematic consequences of the view that sentience is the only valid criterion of moral status. The fourth objection involves some implications of the principle of equal consideration which I argue are impossible to reconcile with the demands of practical necessity.

### *The Environmentalist Objection*

Many environmental ethicists reject the Sentience Only view because it denies moral status to plants, species, and other non-sentient elements of the biosphere.[59] On the Sentience Only view, we may have

---

[57] Ibid. 78.

[58] There are, however, questions about the nutritional adequacy of a vegan diet for pregnant and nursing women, and young children. See Kathryn Paxton George, 'Should Feminists be Vegetarians?', *Signs: Journal of Women in Culture and Society*, 19, No. 2 (Winter 1994), 405–34.

[59] For instance, Rolston, *Environmental Ethics* (Philadelphia, Pa.: Temple

morally sound reasons to protect these things, but these reasons can only be based upon the interests of sentient beings, since non-sentient entities have no interests that can enter directly into our moral calculations. Species, Singer says, 'are not conscious entities and so do not have interests above and beyond the interests of the individual animals that are members of the species'.[60] We have, therefore, no moral obligations to species as such.

In contrast, deep ecologists argue that natural plant and animal species, populations, and habitats can all have moral status. Aldo Leopold, the intellectual founder of the contemporary environmentalist movement, called for an ethic in which human beings are seen as members of the biological community, having moral obligations to the community's other members.[61] Within such an ethic, an organism's moral status is based upon its ecosystemic relationships to the rest of the biosphere. Leopold would probably have agreed, for instance, that it is more important to protect the remaining stands of bishop pines on the California coast than the wild radishes that grow by the roadsides there. For the pines are an important and vulnerable part of the indigenous plant community; while the radishes are hardy European imports which are in no danger of disappearing.[62]

On the Sentience Only view, such considerations are irrelevant to moral status. Trees—however vital to the ecosystem—have no more moral status than wild radishes. To many environmentalists, a theory which allows us to have moral obligations *regarding* the non-sentient elements of the natural world but never *to* them, seems just as inadequate as the Kantian theory, which allows us to have duties regarding animals, but never to them. John Rodman recounts that he first perceived a particular piece of California coastal chaparral 'in terms of sagebrush, scrub oak, and cactus', and only later learned that it was also home to dusky-footed woodrats. 'On reflection,' he

---

University Press, 1988), 94, 146; and J. Baird Callicott, 'On the Intrinsic Value of Nonhuman Species', in Bryan G. Norton (ed.), *The Preservation of Species* (Princeton, NJ: Princeton University Press, 1988), 280–4.

[60] Peter Singer, 'Not for Humans Only: The Place of Nonhumans in Environmental Ethics', in K. E. Goodpaster and K. M. Sayre (eds.), *Ethics and the Problems of the 21st Century* (Notre Dame, Ind.: University of Notre Dame Press, 1979), 203.

[61] Aldo Leopold, *A Sand County Almanac* (New York: Ballantine Books, 1970).

[62] The pine is *Pinus muricata*, the radish, *Raphanus sativus*.

says, 'I find it as odd to think that the plants have value only for the happiness of the dusky-footed woodrats as to think that the dusky-footed woodrats have value only for the happiness of humans.'[63]

J. Baird Callicott argues that, for beings like us, an ethic that ascribes moral status to all of the vulnerable components of the natural world is more rational than one that bids our moral concern to stop at the boundaries of sentience.[64] We are part of a complex and easily damaged community of life, and wholly dependent upon this community for our survival; thus, it behoves us to recognize moral obligations to the community's other members—even those that are not sentient.

Edward O. Wilson argues that human beings have an innate and biologically based 'biophilia', i.e. a natural drive to seek connection with diverse life forms, both plant and animal.[65] Of course, circumstances and cultural influences can limit the extent to which this biophilic urge finds expression. But if humans are naturally biophilic, then ideologies that deny moral status to other living things may be inimical to human well-being. Stephen R. Kellert says:

The biophilia hypothesis suggests that the widest valuational affiliation with life and lifelike processes (ecological functions and structures, for example) has conferred distinctive advantages in the human evolutionary struggle to adapt, persist, and thrive as individuals and as a species. Conversely, this notion intimates that the degradation of this human dependence on nature brings the increased likelihood of a deprived and diminished existence, . . . not just materially, but also in a wide variety of affective, cognitive, and evaluative respects.[66]

Whether or not human beings are naturally biophilic, it is probable that peoples whose ethical and spiritual beliefs imply obligations to the land—including some of its non-sentient elements—are more likely to care for it well, over the millennia, than those who regard themselves as having moral obligations only to sentient beings. The aboriginal people of Australia have won their subsistence from

---

[63] Rodman, 'The Liberation of Nature?', 84.

[64] Callicott, 'On the Intrinsic Value of Nonhuman Species', 161.

[65] Edward O. Wilson, *The Diversity of Life* (Cambridge, Mass.: Harvard University Press, 1992), 350; and 'Biophilia and the Conservation Ethic', in Stephen R. Kellert and Edward O. Wilson (eds.), *The Biophilia Hypothesis* (Washington, DC: Island Press, 1993), 31.

[66] Stephen R. Kellert, 'The Biological Basis for Human Values of Nature', in Kellert and Wilson (eds.), *The Biophilia Hypothesis*, 42–3.

the arid continent for perhaps sixty thousand years, while destroying little of its biological richness and diversity. This impressive
record may be partially explained by the biophilic elements of their
spiritual traditions.[67] Many North American Indian cultures also
possess a view of nature 'that in its practical consequences . . . is on
the whole more productive of a co-operative symbiosis of people
with their environment than is the view of nature predominant in
the Western European tradition'.[68] Within many Native American
world views, plants and other non-sentient entities can sometimes
have moral status.

A land ethic cannot guarantee that natural species and ecosystems will never be endangered by human overexploitation. It cannot, for instance, prevent one's ancestral lands from being seized by
strangers who are less biophilic. But people whose cultural traditions imply moral obligations to the land are more likely to identify
and correct ecological problems resulting from their own activities.
This is an important pragmatic reason for adopting a theory that
permits the extension of moral status not only to sentient beings,
but to other living things as well—and perhaps to some things that
are not themselves alive, such as plant or animal species.

## The Humean/Feminist Objection

Deep ecologists ascribe moral status to individual organisms and
species on the basis of their roles within the biological community.
Feminist ethicists have also argued for the relevance of relationships
to moral status; however, they have usually emphasized social and
emotional relationships rather than ecological ones.[69] Whereas
Singer makes a point of not basing his case for animal liberation
upon appeals to emotion,[70] these ethicists give human emotions a
central place in their moral theory.

[67] See A. W. Reed, *Aboriginal Legends: Animal Tales* (French's Forest, NSW: Reed Books, 1978).

[68] J. Baird Callicott, 'Traditional American Indian and Western European Attitudes Towards Nature: An Overview', *Environmental Ethics*, 4 (1982), 190.

[69] Ecofeminists give more attention to relationships to nature. See Greta Gaard, 'Living Interconnections with Animals and Nature', in Greta Gaard (ed.), *Ecofeminism: Women, Animals, Nature* (Philadelphia, Pa.: Temple University Press, 1993), 1–12; and other articles in this collection; also *Hypatia: Special Issue on Ecological Feminism*, 6, No. 1 (Summer 1991).

[70] Singer, *Animal Liberation*, xi; *Practical Ethics*, 66–7.

Annette Baier points to the affinities between Hume's account of human morality and 'the ethics of care' that moral psychologist Carol Gilligan regards as characteristic of women's moral reasoning.[71] Women, Gilligan maintains, are more likely than men to see their moral obligations as rooted in specific social relationships, rather than in general rules and principles. Within this ethics of care, preserving human relationships, and avoiding harm to those one cares about, take precedence over adherence to abstract principles. Gilligan does not advocate the abandonment of moral rules and principles; rather, she suggests that we give equal time to the other moral 'voice', which speaks not of principles, but of caring.

Some feminist ethicists have argued that a care-based ethics cannot be reconciled with utilitarianism, because utilitarianism requires us objectively to weigh the interests of those we care about against the interests of those we do not know or do not like. Susan Sherwin says:

if a utilitarian can produce the greatest amount of happiness by performing an action that will benefit her enemies rather than her children, she is obligated to do that. Although the individual agent would find it preferable to benefit her loved ones rather than her enemies, and although her own pain at the outcome is an element to be considered in the calculation, the theory says that what is important is the total amount of happiness that will be produced by the act. There is no assurance that this requirement will allow her to act on behalf of those she loves, rather than on behalf of those she fears or loathes.[72]

Nel Noddings also maintains that our moral obligations cannot be understood in isolation from 'our human intuitions and feelings'. In her view, 'natural caring' is the wellspring of the human moral

---

[71] Annette Baier, 'Hume, the Women's Moral Theorist?', *Moral Prejudices: Essays on Ethics* (Cambridge, Mass.: Harvard University Press, 1994), 51–94; Carol Gilligan, *In a Different Voice* (Cambridge, Mass.: Harvard University Press, 1982).

[72] Susan Sherwin, *No Longer Patient* (Philadelphia, Pa.: Temple University Press, 1992), 40. Sherwin's comment applies to act rather than rule utilitarianism. Act utilitarians hold that individual actions are to be evaluated by their consequences. Rule utilitarians hold that actions are to be evaluated by their conformity to certain moral rules, i.e. those that would produce optimum consequences if all moral agents followed them all of the time. Thus, rule utilitarians are free to argue that it is permissible for individuals to show some preference for family members, friends, etc., on the grounds that this will generally produce better consequences than a rule demanding complete impartiality. Rule utilitarianism has its own problems, e.g. of internal consistency. Singer, in any case, is not a rule utilitarian.

impulse.[73] The care of parents for their children is, she says, the clearest example of natural caring. Thus, she objects to Singer's claim that it is always wrong to do to sentient animals what we would not be willing to do to human infants. In her words, 'A philosophical position that has difficulty distinguishing between our obligations to human infants and, say, pigs is in some difficulty straight off. It violates our most deeply cherished feelings about human goodness.'[74]

The conviction that human infants have a moral status different from that of pigs is, in Noddings's view, an entirely appropriate consequence of the fact that human beings care for infants in ways they do not usually care for pigs; and that infants respond to human caring in ways that pigs usually do not. Noddings recognizes that many people care for animals, and she holds that this caring creates moral obligations. She argues, however, that active concern for the interests of animals is ethically optional, whereas concern for children is morally basic: to abandon or weaken it is to undermine the human capacity for moral response.[75]

This is a point with which Hume would probably have agreed. He says that the love of parents for their children 'produces the strongest tie the mind is capable of'.[76] He also observes that the human capacity for empathy initially develops within such close interpersonal relationships. This psychological fact does not suggest that our moral concern should extend only to beings with whom we have close social relationships. But it does suggest that it is not always irrational for human beings to show special concern for members of their social communities. Thus, it may be inappropriate to demand, as Singer does, 'that when we act we assess the moral claims of those affected by our actions independently of our feelings for them'.[77] As Lori Gruen points out,

the beings we are considering are not always just animals; they are Lassie the dog and the family's companion cat, bald eagles and bunnies, snakes and skunks. Similarly, humans are not just humans; they are friends and lovers, family and foe. The emotional force of kinship or closeness to an-

[73] Noddings, *Caring*, 79–80.                    [74] Ibid. 87.
[75] Ibid. 153–4.
[76] David Hume, *A Treatise of Human Nature*, ed. L. A. Selby-Bigge (Oxford: Oxford University Press, 1967), 362.
[77] *Practical Ethics*, 67.

other is a crucial element in . . . moral deliberations. To ignore the reality of this influence in favor of some abstraction such as absolute equality may be not only impossible, but undesirable.[78]

## The Human Rights Objection

Another objection to utilitarianism is that it provides no basis for ascribing strong moral rights to individual human beings—or, for that matter, individual animals. The charge is that utilitarianism regards individual beings as mere 'receptacles' for utility: if a greater quantity of utility can be produced by sacrificing some individuals for the benefit of others, then there is no utilitarian objection to doing this.[79] In contrast, those who believe that persons have moral rights do not believe that these rights may be overridden in order to increase the amount of happiness in the universe. The right to life, for instance, prohibits the act of murder, regardless of how many sentient beings may benefit from it.

Ronald Dworkin argues that the concept of a legal or moral right is, in this sense, non-utilitarian. Rights are traditionally understood to be moral on legal 'trumps', which generally override considerations of utility: 'If someone has a right to something, then it is wrong . . . to deny it to him even though it would be in the general interest to do so.'[80] Rights are not absolute; but they may not justly be set aside just because it is judged—even correctly—that this will produce a net increase in happiness.[81] Perhaps the most important function of moral and legal rights is to protect individuals against unjustified harms that might otherwise be inflicted upon them in the name of the social good.

Singer responds to the human rights objection by pointing to the difference between classical and preference utilitarianism. He agrees that, for a classical utilitarian, sentient beings are just receptacles for

---

[78] Lori Gruen, 'Dismantling Oppression: An Analysis of the Connection Between Women and Animals', in Gaard (ed.), *Ecofeminism*, 79.

[79] That is, no act utilitarian objection. Rule utilitarians can avoid the human rights objection by arguing that respect for basic human moral rights produces the best consequences in the long run, whatever its short-term costs. This is John Stuart Mill's view: *Utilitarianism*, 42–57.

[80] Ronald Dworkin, *Taking Rights Seriously* (Cambridge, Mass.: Harvard University Press, 1978), 269.

[81] Ibid. 191–2.

happiness. This means that any sentient being, even a person, is 're-placeable'. In other words, killing it is morally permissible, provided that its place will be taken by one or more other beings, whose existence will hold at least as much happiness as the victim's future existence would have held. But for a preference utilitarian, Singer says, persons are not replaceable in this way, because they are sufficiently self-aware that they are likely to fear death, and greatly prefer their own continued existence.[82]

Other philosophers have pointed out that this argument does not show that persons are not receptacles on the preference utilitarian theory; what it shows is that they are receptacles for both pleasure and preference satisfaction, rather than merely for pleasure.[83] Consequently, the utility of satisfying one person's preference for survival can still be overridden by the utility of satisfying the preferences of other persons—provided that these others are sufficiently numerous, and their preferences sufficiently strong. This result is incompatible with a belief in individual moral rights.

Singer doubts that this is a problem for his theory, since he doubts the usefulness of the concept of a moral right, except as a rhetorical device. Strictly speaking, he says, the only right his theory attributes to animals is the right to equal consideration of comparable interests.[84] This is also the only right this theory can consistently attribute to human beings. The principle of equal consideration protects the lives, liberty, and well-being of sentient individuals only so long as this will maximize overall utility; and that may not be long enough. As I argue in Chapter 4, there are sound reasons for upholding stronger rights for human beings than can be derived from the principle of equal consideration.

## The Comparable Interests Dilemma

Singer's principle of equal consideration requires us to weigh equally the equally strong interests of all sentient beings. Yet it does not require us to attribute to all sentient beings an equally strong in-

---

[82] *Practical Ethics*, 79–81.

[83] H. L. A. Hart makes this point in 'Death and Utility', *New York Review of Books*, 27, No. 8 (15 Nov. 1980), 30; as does Tom Regan, *The Case for Animal Rights* (Berkeley and Los Angeles: University of California Press), 209.

[84] Peter Singer, 'The Fable of the Fox and the Unliberated Animals', *Ethics*, 88, No. 2 (Jan. 1978), 122.

terest in life, pleasure, freedom from pain, or any other specific good. Moreover, it does not require us to regard each sentient being as possessing an 'interest package' with the same total value as that of any other sentient being. The preference utilitarian is free to claim that the interest packages of some sentient beings are smaller than those of others, e.g. because some sentient beings have no conscious interest in continued life; or because some are only minimally sensitive to pleasure or pain. Indeed, a preference utilitarian must assume that some sentient beings have very small interest packages. For, as we shall see, the view that all sentient beings have interest packages of equal weight leads to the conclusion that we have many moral obligations to non-human beings that we cannot possibly fulfil—at least not without making our own survival all but impossible.

This problem is particularly acute with respect to many small invertebrate animals, such as insects, spiders, and mites. I argued in Chapter 2 that many of these animals are probably sentient. In tropical and temperate climates, these animals are often extremely numerous and virtually ubiquitous. Many, such as the dust mites that colonize human habitations, are so small as to be almost invisible. Thus, it is often impossible to carry out such essential activities as cleaning one's house or cultivating food crops, without harming many such animals.

Consider, for instance, what happens when a field is ploughed, planted, and harvested. These disruptions are bound to cause death or injury to an enormous number of spiders, insects, mites, snails, slugs, worms, or other small invertebrates. This is particularly true if heavy equipment is used; but even one person pushing a wooden plough is likely to inadvertently harm many sentient invertebrates. Moreover, it is sometimes necessary deliberately to destroy insects, mites, or other small creatures that would otherwise decimate the crop.[85]

These are some of the reasons why the Jain faithful prefer not to engage in agriculture. But are they reasons why no one should? If all sentient beings have interest packages of equal value, then they are. For the number of sentient beings that a farmer deliberately or inadvertently kills is always greater than the number of humans who benefit from what the farmer grows—often by a factor of millions.

---

[85] Not necessarily through the use of chemical pesticides, of course. Encouraging natural predators is often less destructive of harmless animal life.

The replaceability argument cannot justify these killings, since there is no reason to suppose that these sentient beings will be replaced by others that will jointly enjoy at least as much happiness. On the contrary, the cultivation of land is likely to reduce the number of sentient animal inhabitants. Nor can we assume that the pleasures which humans derive from what the farmer grows are great enough to outweigh the pain caused to sentient beings that the farmer injures but does not kill. Thus, a utilitarian who held that the lives and happiness of all sentient beings have the same value as those of human beings—or even a significant fraction of that value—would be forced to condemn the practice of cultivating crops. Even gathering wild plant food would probably have to be condemned, since this practice also supports fewer human lives than it is apt to cost in invertebrate lives.

As we have seen, Singer does maintain that the lives of sentient non-persons are worth less than the lives of persons. But how much less? Without a numerical estimate of magnitude of the difference, we can have no idea how much weight to give to the lives of sentient beings that are not persons. In some passages, Singer appears to endorse a stronger claim, i.e. that only self-aware beings can have any interest at all in their own continued existence.[86] If this stronger claim is true, and if invertebrate animals are not self-aware, then we need not worry about how much their lives are worth in the utilitarian calculus, since their lives as such are worth nothing; only their pleasures and pains have moral weight. But this stronger claim is difficult to justify. Non-self-aware beings may not consciously *take* an interest in their own survival, but it does not follow that they cannot *have* such an interest. Having an interest in something does not require a conscious desire for it, but only the potential to experience some benefit from it. Thus, it seems plausible that if a spider has an interest in anything, then it has an interest in not being smashed flat—even if the process is quite painless. Because continued life is necessary for the spider's future enjoyment of whatever pleasures it has enjoyed in the past, it seems obvious that it has an interest in survival.

Dale Jamieson argues that the life of a sentient organism has value for it even if it is not self-aware. His view is that 'consciousness itself is a good, whatever its object, and whatever the pleasantness

---

[86] *Practical Ethics*, 94.

of a particular experience'.[87] Human beings, he notes, normally prefer life to death; and this is true precisely because they normally prefer consciousness to its permanent extinction. Although we can experience suffering so severe that we come to regard death as a lesser evil, we normally regard consciousness as an intrinsic good. Because consciousness is itself a good, Jamieson says, we are under a *prima facie* obligation not to kill its subjects.[88]

In response to Jamieson, it might be said that what we value is not consciousness *per se*, but existence as a thinking, self-aware being. But this is not universally true. Some people might prefer to die rather than live without the capacity for thought and self-awareness; but others might prefer that sort of life to no life at all—at least on the provision that their existence would not be excessively burdensome to others. In any case, these human preferences have little relevance to the value of a spider's life to the spider. The cases are different, in that an adult human being with no capacity for thought or self-awareness is a being that is deprived of many of the pleasures natural to its kind; but a spider that lacks these capacities is probably not similarly deprived.

If a spider is not self-aware, then the value that its life has for it is based upon the enjoyment of its natural pleasures, and perhaps of consciousness itself. It is possible that invertebrate animals are less sensitive to pleasure and pain than human beings are. If this is so, and if the difference is great enough, then perhaps we can accept the principle of equal consideration and still not worry much about harming such animals. But can we assume that spiders can feel pain or pleasure only very dimly? I think not. A capacity to experience only mild pain would have less survival value than a capacity to experience a range of pains from mild to severe. A highly mobile animal that could feel only slight discomfort would be likely to respond too slowly to incipient disasters. Similarly, an animal that could experience only slight enjoyment might be insufficiently motivated to do what it must to survive and reproduce. It is possible, therefore, that the most severe pain that a spider experiences feels about as bad as the most severe pain that a human being experiences;

---

[87] Dale Jamieson, 'Killing Persons and Other Beings', in Harlan B. Miller and William H. Williams (eds.), *Ethics and Animals* (Clifton, NJ: Humana Press, 1983), 145.

[88] Ibid.

and it is also possible that the spider's pleasures are comparable in intensity to ours.

This, of course, is pure speculation. But it is no more speculative than the view that the experiential world of invertebrate animals must lack intensity, compared to our own. Although Rosemary Rodd was probably thinking of vertebrates when she wrote the following passage, her point is also applicable to sentient invertebrates:

> If some animals are conscious, but less self-conscious than we are, this does not mean that their feelings must be less intense than ours. It is difficult for us to imagine what consciousness without awareness of ourselves watching would be like. Some idea can perhaps be gained by remembering how it feels to watch or feel with such involvement that we 'lose ourselves' in the action. We forget to think about ourselves watching. Thus the experience of animals may be more rather than less intense than ours. They have less capacity for distancing themselves.[89]

Some invertebrate animals appear to have more sophisticated minds than most people imagine. The more one studies spiders, the more one is apt to gain the impression that they are intelligent animals. They are purposeful, skilled, and alert. Moreover, they often seem to approach problems (e.g. repairing damage to their webs or tunnels) in ways that are too responsive to the demands of the particular situation to be merely mindless reflexes. It is possible that such animals have a degree of self-awareness. Some philosophers argue that self-awareness requires the use of a human-style language—a claim that will be considered in Chapter 4. If they are right, then the spider is presumably not self-aware. But if there are forms of self-awareness that do not require the use of language, then the spider's behaviour might make it about as good a candidate for self-awareness as, say, a rabbit or an opossum.

Let me summarize the argument thus far. Singer's theory of moral status faces the following dilemma. Unless the lives and happiness of beings that are not self-aware are worth little or nothing to them, giving equal consideration to their interests precludes activities essential to human health and survival. But the claim that the lives and happiness of non-self-aware beings are worth very little to them is implausible. Even if their lives are worth less to them than ours are worth to us, and even if their pleasures and pains are some-

---

[89] Rodd, *Biology, Ethics, and Animals*, 73.

what less intense, it is unlikely that the differences are sufficiently great to allow a preference utilitarian to avoid this dilemma. For instance, unless human lives and happiness are worth millions of times more than the lives and happiness of small invertebrates, the principle of equal consideration prohibits the cultivation of crops. A moral principle with such impractical consequences cannot gain general acceptance—unless, of course, those consequences go unnoticed.

One reason that the more impractical implications of the principle of equal consideration have gone largely unnoticed is that Singer is not especially interested in small invertebrate animals. His primary concern, like that of most animal welfare activists, is with the abuses that human beings inflict upon vertebrate animals. But, although some philosophers make the assumption that only vertebrate animals are sentient,[90] Singer does not. Moreover, that assumption is probably false.

It is not an accident that the Sentience Only view generates particularly implausible consequences in connection with small sentient invertebrates. These animals represent an unusually clear test case for this view. For although they are probably sentient, they lack most of the other features that are apt to lead human beings to ascribe a relatively high moral status to certain animals. Most invertebrates appear to be somewhat less intelligent and self-aware than most birds and mammals. Most are neither cute nor cuddly; and they rarely make eye contact with humans. Consequently, they tend not to arouse human sympathies in the ways that warm-blooded vertebrate animals often do. Unlike dogs and cats, they rarely become members of our social communities, or we of theirs. And, although many thousands of invertebrate species are now endangered—particularly in the vanishing rainforests—most of the invertebrate animals that human beings harm through their ordinary domestic and agricultural activities are not members of endangered species.

In short, sentience is probably the only plausible criterion of strong moral status that most common sentient invertebrate animals meet. If *their* sentience is not sufficient for full moral status, then the Sentience Only view cannot be right. And it is not sufficient, for the

---

[90] See, for instance, L. W. Sumner, *Abortion and Moral Theory* (Princeton, NJ: Princeton University Press, 1981), 143.

compelling reason that human beings cannot exist—even as peaceful gatherers of wild plant foods—without sometimes putting their own interests ahead of those of other sentient animals. On a world with no sentient animals as small, numerous, and ubiquitous as terrestrial invertebrates, it might be possible for moral agents to follow the principle of equal consideration for all sentient beings, and still earn their own subsistence. On earth, any human society which seriously sought to accord equal moral status to all sentient beings would severely endanger its own survival.

### 3.5. *The Sentience Plus View*

The Sentience Plus view avoids these objections by treating sentience as a sufficient, but not necessary, condition for having a certain sort of moral status, while denying that it is a sufficient condition for having full moral status. The particular sort of moral status for which sentience suffices is indicated by the common-sense objection to cruelty.

### *What's Wrong With Cruelty?*

Utilitarians are right to hold that pain is intrinsically bad. Sentient beings *mind* being subjected to pain. Although animals gain survival advantages from the capacity to experience pain, pain itself is harmful to them. Animals benefit from the capacity to feel pain precisely because pain is an experiential harm—one that, by calling attention to itself, sometimes enables the animal to avoid a much greater harm. Conversely, pleasure is an experiential benefit.

Because pain is intrinsically bad for the being that feels it, and pleasure intrinsically good, sentience gives a being a distinctive moral status. Moral common sense assumes that no sentient being should be killed or subjected to pain without good reason. It also presumes that cruelty to animals is a wrong against its victims. It presumes that we owe it to sentient beings either to leave them alone or to interact with them in ways that are not cruel.

Tom Regan argues that the obligation not to be cruel to animals cannot be an obligation *to* them, because cruelty is the disposition to inflict pain *either maliciously or with indifference*; and because our moral obligations towards animals involve our actions, not our mental states.[91] This argument may be valid if cruelty is defined as necessarily involving malice or indifference. However, it is possible to judge that an action or practice is cruel without presupposing such attitudes on the part of the agent. If a researcher inflicts severe pain upon laboratory animals in the mistaken belief that anaesthetizing them would invalidate the experiment, then that action may be considered cruel, even though the researcher is neither indifferent nor malicious.

The common-sense objection to cruelty does not require moral agents to treat all sentient beings as moral equals. It precludes killing sentient beings or making them suffer without good reason, but it leaves room for the possibility that what counts as a good reason depends upon the being's other properties. There is room to argue, for instance, that harming sentient human beings normally requires a stronger justification than does harming sentient invertebrates, even when the interests infringed upon appear to be comparably strong.

## Two Levels of Moral Status

One way for a utilitarian to avoid the comparable interests dilemma is to retain the objection to cruelty, while rejecting the principle of equal consideration. A utilitarian may hold, for instance, that all sentient beings are entitled to moral consideration, but that persons are entitled to substantially more consideration than are sentient beings that are not persons. Martin Benjamin proposes such a bi-level sentience-based theory of moral status. He suggests that both persons and 'simple beings' (sentient beings that are not persons) have moral status, but that 'persons, who are characterized as possessing reflexive consciousness, may have a higher status than beings having only simple consciousness'.[92] In his view, we are obliged to take the interests of simple beings into account, but not on an equal basis with those of persons:

To the extent that persons reluctantly cause pain, suffering and even death to beings possessing simple consciousness in order to meet *important needs*,

[91] *The Case for Animal Rights*, 199.
[92] Martin Benjamin, 'Ethics and Animal Consciousness', in Thomas A. Mappes and Jane S. Zembaty (eds.), *Social Ethics: Morality and Social Policy* (New York: McGraw-Hill, 1987), 483.

what they do may be justified by appeal to their higher status or greater worth. But, to the extent that persons inflict avoidable pain and suffering on such beings merely to satisfy *trivial tastes or desires*, they pervert their greater capacities.[93]

Such a bi-level theory does a better job of capturing some of the convictions shared by many animal liberationists than does preference utilitarianism. For instance, it provides a more persuasive account of what is morally objectionable about farming methods that subject animals to protracted misery, or experiments that inflict suffering upon animals in the service of trivial human interests (e.g. the development of new cosmetics): sentient beings should not be subjected to pain or suffering, except in the service of needs that are important, and that cannot otherwise be served. In contrast, preference utilitarianism permits the infliction of pain upon animals to be justified by trivial human interests, provided that there are enough humans who benefit in trivial ways. For instance, dog fights—especially if widely broadcast and enormously enjoyed by the spectators—might be justifiable on the basis of the principle of equal consideration. Such spectacles cannot so easily be justified on Benjamin's bi-level theory, since the human interests served (e.g. in profit or entertainment) could probably be as well served in other ways.

At the same time, a bi-level theory implies a more lenient moral test for the use of animals in scientific research than does the principle of equal consideration. Because most animals are not persons, the human interests served by an experiment may sometimes be important enough to justify the infliction of pain or death upon a small number of sentient animals, yet not important enough to justify doing this to unconsenting persons.

A bi-level theory which incorporates the common-sense objection to cruelty is also more consistent with the moral judgements that most people make about the treatment of invertebrate animals than is the principle of equal consideration. People who inadvertently harm spiders or insects in the course of walking about, tilling the soil, or sweeping out the kitchen are not usually regarded as cruel, because what they do serves important human needs, and because these needs often cannot be served without causing harm to

---

[93]    'Ethics and Animal Consciousness', 483.

invertebrate animals. However, when a child pulls the legs off a grasshopper in order to watch it struggle, adults are right to interfere, because this activity serves no important human interest that could not be served in other ways.

## Degrees of Moral Status

A sentience-based bi-level theory of moral status is more consistent with moral common sense than is the Sentience Only view. However, the bi-level theory has serious shortcomings. It is implausible to suppose that all sentient beings can be fitted into just two categories of moral status, one for persons and another for all the rest. The mental differences between animals of different species are very often differences in degree. There is no obvious place on the phylogenetic scale to draw a line between self-aware beings and those that are not self-aware; or between minimally sentient organisms and those that are wholly non-sentient. A sliding scale of moral status enables us to avoid the distasteful task of sorting animals into those that have first-class status, those that have second-class status, and those that have no moral status at all. It also reduces the need to determine the precise location of the sentience line, since on a sliding scale the moral status of minimally sentient beings may be only slightly different from that of non-sentient organisms.

L. W. Sumner is a utilitarian who argues for such a sliding scale of moral status. He holds that sentience is a necessary and sufficient condition for moral status; he argues, however, that both sentience and moral status come in degrees, such that the strength of a being's moral status is proportional to its degree of sentience. He says: 'The animal kingdom presents us with a hierarchy of sentience. Non-sentient beings have no moral standing; among sentient beings the more developed have greater standing than the less developed, the upper limit being occupied by the paradigm of a normal adult human being.'[94]

The hypothesis that the moral status of a being is proportional to its degree of sentience helps to explain why it is reasonable to distinguish between the moral status of (for instance) fleas, sparrows, and human beings. It enables us to say that, because a flea is not very highly sentient, harming it requires little justification; but because

[94] Sumner, *Abortion and Moral Theory*, 143–4.

sparrows are probably more highly sentient, harming them requires stronger reasons; and because human beings have a still higher form of sentience, harming them requires reasons that are still more compelling. The arguments for such distinctions will be explored in the next two chapters. However, it is an advantage of the Sentience Plus view that it does not declare all such arguments out of order.

## *Relational Criteria*

A sliding scale of moral status, based upon degrees of sentience, helps to avoid the comparable interests dilemma, and requires fewer arbitrary distinctions than does a bi-level theory. However, it is incompatible with the common-sense view that human infants and mentally disabled human beings have a stronger moral status than do most comparably sentient non-human animals. Moreover, a sliding scale based solely upon sentience does not permit us to ascribe stronger moral status to animals that belong to species that are endangered by human activities than to comparably sentient animals that are not in danger of extinction—a result that environmentalists will find unacceptable.

The Sentience Plus view permits us to use a sentience-based sliding scale, but not as the sole criterion of moral status. For instance, it permits social and ecosystemic relationships also to be taken into account in the ascription of moral status. It permits us to argue that human infants and mentally impaired human beings have a stronger moral status than many equally sentient animals, by virtue of their social relationships to other human beings. It also permits our obligations towards non-humans to depend in part upon whether theirs is an endangered species. As we shall see in Chapter 5, there are many wrong ways to take account of relationships in the ascription of moral status. However, there are also right ways to take account of relationships; according full moral status to human infants need not diminish our abhorrence of cruelty to non-human beings.

## 3.6. *Conclusions*

The Sentience Only view is somewhat more tenable than the Life Only view. It does not lead to the absurd consequence that brushing one's teeth is the moral equivalent of mass homicide. However, it has serious weaknesses. It is too narrow, in that it excludes all non-sentient organisms, as well as species and ecosystems, from direct moral consideration. Because it denies the relevance of social relationships to moral status, it conflicts with important moral convictions that most thoughtful human beings share; e.g. that we owe more to human infants than to most non-human animals that display a comparable level of sentience. Moreover, because it explicates the moral status of all sentient beings—including persons—solely in terms of the utilitarian calculus, it precludes strong moral rights for individuals. Finally, it cannot be made consistent with such practical necessities as growing food, except through the dubious claim that the lives and happiness of sentient beings that are not self-aware are worth very little to them.

Singer's utilitarian theory is not the only possible philosophical defence of the Sentience Only view. It might be possible, for instance, to develop a neo-Kantian deontology that makes sentience, rather than rationality, the basis of full moral status. But, as we shall see in the next chapter, philosophers who use deontological arguments to support animal rights tend to support rights for only some sentient beings. The reason for this is clear. Deontological theories yield a moral status for individuals that is stronger, in certain respects, than that yielded by utilitarian theories; but the utilitarian version of the Sentience Only view already accords to some animals a status that is too strong to be compatible with human practical necessities. Thus, a deontological version of the Sentience Only view would generate even more problems.

The Sentience Plus view avoids the major objections to the Sentience Only view. While it offers no account of the relevance of social or ecosystemic relationships to moral status, it erects no obstacle to the environmentalist, Humean/feminist, or other approaches to the construction of such an account. It also leaves room for an understanding of moral rights that provides sentient human beings with stronger protections than can be derived from the utilitarian principle of equal consideration.

# 4

## *Personhood and Moral Rights*

I have argued that neither life nor sentience can successfully serve as the sole criterion of moral status. Philosophers who have sought such a solitary criterion have often found a more promising candidate in personhood. Whatever else we are, we are persons; and it seems likely that this fact will prove fundamental to the justification of the strong moral status that most of us want for ourselves and those we care about.

This chapter begins with an examination of the concept of personhood. A distinction is made between (1) 'maximalist' definitions of personhood, which make moral agency—or at least the potential for it—a necessary condition for being a person; and (2) 'minimalist' definitions, which do not require moral agency, but only some capacity for thought and self-awareness.

Kant's definition of 'person' is a maximalist one; he holds that personhood consists in rational moral agency. His theory is that being a moral agent is (1) a necessary condition for any moral status; and (2) a necessary and sufficient condition for full moral status. I call this the Personhood Only view. If the conclusions drawn in Chapter 3 are correct, then the first part of this view is false; moral agency is not a necessary condition for having moral status, since we have moral obligations towards all sentient beings—including those that are not, never have been, and never will be moral agents. However, moral agency might still be a necessary and sufficient condition for *full* moral status. I argue that this claim is also false. On the Personhood Plus view, which I defend, being a moral agent is sufficient for full moral status, but it is not necessary. On this view, there may be sound reasons for extending full moral status to some sentient beings that are not moral agents.

Tom Regan defends another form of the Personhood Only view, based upon what amounts to a minimalist definition of personhood. He holds that all (and probably only) 'subjects-of-a-life' have moral status, and that all of them have the same moral status. In his view, normal mammals over a year of age are subjects-of-a-life, and thus have the same moral rights as human beings. This version of the Personhood Only view accords strong moral status to many sentient beings, but withholds all moral status from many others. Like the Sentience Only view, it denies moral status to non-sentient organisms, biological species, and the non-living elements of the natural world. I argue that, for these and other reasons, being a subject-of-a-life cannot be the only valid criterion of moral status.

### 4.1. Defining 'Personhood'

Personhood is more difficult to define than life or sentience, in part because there is a strong conceptual link between being a person and having full moral status. Thus, those who advocate equal moral status for animals of particular types often maintain that these animals are persons,[1] while their opponents maintain the opposite. Similarly, abortion opponents often claim that human embryos are persons from conception onwards, while those who believe that women have the right to choose abortion are likely to maintain that foetuses do not become persons until some later stage of development, e.g. when they become viable, or when they are born. These disputes about the boundaries of personhood arise not only because the protagonists hold different beliefs about the mental capacities of non-human animals or human foetuses, but also because they have prior and conflicting beliefs about the moral status of these entities.

### 'Person' as an Honorific Term

Such considerations have led some philosophers to conclude that the term 'person' is strictly an honorific one, indicating only that the entity in question has a special moral status. On this view, the concept of a person has important ethical content, but no descriptive content. Thus, the claim that something is a person implies that it has a strong moral status, but not that it has any empirically observable property, such as life, sentience, or rationality.

---

[1] See, for instance, Francine Patterson and Wendy Gordon, 'The Case for the Personhood of Gorillas', in Cavalieri and Singer (eds.), *The Great Ape Project*, 58–79.

Michael Tooley adopts this approach in his 1972 article 'Abortion and Infanticide'. There he says that the concept of a person is 'a purely moral concept, free of all descriptive content'. He suggests that 'the sentence, "x is a person" . . . [is] synonymous with the sentence "x has a (serious) moral right to life." '[2] But in his 1983 book of the same title, Tooley concludes that the ordinary concept of a person does have descriptive content.[3] He notes that even philosophers who deny that persons have a special moral status regard the term 'person' as meaningful, and use it to refer to much the same entities that others refer to as persons. Nevertheless, Tooley points out, 'the assignment of descriptive content to the term "person" is ordinarily guided by moral considerations'.[4] In other words, our willingness to regard a particular entity as a person often depends in part upon our prior beliefs about its moral status.

## Personhood and Genetic Humanity

Those who believe that only human beings can be persons sometimes deny that it is even logically possible for a non-human being to be a person. For instance, some animal rights advocates argue that personhood cannot be a valid criterion of moral status, because the concept of a person presupposes membership in the human species. S. F. Sapontzis argues that in ordinary usage the term 'person' necessarily denotes a being that has a human body. He says:

The behavior of a normal, adult dog is more . . . intelligent, and self-aware than that of a human infant or a human adult suffering some severe muscular, neurological, or mental disorders; yet a dog is still not considered a person . . . while these humans are. No matter how superior its behavior, a dog can never be a person . . . because it does not have a human body.[5]

I believe that the ordinary concept of a person is less closely linked to the possession of a human body than Sapontzis supposes. Children's books often depict animals as persons, who speak, wear clothes, drive cars, and live exactly like human beings. While this is

---

[2] Michael Tooley, 'Abortion and Infanticide', *Philosophy and Public Affairs*, 2 (Fall 1972), 37–56.
[3] Michael Tooley, *Abortion and Infanticide* (Oxford: Oxford University Press, 1983), 35.
[4] Ibid.
[5] S. F. Sapontzis, 'A Critique of Personhood', *Ethics*, 91 (July 1981), 608.

fantasy, it demonstrates that the existence of non-human persons is not inconceivable. Similarly, gods and goddesses are usually thought of as persons, even when their visible forms are those of animals or chimeras, or when they have no visible forms. Many people believe in ghosts, angels, or other immaterial spirits. Although they often lack either tangible or visible human bodies, spirits are typically regarded as persons; they may be thought to have individual personalities, and to be capable of holding intelligent conversations with human beings.[6]

Other evidence that the term 'person' does not necessarily apply only to human beings can be found in science fiction. A popular theme is that of an initial encounter between human beings and extraterrestrials. At first, the members of one or both species fail to recognize members of the other species as persons. Often this recognition comes about through the determined efforts of a few humans or extraterrestrials who have learned to sympathize and communicate with members of the other species.[7] To win full moral status for the 'aliens', these individuals must persuade their conspecifics that the aliens are people too. Sometimes the aliens are not extraterrestrials, but sapient machines that have been constructed by human or other beings, who initially fail to recognize the personhood of their creations.[8]

The philosophical lesson of these stories is that, just as a being need not belong to one's own sex, race, or tribe in order to be a person, neither need it be biologically human, or of terrestrial origin. It need not even be a living organism. Personhood is a psychological concept, not a biological one. It is a being's mental and behavioural capacities that make it a person, not the shape of its body, the microstructure of its chromosomes, or any other strictly physiological

[6] Kant was interested in Emanuel Swedenborg, a mystic who claimed to be in psychic communication with immaterial spirits throughout the universe. Kant eventually concluded that 'all stories about apparitions of departed souls or about influences from spirits . . . have appreciable weight only in the scale of *hope*, while in the scale of speculation they seem to consist of nothing but air'. He held, however, that the *idea* of a disembodied person is neither incoherent nor meaningless. *Dreams of a Spirit-Seer, Illustrated by Dreams of Metaphysics*, trans. Emanuel F. Goerwitz (London: Swan Sonnenschein, 1990), 86–7.

[7] See, for instance, H. Beam Piper, *Little Fuzzy* (New York: Ace, 1976), and *Fuzzy Sapiens* (New York: Ace, 1983); Janet Kagan, *Hellspark* (New York: Tom Doherty, 1988); and Anne McCaffrey, *Decision at Doona* (New York: Ballantine, 1969).

[8] For instance, Tannith Lee, *The Silver Metal Lover* (New York: Doubleday, 1991).

characteristic. It is not surprising that the terms 'human being' and 'person' are often used more or less interchangeably, since in the real world all of the persons with whom most human beings are acquainted are members of the human species. Nevertheless, the terms have different meanings. Were it to be to discovered that some of the members of our community who have long been accepted as biologically human are in fact the descendants of visiting extraterrestrials, that in itself should make no difference to our belief that they are persons.

### Personhood and Sentience

But which mental or behavioural capacities are relevant to being a person? Some capacities are obviously inessential: one need not be capable of doing higher mathematics, or playing the flute, to be a person. Other capacities are more basic to personhood. Of these, the capacity to have conscious experiences is perhaps the most fundamental. A person is necessarily a being, i.e. an entity that has conscious experiences.

Are all beings persons, or only some of them? Some philosophers maintain that any being that can experience pain or pleasure is a person.[9] But most hold that personhood requires something additional to the capacity for sentience. Moreover, while the capacity for conscious experience is necessary for personhood, the capacity for sentience may not be. A conscious being that is incapable of experiencing pleasure or pain, but that clearly demonstrates self-awareness and moral agency, probably ought to be considered a person. Conversely, mere sentience is insufficient for personhood; aphids probably possess a degree of sentience, but they appear to lack most of the other mental and behavioural capacities that are essential to personhood.

### Maximalist and Minimalist Definitions of Personhood

John Locke's well-known definition of the term 'person' presupposes that persons are conscious beings, and seeks to capture that

---

[9] One example is Leonard Nelson, who defines a person as a 'being that has interests', and argues that all sentient beings are persons: *System of Ethics*, trans. Norbert Guterman (New Haven, Conn.: Yale University Press, 1956), 99.

which is additionally necessary for being a person. 'Person', Locke says, 'stands for . . . a thinking intelligent being, that has reason and reflection, and can consider itself as itself, the same thinking thing, in different times and places.'[10] This definition is species-neutral; it leaves room for the logical possibility that there can be persons that are not human beings, or human beings that are not persons. What makes a being a person, on this definition, is not its biological humanity, but its intelligence, and its capacity for thought, reason, reflection, and self-awareness.

On one view, the capacity for reason and self-awareness that is required for personhood need not include the capacity for moral agency.[11] On such a minimalist definition of personhood it is reasonable to conclude, as Peter Singer does, that animals of many terrestrial species may be persons.[12] But Locke's is not such a minimalist definition; for Locke also says that 'person is a forensic term, appropriating actions and their merit, and so belongs only to intelligent agents, capable of a law'.[13] On his view, a person is essentially a moral agent: a being that is 'capable of a law', and that may therefore be held morally or legally responsible for its actions. This is what I call a maximalist definition of personhood.

Most of our ordinary talk about persons does not exclusively presuppose either a minimalist or a maximalist definition of personhood. On the one hand, we often think of human beings as persons before they have developed a capacity for moral agency, or after they have irreparably lost it. On the other hand, most of us assume that non-human animals are not persons, in part because we assume that they are incapable of moral agency. Even if one of these definitions were truer to the ordinary concept of a person than the other, that would not show that the alternative concept of personhood cannot legitimately serve as a criterion of moral status. Thus, rather than choosing one of these definitions to the exclusion of the other, we shall need to explore both versions of the Personhood Only view.

[10] John Locke, *An Essay Concerning Human Understanding*, ed. A. D. Woozley (Cleveland, Ohio: World, 1964), 211.
[11] Singer, *Practical Ethics*, 79.
[12] Ibid. 98.
[13] Locke, *Essay Concerning Human Understanding*, 220.

## 4.2. *Immanuel Kant's Personhood Only View*

In the conclusion to his *Critique of Practical Reason*, Kant says, 'Two things fill the mind with ever new and increasing admiration and awe, the oftener and more steadily we reflect upon them: the starry heavens above me and the moral law within me.'[14] The 'moral law within' is what, in his view, makes us persons. It is also what makes persons the only things in the universe that can have moral worth. Only persons can have moral obligations. Persons are also the only entities towards whom moral agents can have moral obligations. Entities that are not persons, Kant says, have 'only a relative value as means, and are consequently called things'.[15] While we are morally obliged not to be cruel to sentient animals that are not persons, this is not an obligation to these animals, but rather to other persons.

### Duty and the Moral Law

To understand the case that Kant makes for these claims, we need to place them in the context of his deontological, or duty-based, moral theory. This theory is an attempt to demonstrate that sound moral principles are fully objective and universally valid. Towards this end, Kant sought to derive the most fundamental moral principles from reason alone, rather than from unprovable religious doctrines, or from the uncertain and changing realities of the natural world.

Kant argues that, contrary to utilitarian theories, the moral rightness of an action does not depend upon the production of happiness, or other good consequences. Happiness is a moral good, and one that we are obliged to promote; but its goodness is contingent upon the moral rightness of the means by which it is produced. The moral rightness of an action depends entirely upon the good will of the agent. To have a good will is to be motivated to do one's moral duty, and to do it simply because it is one's duty.[16] This does not mean that in order to act from a good will one must suppress all

---

[14] Immanuel Kant, *Critique of Practical Reason*, trans. Lewis White Beck (Indianapolis, Ind.: Bobbs-Merrill, 1956), 166.

[15] Immanuel Kant, *The Moral Law: Kant's Groundwork of the Metaphysics of Morals*, trans. H. J. Paton (London: Hutchinson, 1948), 91.

[16] Ibid. 66.

kindly or benevolent feelings, but rather that such emotions must not be what directs the will towards the performance of duty. To act from a good will is to act from morally sound principles, and to do this because it is what reason requires.

But how are we to know which principles of action are morally sound? Kant proposes a single universal principle, from which all other moral principles may be derived. This principle, he says, 'is of such widespread significance as to hold, not merely for men, but for *all rational beings as such*—not merely subject to contingent conditions and expectations, but with absolute necessity'.[17] He calls this principle the Categorical Imperative, by contrast with those imperatives that are hypothetical, i.e. that hold only when the agent has certain goals.

Kant offers several formulations of the Categorical Imperative, which he regards as logically equivalent. One of the most important of these is the Formula of Universal Law, which requires that we act only upon principles that it is rational to want everyone to act upon at all times. In Kant's words, 'I ought never to act except in such a way that I can also will that my maxim should become a universal law.'[18] The 'maxim' is the principle upon which one acts, whether or not one has ever consciously formulated that principle. The Categorical Imperative requires us to act only upon maxims which any rational being could, without contradiction, agree to act upon all of the time.

One example which Kant uses to illustrate the universalizability requirement is of a person who obtains money by making a false promise of repayment. The maxim of such an action, Kant says, contradicts itself when proposed as a universal moral law, because if everyone made false promises for personal gain, the very institution of promising would be destroyed.[19] Since it is irrational to will the universalization of a self-contradictory maxim, we must conclude that it is always morally wrong to make a false promise.

This formulation of the Categorical Imperative has faced serious objections. Perhaps the most damaging is that Kant provides no principled way of determining which elements of the situation may legitimately be included within our formulation of the maxim of an action. Thus, it is nearly always possible to formulate a maxim under

---

[17] Ibid. 67.    [18] Ibid.    [19] Ibid. 85.

which an action falls, which a rational being could without self-contradiction will to become universal law. For instance, if you wish to make a false promise in order to obtain money, you may formulate the maxim that it is permissible to make a false promise when the circumstances are *exactly* like the ones in which you find yourself. This is a maxim that could be universalized without self-contradiction, since there will be very few cases in which a rational being is in exactly the same situation that you are; hence the institution of promise making would be in little danger if that maxim were universally followed. But the objections to this formulation of the Categorical Imperative need not concern us further, since there is another formulation which is more directly relevant to Kant's defence of the Personhood Only view.

## Persons as Ends in Themselves

A second formulation of the Categorical Imperative is what Kant calls the Formula of the End in Itself. In his words,

man, and in general every rational being, *exists* as an end in himself, *not merely as a means* for arbitrary use by this or that will: he must in all his actions, whether they are directed to himself or to other rational beings, always be viewed *at the same time as an end*.[20]

To treat persons as ends in themselves is to treat them as having 'dignity', or 'intrinsic value'. This is a value 'which is exalted above all price, and so admits of no equivalent'.[21] Because persons are ends in themselves, their autonomy must be respected, not just as one component of utility, but as something that imposes strict constraints upon the ways in which they may be treated. There is nothing wrong with treating persons as means to ends that they have accepted; we do this in all co-operative human activities. It is, however, wrong to treat persons as if they were *mere* means, things that we are entitled to use towards ends that are not their own. Because we could not rationally agree to being treated as mere means, maxims that allow us to treat other persons as mere means cannot consistently be willed to become universal law; thus, the two formulations of the Categorical Imperative turn out to be substantially equivalent.

---

[20] *The Moral Law*, 90.     [21] Ibid. 96.

Because they are ends in themselves, persons have moral rights, which all moral agents are morally obliged to respect. The most fundamental of these is the right to freedom. Freedom is the only right that is innate, i.e. that belongs 'to every man by virtue of his humanity'.[22] Every moral agent is entitled to as much freedom as 'can coexist with the freedom of every other in accordance with a universal law'.[23] The right to freedom encompasses the right to life, since life is a precondition for freedom.

Treating persons as ends in themselves requires that we treat their ends as important, and that we sometimes act on maxims that will promote their happiness and fulfilment. However, we cannot act benevolently towards every person we may meet; it is necessary to be selective in our benevolence. Benevolence is, then, an 'imperfect' duty; whereas the duty not to treat others as mere means is a 'perfect' duty, that is, one that is binding at all times.

Just as our duties to others include acts of benevolence, so our duties to ourselves include the promotion of our own happiness, and the development of our talents and abilities. And, just as we may not kill other persons to promote a greater sum of happiness, so we may not kill ourselves, for that or any other reason. Suicide is the denial of one's own human dignity:

> Man can only dispose over things; beasts are things in this sense; but man is not a thing, not a beast. If he disposes over himself, he treats his value as that of a beast. He who so behaves . . . has no respect for human nature and makes a thing of himself.[24]

## Kant's Metaphysics of Freedom

Kant's arguments for the claim that all and only rational beings are ends in themselves are notoriously difficult to interpret. Some commentators have held that he never seriously sought to prove this claim, since he believed that the light of reason reveals its truth to each rational being.[25] It is clear, however, that Kant credits rational

---

[22] Immanuel Kant, *The Metaphysics of Morals*, trans. Mary Gregor (Cambridge: Cambridge University Press, 1991), 63.

[23] Ibid.          [24] Kant, *Lectures on Ethics*, 151.

[25] See Pepita Haezrahi, 'The Concept of Man as an End-in-Himself', in Robert Paul Wolff (ed.), *Kant: A Collection of Essays* (Garden City, NY: Doubleday, 1967), 293.

beings with this unique                    pacity for
moral agency. He says,                 nly condition under which a rat                 nself . . .
Therefore morality, *and*              *morality*,
is the only thing which

For Kant, the moral                    f a metaphysical difference betw                          . Persons
are, in his view, the only earthly beings that are free of causal determination. Persons are not free in the 'sensible' world—the world to
which perception gives us access. There, deterministic causal laws
prevail. Rather, we are free in the 'intelligible' world—the world of
things as they are in themselves. To that world, we have no perceptual access. As long as we regard ourselves solely as parts of the sensible world, our actions will appear to be governed by causal laws,
and thus to be unfree. Yet we know that, as moral agents, we are free
to act upon the deliverances of reason, rather than merely from natural causes. Unlike other animals, we are not motivated solely by
emotion, instinct, and other non-rational forces.[27] Because we can
neither doubt our freedom, nor find room for it in the natural world,
we must locate it within the realm of things in themselves, where
causal laws do not apply.

Today, most philosophers reject this dualistic metaphysics of
freedom. Soft determinists argue that we may consistently believe
both that some human beings are capable of moral agency, and that
all human behaviour has natural causes. On this view, the difference
between voluntary actions, for which we may be held morally ac-
countable, and actions that are not voluntary, lies not in *whether*
they are caused, but rather in *how* they are caused.[28] Generally
speaking, an action may be regarded as voluntary if it results from
the agent's informed and uncoerced decision, rather than from ignorance, confusion, external coercion, or psychological compulsion.

In evaluating the Kantian version of the Personhood Only view,
we need to ask how much plausibility it retains, once divorced from
Kant's dualistic metaphysics of freedom. If the freedom of moral

[26] *The Moral Law*, 96–7.

[27] *Critique of Practical Reason*, 63, 77.

[28] For example, Robert Olson, 'Freedom, Selfhood, and Moral Responsibility', in
A. K. Bierman and James A. Gould (eds.), *Philosophy for a New Generation* (New
York: Macmillan, 1977), 534–48.

agents is not the mark of a fundamental metaphysical difference between moral agents and all other beings, then what reason do we have for accepting moral obligations only towards moral agents?

## 4.3. *Objections to Kant's Personhood Only View*

The primary advantage of Kant's deontological theory over Singer's preference utilitarianism is that it provides individual persons with stronger moral rights. Like utilitarianism, it requires each moral agent to contribute to human happiness; but unlike utilitarianism it places limits upon what may be done to individuals in the name of increasing the total amount of happiness. A moral theory that demands a categorical respect for the moral rights of individuals is truer to the convictions that most of us hold than one that permits those rights to be sacrificed to the goal of maximizing utility. It is also truer to the spirit of the Golden Rule, which speaks not of maximizing total happiness, but of treating other persons as we would like to be treated.

Despite these virtues, Kant's theory is vulnerable to a number of objections. In the first place, moral agency is not plausibly construed as a necessary condition for any moral status, since (as was argued in Chapter 3) mere sentience is a sound basis for the ascription of some moral status.

There are also grounds for rejecting the view that moral agency is a necessary condition for full moral status. If we take literally Kant's claim that only rational beings are ends in themselves, then it would seem to follow that human beings who are not moral agents are not ends in themselves, and do not have moral rights. Thus, the Personhood Only view threatens to lead to a troubling constriction of the community of moral equals.

### Constricting the Moral Community

Kant ascribes full moral status only to rational moral agents; thus, his community of moral equals would appear to exclude not only animals, but also human infants, young children, and human beings who are severely mentally disabled. Infants and young children are not yet capable of acting on general moral principles. Some human beings suffer from genetic or developmental abnormalities that preclude their ever becoming moral agents. And some persons suffer injury or illness that permanently robs them of the capacity for rational moral agency.

Kant says very little about such human beings. Nevertheless, what he says about the moral status of animals raises vexing questions about the status of these human beings. 'Animals', he says, 'are not self-conscious and [thus] are there only as a means to an end.'[29] If the premiss that non-human animals are not self-conscious implies that we cannot have moral duties towards them, then we are owed an explanation of how we can have moral duties towards human beings who are not self-conscious. Otherwise, in Tom Regan's words,

All that can be said about our dealings with such humans [on Kant's theory] is that our duties involving them are indirect duties to rational beings. Thus, I do no moral wrong *to a child* if I torture her for hours on end. The moral grounds for objecting to what I do must be looked for elsewhere— namely, in the effects doing this will have on my character.[30]

Regan's point here is that any theory which implies that we cannot have moral obligations towards human beings who are not moral agents clashes with moral convictions that are too fundamental to be surrendered. To be fair, Kant probably did not believe that such human beings ought to be treated as mere things. In speaking of the suicide, he says, 'Even when a man is a bad man, humanity in his person is worthy of esteem.'[31] It seems likely that he would have said that humanity in the person of a young child or a mentally disabled adult is also worthy of esteem. He might, for instance, have argued that young children are ends in themselves by virtue of their *potential* for moral agency. (The problems with this response will be considered presently.) The problem, then, is not that Kant explicitly denies that we can have moral obligations towards human beings who are not moral agents, but rather that his claim that the moral status of human beings springs solely from their moral agency leaves us in the dark about *why* we have such obligations.

The human rights problems generated by Kant's theory do not end here. If Kant's view is that only the (actual or potential) cap-

---

[29] *Lectures on Ethics*, 151.
[30] Regan, *The Case for Animal Rights*, 182.
[31] *Lectures on Ethics*, 239.

acity for a certain kind of moral reasoning gives rise to moral status, then his theory may exclude many mentally normal human adults. For the type of moral reasoning that Kant requires is so intellectually demanding, and so contingent upon a particular type of education, as to be arguably beyond the reach of many mentally normal adults. Even if all normal adults are moral agents, rational moral agency is unsatisfactory in practice as the sole criterion for full moral status, because it can too readily be used to deny moral status to persons whom others consider less than fully rational.

It is always difficult for powerless or socially stigmatized persons successfully to demonstrate their rationality to their social superiors, who often have strong incentives to deny it. Powerless persons often cannot speak freely, except at great risk to themselves and others. Moreover, whatever they say can easily be interpreted as evidence that they are governed by instinct and emotion, rather than reason. Women, slaves, servants, poor people, racial, religious, and ethnic minorities, colonized people, children past infancy, and people with mental or physical disabilities all experience such treatment. Thus, to make rational moral agency the only basis for having moral rights is to risk rendering the rights of all but the most powerful persons perpetually vulnerable to challenge.

Kant's own work provides embarrassing illustrations of the tendency of members of elite groups to view other human beings as incapable of reason. In an early essay, *Observations on the Feeling of the Beautiful and the Sublime*, he opines that women are incapable of abstract reasoning, and should therefore be educated primarily in domestic skills and art appreciation—not geography, history, mathematics, philosophy, or other mentally taxing subjects. As for acting on moral principles, he says, '[Women] . . . do something only because it pleases them . . . I hardly believe that the fair sex is capable of principles, and I hope by that not to offend, for these are also extremely rare in the male.'[32]

At the time he penned these remarks, Kant believed that moral principles can be derived from 'a feeling that lives within every human breast', namely, 'the feeling of the beauty and dignity of human nature'.[33] Because he considered women to be capable of this feeling, he did not conclude that their intellectual inferiority

[32] Kant, *Observations on the Feeling of the Beautiful and the Sublime*, 81.
[33] Ibid. 60.

renders them incapable of moral virtue. However, he considered women's virtue to be based *only* upon feelings, and thus to be inferior to the virtue of which (some) men are capable, which is based upon an intellectual understanding of moral principles.[34] Nevertheless, he says, it is fortunate that women—and most men—act on the basis of feelings rather than principles, since most human beings act reasonably well when guided by morally desirable feelings, including 'kind and benevolent sensations, [and] a fine feeling for propriety'.[35] On the other hand, he says, when one acts solely upon moral principles, 'it can so easily happen that one errs in these principles, and then the resulting disadvantage extends all the further, the more universal the principle and the more resolute the person who has set it before himself'.[36]

This early view is different from that of the *Groundwork of the Metaphysics of Morals* and later works, wherein Kant denies that acting upon feelings ever constitutes genuine moral agency. By moving towards a strictly rationalist model of moral agency, while at the same time making moral agency the sole criterion of moral status, Kant arrived at a theory which tends to undermine the moral status of persons who are unable to demonstrate their rational moral agency to the satisfaction of those who have the power to deny them basic moral rights. Even human beings who *are* moral agents cannot be secure in these rights unless the criterion for having full moral status is one the fulfilment of which can readily be demonstrated, even to an unsympathetic audience.

## Responses to the Human Rights Objections

Philosophers who regard moral agency as the sole criterion of moral status have suggested a number of ways of avoiding these objections. One strategy is to employ a less restrictive definition of moral agency. For instance, John Rawls characterizes 'moral persons'—individuals to whom justice is owed—as 'rational beings with their own ends and capable of a sense of justice'.[37] To avoid the implication that young children and the mentally impaired are not moral persons, Rawls stipulates that having one's own ends and being

[34] *Observations on the Feeling of the Beautiful and the Sublime*, 60.
[35] Ibid.                                        [36] Ibid. 74.
[37] John Rawls, *A Theory of Justice* (Cambridge, Mass.: Harvard University Press, 1971), 12.

capable of a sense of justice are 'range properties'.[38] This means that individuals need not have equally refined ends, or an equally excellent sense of justice, in order to be moral persons. For that, it is enough that they possess these properties to some degree.

But what about infants who have scarcely begun to develop a set of individual ends, let alone a sense of justice? Rawls says that these individuals have the *capacity for developing* these capacities, and that this is enough:

the minimal requirements defining moral personality refer to a capacity and not to the realization of it. A being that has this capacity, *whether or not it is yet developed*, is to receive the full protection of the principles of justice. Since infants and children are thought to have basic rights (normally exercised on their behalf by parents and guardians), this interpretation of the requisite conditions seems necessary to match our considered judgments.[39]

The hypothesis that the potential to develop one's own ends and a sense of justice is sufficient for moral personhood enables Rawls to gather normal infants and young children into the fold. However, it appears to do this at the cost of also admitting fertilized or unfertilized human ova—which also have the potential, under the right circumstances, eventually to develop the capacities in question.

A proponent of the Personhood Only view might respond to this objection by reminding us that persons are conscious beings, entities that have the capacity to have experiences, and not merely the potential to develop that capacity at a later time. Thus, it might be suggested that a person is a conscious being who is either actually or potentially capable of moral agency. This definition of personhood blocks the admission of human ova and presentient foetuses, while admitting infants and young children, and possibly third-trimester foetuses, which may already be sentient. (This point is discussed in Chapter 9.)

But the appeal to potential capacities cannot salvage the personhood of human beings who lack even the potential to develop individual ends and a sense of justice. Recognizing that the moral status of these individuals will otherwise be problematic, Rawls ultimately rejects the claim that personhood is a necessary condition for having moral rights, holding only that it is sufficient.[40]

In contrast, H. J. McCloskey resolutely defends the claim that

---

[38] Ibid. 508–10.
[40] Ibid. 505–6.

[39] Ibid. 509 (my italics).

actual or potential moral agency is a necessary condition for full moral status. He suggests that when we ascribe moral rights to human beings who are not even potential moral agents,

> we are doing something akin to what we are doing when we describe a cat as a quadruped, knowing that some cats are born with more and others with fewer than four legs. *Qua* cat, an animal, even this animal with only three legs, is naturally a quadruped. *Qua* human being, where human beings normally become persons, human beings are possessors of rights. However, if we are to speak with strict accuracy, we must deny rights and the possibility of the possession of rights to ex-persons [and] non-persons who have no potentiality to become persons.[41]

McCloskey says that, although such human beings have no moral rights, we often assume that they do, because this assumption is useful:

> With those born of human parents, even the most inferior beings, it may be a *useful lie* to attribute rights where they are not and cannot be possessed, since to deny the very inferior beings born of human parents rights, opens the way to a dangerous slide. But whether useful or not, it is a lie or a mistake to attribute rights or the possibility of rights to such beings.[42]

While I agree about the dangerous slide, I would deny that it is either a lie or a mistake to ascribe moral rights to sentient human beings who are not moral agents, even potentially. As I argue in Chapters 5, 6, and 7, there are sound reasons for according moral rights to such individuals. If so, then we must reject those forms of the Personhood Only view that employ a maximalist definition of personhood.

### 4.4. *Tom Regan's Animal Rights View*

If personhood requires actual moral agency, then the Personhood Only view leaves many sentient human beings with no moral status. Even if potential moral agency is treated as sufficient for personhood, the Personhood Only view forces us to deny that we can have moral obligations to human beings whose mental or physical impairments preclude their becoming rational moral agents.

---

[41] H. J. McCloskey, 'Moral Rights and Animals', *Inquiry*, 22 (1979), 31.
[42] H. J. McCloskey, 'Rights', *Philosophical Quarterly*, 16 (1965), 118.

Tom Regan defends a version of the Personhood Only view which at least partially avoids this objection. On his view, most sentient human beings—including some who are not even potentially capable of moral agency—have full moral status; and so do many non-human animals. All beings that are subjects-of-a-life—whether or not they are human—have moral rights; and all of them have the same basic moral rights. Thus, subjecthood plays much the same role in Regan's theory as rational moral agency plays in Kant's.

## Being a Subject-of-a-Life

Subjects-of-a-life are beings that possess certain mental and behavioural capacities, in addition to the capacity for conscious experience. These include the capacities to have

beliefs and desires; perception, memory, and a sense of the future, including their own future; an emotional life together with feelings of pleasure and pain; preference- and welfare-interests; the ability to initiate action in pursuit of their desires and goals; a psychophysical identity over time; and an individual welfare in the sense that their experiential life fares well or ill for them, logically independently of their utility for others and . . . of their being the object of anyone else's interests.[43]

Regan's subjects-of-lives have many of the mental and behavioural capacities of Kantian persons, but differ in that they need not be even potentially capable of rational moral agency. Although Regan claims only that subjecthood is a sufficient condition for moral status, he is all but convinced that it is also necessary. 'As in the case of non-conscious natural objects or collections of such objects,' he says, 'it is radically unclear how the attribution of inherent value to . . . individuals [that are not subjects] can be made intelligible and nonarbitrary.'[44]

## Which Animals are Subjects-of-a-Life?

Some philosophers argue that only beings that use a human-style language can have such mental states as beliefs and desires.[45] But Regan points out that the behaviour of many animals provides

---

[43] *The Case for Animal Rights*, 243.   [44] Ibid. 246.
[45] See Frey, *Interests and Rights*, esp. chs. 6 and 7.

ample evidence that they too have desires and beliefs. The behaviour of cats and dogs, for instance, is often comprehensible on that assumption, and incomprehensible without it. For instance, when Fido sees a meaty bone in his dish and bounds over to grab it, it is reasonable to explain his behaviour by saying that he wants the bone, and believes that it will taste good. Fido's concept of a bone is probably not identical to ours; for instance, his concept might not apply to a fossilized bone, or one that has been preserved in formaldehyde. But the differences between Fido's concept of a bone and ours do not show that Fido is incapable of desiring bones, and having beliefs about them. While it may be necessary to have concepts in order to have beliefs, it is surely not necessary to have concepts identical to those that humans have.[46]

A second argument against the claim that a being must use a human-style language in order to have beliefs and desires is that, on this hypothesis, pre-linguistic children cannot have beliefs and desires. But if that were so, then it would be impossible for children ever to *learn* a language. For,

unless Baby Jane comes to believe that there is a particular thing we are referring to, when we say the word *ball*, all manner of instruction in the use of the word *ball* will be for naught. She simply will not come to learn the meaning of the word.[47]

Regan ventures no opinion respecting the location of the line between animals that are subjects-of-lives and animals that are not. He claims only that all mentally normal mammals of a year or more of age have the requisite mental capacities.[48] This, he says, is a conservative claim, involving only 'individuals [who are] *well beyond* the point where anyone could reasonably "draw the line" separating those who have the mental abilities in question from those who lack them'.[49] He is aware that there may be non-mammalian animals that are subjects-of-a-life, and that some animals (or humans) may become subjects before the age of one year. His suggestion is that, in dealing with sentient beings that may or may not be subjects, we ought to apply the principle of the benefit of the doubt. That is, we should behave towards such beings '*as if* they are subjects, due our

---

[46] This is a point that Peter Carruthers makes, in *The Animals Issue*, 130–3.
[47] Regan, *The Case for Animal Rights*, 45.
[48] Ibid. 78.                                                                    [49] Ibid.

respectful treatment, especially when doing so causes no harm to us'.[50]

## The Inherent Value of Subjects

The moral status that Regan claims for all subjects-of-a-life is similar to that which Kant claims for all rational beings. Subjects are ends in themselves, and thus have basic moral rights. These include the rights to life, to liberty, and not to be harmed. These rights, Regan says, 'do not arise as a result of the creative acts of any one individual . . . or any group'.[51] Rather, they follow from the postulate that all subjects-of-a-life have inherent value. This postulate expresses the conviction that individual subjects are more than receptacles for utility. Subjects have a value that is distinct from the value of their pains and pleasures, and independent of the instrumental value that they may have for other subjects. Consequently, they may not be used as mere means to any end—even their own happiness, or that of other subjects.

Regan says that inherent value is 'a categorical concept', i.e. one that does not come in degrees.[52] The only alternative to this view, he says, is a 'perfectionist' theory of justice. He argues that a perfectionist theory of justice is unacceptable because, on such a theory, 'what individuals are due, as a matter of justice, depends on the degree to which they possess a certain cluster of virtues or excellences'.[53] Such theories are 'morally pernicious, providing, as they do, the foundation of the most objectionable forms of social, political, and legal discrimination'.[54] At the very least, all moral agents must have equal inherent value. For,

If moral agents are viewed as having inherent value to varying degrees, then there would have to be some basis for determining how much inherent value any given moral agent has. Theoretically, the basis could be claimed to be anything—such as wealth or belonging to the 'right' race or sex. . . . To accept this view of the inherent value of moral agents is to pave the way for a perfectionist theory of justice: those with less inherent value could *justly* be required to serve the needs and interests of those with more, even if it is not in the interests of those who serve to do so.[55]

---

| | | |
|---|---|---|
| [50] Ibid. 367. | [51] Ibid. 268. | [52] Ibid. 240–1. |
| [53] Ibid. 233–4. | [54] Ibid. 234. | [55] Ibid. 236–7. |

## Moral Agents and Moral Patients

Moral patients are subjects-of-a-life that are not moral agents.[56] Regan argues that there is no sound basis for holding that moral agents have inherent value, but that moral patients do not. To make this point, he sometimes relies upon what has been called the 'argument from marginal cases'. This argument begins with the observation that if we hold that the capacity for moral agency is a necessary condition for having inherent value, then we are forced to deny that infants, young children, and mentally disabled human beings have inherent value. Since this is unacceptable, we might look for another mental capacity to serve as a necessary and sufficient condition for inherent value, e.g. a certain type of intelligence or self-awareness. But no such criterion will enable us to ascribe inherent value to all and only *human* moral patients. Any such criterion will either (1) exclude non-human moral patients, along with many human ones; or (2) include human moral patients, along with many non-human ones. Thus, Regan concludes, if we wish to ascribe inherent value to human moral patients, then we cannot consistently withhold it from moral patients of other species.[57]

The argument from marginal cases presupposes that human moral patients have inherent value. Regan's second argument for the moral equality of moral agents and moral patients does not rely upon this assumption. The argument is that moral agents and moral patients are alike in respects that are relevant to the possession of inherent value. Both have experiential lives that can go better or worse; both can be harmed by pain, injury, or the loss of freedom. For both, death is the ultimate loss because it frustrates any future-oriented desires that they have, and deprives them of a future.[58] Because both moral agents and moral patients can be harmed in these ways, both are protected by the harm principle, which states that we have 'a . . . *prima facie* duty not to harm individuals'.[59] This is a duty to all subjects-of-a-life, based upon their equal inherent value.

---

[56] *The Case for Animal Rights*, 152.
[57] Tom Regan, *All that Dwell Within: Essays on Animal Liberation and Environmental Ethics* (Berkeley and Los Angeles: University of California Press, 1982), 27–8.
[58] *The Case for Animal Rights*, 101–2.
[59] Ibid. 187.

## Practical Conclusions

In Regan's view, animals that are subjects-of-a-life may never be killed for food, or for any reason that would be insufficient to justify killing a human being. Nor may they be used in scientific research that will harm them, or be exploited in any other way that would be morally objectionable if they were human beings. If ceasing to exploit animals causes inconvenience or even hardship to us, this is irrelevant; the moral rights of non-human subjects-of-a-life may not be overridden just to avoid hardship to human beings.

Consequently, Regan takes Singer to task for producing a theory that does not yield sufficiently strong protections for individual animals.[60] He points out that almost any use of animals might sometimes be justified on utilitarian grounds. For instance, if some people need meat in order to be well nourished, then a utilitarian may have to condone their meat-eating—especially if the animals that they eat lead good lives, and are killed in a fairly painless way. On the Animal Rights view, killing animals cannot be justified by any nutritional or other benefits that human beings gain from eating meat. Similarly, no experimentation that harms animal subjects-of-a-life can be justified by the medical or other benefits to humans. Killing or otherwise harming animals for food or any other use violates their rights, just as it would if they were human beings.

### 4.5. *Objections to Regan's Animal Rights View*

Regan's theory of moral status generates a somewhat different set of problems from those raised by Kant's Personhood Only view. I shall consider four objections: first, two environmentalist objections, involving human interference with natural predation, and the protection of species and ecosystems; next, a pragmatic objection, involving the moral status of rats and mice; and lastly, an objection involving the absence of a sharp line between those animals that are subjects and those that are not.

## The Objection from Natural Predation

The Animal Rights view would appear to imply that we have a moral obligation to protect not only domestic but also wild animals

---

[60] Ibid. 218–24.

from natural predators, whenever we reasonably can. If deer and rabbits have the same moral rights as us, then how can we refuse to intervene when their lives are threatened by cougars or bears? We surely would not refuse protection to human beings whose lives were similarly threatened.

Many environmentalists consider this a *reductio* of the Animal Rights view.[61] Human interference with natural predation is apt to cause serious ecosystemic disturbances. For instance, without wolves or other large predators to limit their numbers, deer populations in North America often outstrip the carrying capacity of the land, resulting in starving deer and damage to vegetation that cannot readily recover. In 'Thinking Like a Mountain', Aldo Leopold writes,

I have lived to see state after state extirpate its wolves. I have watched the face of many a newly wolfless mountain, and seen the south-facing slopes wrinkle with a maze of new deer trails. I have seen every edible bush and seedling broused, first to anaemic desuetude, and then to death. I have seen every edible tree defoliated to the height of a saddlehorn . . . In the end the starved bones of the hoped-for deer herd, dead of its own too-much, bleach with the bones of the dead sage, or . . . under the high-lined junipers.[62]

Regan's response to the objection that the Animal Rights view requires us to interfere with natural predation is that non-human predators are not moral agents, and thus cannot violate the rights of the animals that they kill. Consequently, he says, there is no obligation on our part to protect wild animals from natural predation.[63] In his words, 'The suffering . . . animals cause one another in the wild is not the concern of morally enlightened wildlife management . . . [which] should be principally concerned with *letting animals be*, keeping human predators out of their affairs.'[64]

This response is unsatisfactory. If human beings are threatened by wolves, we do not assume that the wolves' lack of moral agency relieves us of any moral obligation to help; for it is not the moral

---

[61] See J. Baird Callicott, 'Animal Liberation: A Triangular Affair', *In Defense of the Land Ethic: Essays in Environmental Philosophy* (Albany, NY: State University of New York Press, 1989), 57; and D. G. Ritchie, 'Why Animals Do Not Have Rights', in Tom Regan and Peter Singer (eds.), *Animal Rights and Human Obligations* (Englewood Cliffs, NJ: Prentice-Hall, 1976), 183.

[62] Leopold, *A Sand County Almanac*, 139–40.

[63] *The Case for Animal Rights*, 285, 357.          [64] Ibid. 357.

obligations of wolves that are in question, but our own. If animals have the same rights as human beings, then we should seek to protect them even from attackers that are not moral agents. By the same token, we ought to prevent human beings who are not moral agents from harming other human beings, or behaving cruelly towards animals. As Steve Sapontzis remarks, the fact 'that a young child "doesn't know any better" does not prevent us from being morally obligated to stop him from tormenting the cat'.[65]

Sapontzis agrees that the Animal Rights view implies a *prima facie* obligation to prevent natural predation, but argues that this does not reduce the view to absurdity. He points out that the Animal Rights view does not require us to prevent natural predation *at any cost to the animals themselves*. If deer will suffer even more in the absence of wolves, then we ought not to interfere with wolf predation. We should prevent natural predation only when doing so 'would not occasion as much or more suffering than it would prevent'.[66] For instance, he says, we ought to prevent our pet cats from killing birds and other small animals. In his view,

working toward preventing natural predation would merely be an extension of a common human activity that is not ordinarily regarded as unnatural or as an expression of the sin of pride. We routinely interfere with nature in order to protect ourselves (and animals too) from such threats to (the quality of) life as flooding rivers, storms, avalanches, erosion, pestilence, diseases, birth defects, infections, and decay.[67]

Environmentalists will reply that predation is an essential part of every natural terrestrial ecosystem, and therefore cannot be regarded an evil to be eliminated whenever possible. Natural predation is vital to the integrity, stability, and beauty of the natural world. To object to it is to suppose that the fundamental design of all terrestrial ecosystems is morally wrong, and that we ought to strive to change it. This is why Callicott says (somewhat hyperbolically), 'the value commitments of the humane movement seem at bottom to betray a world-denying or rather a life-loathing philosophy'.[68] Like other animals, we human beings naturally wish to protect ourselves from our natural predators, and we are entitled to

---

[65] Sapontzis, *Morals, Reason, and Animals*, 230.
[66] Ibid. 233.                                    [67] Ibid. 237.
[68] J. Baird Callicott, 'Animal Liberation: A Triangular Affair', 33.

do this, within the limits of respect for the health of the ecosystem as a whole; but it would be 'biologically ruinous'[69] to extend the same level of protection to all non-human subjects-of-a-life.

## Protecting Species and Ecosystems

Regan considers it possible—though doubtful—that an environmental ethic could be produced that demonstrates that plant and animal species and other elements of the natural world that are not subjects-of-a-life can have inherent value.[70] It would be difficult, however, to reconcile such an environmental ethic with Regan's Animal Rights view. For the rights which this theory ascribes to all mammals over a year of age preclude measures that most ecologists consider essential, in some cases, to the preservation or restoration of natural biodiversity.

Many of these cases involve ecosystems that have been damaged by animals of non-indigenous species. For instance, plants that have evolved in relative isolation (e.g. on islands) are often highly vulnerable to browsing, rooting, and trampling by introduced herbivores, such as pigs, goats, sheep, cattle, rabbits, horses, and donkeys. Similarly, endemic bird and animal populations are often vulnerable to introduced predators, such as cats, dogs, rats, mongooses, ferrets, foxes, and snakes. Endemic birds can also be endangered by competition from introduced species, such as English sparrows, mynahs, and starlings.[71] Killing or deporting introduced animals is sometimes the only way to prevent the extinction of indigenous plant and animal species.

In much of Australia, feral cats, dogs, and foxes have been responsible for the near-extinction of many small native marsupials, even in parks and preserves where grazing by domestic animals is prevented and other human interventions are minimal. Researchers have reported that in New South Wales feral cats kill about 400 million native mammals, birds, and reptiles annually.[72] The consensus

---

[69] 'Animal Liberation: A Triangular Affair', 33.

[70] *The Case for Animal Rights*, 245.

[71] For a lively account of the impoverishment of many island ecosystems through the introduction of non-indigenous animals and plants, see David Quammen, *The Song of the Dodo: Island Biogeography in an Age of Extinction* (New York: Scribner, 1996).

[72] Ian Anderson, 'Alien Predators Devastate Australian Wildlife', *New Scientist* (12 Sept. 1992), 9.

amongst ecologists is that, to protect endangered native species, it is necessary to control introduced predators—sometimes by lethal means. Introduced herbivores (including an estimated 300 million rabbits) also contribute to the loss of indigenous Australian flora and fauna, even where cattle and sheep are excluded.[73]

The Animal Rights view prohibits killing introduced mammals in order to protect native flora and fauna. It is, Regan says, a form of 'environmental fascism' to seek to determine 'what should be done to individuals who have rights by appeal to . . . what will or will not maximally contribute to the integrity, stability, and beauty of the biotic community'.[74]

This view has led to confrontations between environmentalists and animal rights activists. For instance, People for the Ethical Treatment of Animals has demonstrated against the Nature Conservancy's policy of killing feral pigs on Conservancy lands in Hawaii. The pigs are destructive to many endemic species of plants, birds, and molluscs. Trapping the pigs alive might be feasible, but maintaining them in captivity for the rest of their natural lives is not. Releasing them elsewhere is not an option either, since pigs are apt to be destructive to any ecosystem of which they are not a natural part. Moreover, they can spread deadly diseases to domestic and wild animals. Administering contraceptives to the pigs would be morally preferable to killing them; but effectively deliverable porcine contraceptives are not presently available.

Common sense backs the land ethic in this dispute. Plant and animal species, once pushed to extinction, do not return. If it is wrong for us to demolish the few remnants of original Hawaiian ecosystems, then it is wrong for us to permit feral pigs to demolish them. The pigs are a human-caused problem, and one that will not disappear spontaneously. If pigs were moral agents, then a peaceful solution might be negotiated. As it is, there may be no feasible alternative to killing them. If so, then this course of action is justified, even though it deviates from the moral ideal of never harming subjects-of-a-life. It is not the moral equivalent of murdering human beings found wandering on Conservancy land.

---

[73] Ian Anderson, 'Rabbit Virus to be let Loose?', *New Scientist* (25 Sept. 1993), 5.

[74] *The Case for Animal Rights*, 362.

## A Pragmatic Objection

Like the Life Only and Sentience Only views, the Animal Rights view generates moral obligations that cannot be fulfilled without jeopardizing human well-being. There are, for instance, intractable obstacles to always treating mice and rats as our moral equals.[75] Rodents of several species habitually live in proximity to humans. In so doing, they consume or contaminate food, and sometimes spread lethal diseases, such as bubonic plague—the 'Black Death' of the Middle Ages, which is carried by fleas that live on rats. Rodents also have extraordinarily high reproductive rates. Thus, while we may be able to tolerate a few rodents in our homes and granaries, a policy of complete tolerance would often lead to disaster. For these reasons, human beings cannot always treat the lives of rodents as sacrosanct. Even in India, where many people regard rats as sacred animals, rats are routinely killed to protect human health and the human food supply.

Adequate control of rodent populations can sometimes be achieved by non-lethal means; for instance, by live-trapping the animals and releasing them elsewhere. But this is not always feasible. The number of animals may be too great, and the task unmanageable. To avoid cruelty, the traps must be checked frequently, lest the captives suffer from dehydration and hunger, or attack one another in their panic. It is also necessary periodically to transport them to a location where they will have a chance to survive, and where they will not cause problems for other people. When humane live-trapping is not an option, there may be no alternative to such lethal methods as the introduction of cats or other predators, the use of spring-loaded traps, or—always as a last resort—setting out poison.

None of the last three options is defensible on the Animal Rights view. Indeed, if mice and rats have the same basic moral rights that humans do, then even the trap-and-deport method is a wrongful infringement of their rights to life and liberty. Trapping and relocation cause physical and emotional trauma, and the deportees often do not survive long in their new location. Small animals live by knowing their territory: where to take shelter, where to hide, where to find

---

[75] Since mice and rats have short lifespans and mature rapidly, it is probable that they become subjects-of-a-life before they are a year of age. This means that even if most rodents killed by pest control measures are under a year old, they probably have equal rights on the Animal Rights view.

food, where danger lurks. Transporting them to a strange environment can be a virtual death sentence.

A defender of the Animal Rights view might reply that, even though rodents are our moral equals, we are sometimes justified in killing them. If they are dangerous to human well-being, then surely we may kill them in self-defence. But this response is unpersuasive. Lethal self-defence against another sentient human being is rarely permissible, unless that individual is engaging (perhaps innocently) in some immediately life-threatening activity. Rodents threaten human well-being through their very existence and mode of life: where they live, what they eat, and the pathogenic micro-organisms that they can carry. Comparable considerations would not justify launching a homicidal pogrom against one's human neighbours. If human neighbours unintentionally endanger our well-being through their mode of life, or the micro-organisms that they harbour, then we ought to discuss the problem with them, seek a mediator, or appeal to legal or moral authorities to enforce the standards of behaviour that have been breached. But, in Bonnie Steinbock's words,

If rats invade our houses, carrying disease and biting our children, we cannot reason with them, hoping to persuade them of the injustice they do us. We can only attempt to get rid of them. And it is this that makes it reasonable for us to accord them a separate and not equal status.[76]

Steinbock's point goes to the heart of the matter. It is because we cannot reason with rodents that we cannot always resolve our conflicts with them non-violently. Because we cannot always do this, it is futile to insist that we are morally obliged to. No theory of moral status can hope to win general acceptance if its implementation would severely jeopardize human lives and health. The enforcement of equal moral rights for rodents would inevitably cause widespread human suffering. Morality may reasonably demand some sacrifice of individual or group interests. But a moral theory that demands such extreme sacrifices is not a serious candidate for general acceptance.

Just as proponents of the view that moral agency is the only valid criterion of moral status often fail to notice the inconsistency between that view and the common-sense view that infants and

[76] Bonnie Steinbock, 'Speciesism and the Idea of Equality', *Philosophy*, 53 (1978), 253.

mentally impaired persons are part of the human moral community, so proponents of the Animal Rights view rarely notice the impractical implications of the view that all subjects-of-a-life have equal moral rights. Activists who work for better treatment of animals are usually concerned about larger animals than mice and rats. The welfare of rodents sometimes becomes a topic of ethical debate in the context of biomedical research, but rarely in ordinary domestic contexts. The animal rights position is more often defensible in the first context, because some research projects are not important enough to justify the infliction of suffering and death upon highly sentient beings; but it is difficult to deny the importance of not being forced to share one's living quarters with large numbers of rodents.

## The Line-Drawing Problem

Although Regan does not attempt to locate the line between animals that are subjects and those that are not, his theory presupposes that a sharp line can non-arbitrarily be drawn somewhere; for all subjects have inherent value, and inherent value does not come in degrees. But is it likely that all sentient animals fall neatly into two distinct categories: those that are capable of having 'beliefs and desires, memory and a sense of the future, an emotional life, . . . intentionality, and self-awareness', and those that are not?

Human infants are not born with all of these mental abilities; nor is there a magic moment at which the missing abilities spring into being. Sentience and emotion are normally present at birth, and perhaps earlier. But memory, anticipation of the future, a sense of self, and other mental abilities required for being a subject-of-a-life, can develop only during the months and years after the child is born. Thus, there is no uniquely objective way to draw a line between those infants who have become subjects, and those that have not. Similarly, there is no scientific way to sort sentient animals into those that have (enough of) the mental capacities in question, and those that do not.

The problem here is not that we know too little of the experiential lives of animals. It is, rather, that what we know suggests that the subjecthood of non-humans is almost certainly a matter of degree. Even such invertebrate animals as spiders may possess to some degree the mental abilities constitutive of subjecthood. Fish, reptiles, and amphibians display more impressive mental capacities, and birds[77] and mammals still more. It is possible that some animals, such as cetaceans and apes, are about as mentally sophisticated as humans, albeit in somewhat different ways.

The absence of a sharp line between subjects and non-subjects makes the Animal Rights view difficult to apply in everyday life. However, if subjecthood is sufficient for full moral status, then we ought to be careful not to deny the moral rights of any subject. Consequently, we ought to give the benefit of the doubt to sentient beings that *may* be subjects. Moreover, we should do this not only when it costs us little, but also when it costs us a great deal. For, as Regan reminds us, basic moral rights cannot justly be ignored whenever respecting them would cause hardship. This means that, in addition to the problems already discussed, the Animal Rights view inherits those of the Sentience Only view. If we take the principle of the benefit of the doubt seriously, then we probably ought to refrain from ploughing, planting, and harvesting crops, since these activities cause harm to many sentient invertebrates that may be subjects-of-a-life.

### 4.6. *The Case for the Personhood Plus View*

As moral theorists, Kant and Regan have much in common. Each holds that all and only beings that conform to a certain definition of personhood have full and equal moral status. But, while Kant identifies moral agency as the essence of personhood, Regan's criterion includes only those mental capacities that he says can be found in all normal mammals over a year of age. Both theories fail, for different but complementary reasons. Even if we take Kant's criterion of personhood to include potential as well as actual moral agency, his theory excludes many sentient human beings, to whom (as I argue in Chapter 5) we have good reason to accord full moral status. Regan's theory includes all human individuals that are, or may be, subjects-of-a-life. However, it also includes many non-human animals that we cannot always treat as our moral equals.

One might suppose that, if the maximalist personhood criterion is too exclusive, while the minimalist personhood criterion is too

---

[77] See Theodore Xenophon Barber, *The Human Nature of Birds* (New York: Penguin Books, 1993).

inclusive, then a personhood criterion that is intermediate between the two might be just right.[78] But this is probably a false hope. It is highly unlikely that there is any single capacity or set of capacities that is possessed by all of the sentient human beings whom most of us want to treat as having equal basic moral rights, and by none of the animals that human moral agents cannot—without disaster—always treat as if they had such rights.

On the Personhood Plus view, being a subject-of-a-life is neither a necessary nor a sufficient condition for full moral status. We are free to extend full moral status to some beings who do not have all of the capacities constitutive of subjecthood. Conversely, we are free to deny full moral status to some animals that are probably subjects-of-a-life. Their subjecthood is, however, relevant to what we owe to them. Animals that are as mentally sophisticated as most mammals can suffer not only from physical pain, but also from boredom, lack of exercise, or social isolation. As will be argued in Chapter 10, the ethical treatment of captive and domesticated animals requires that these forms of suffering be prevented or ameliorated, through the provision of an environment adequate to their specific needs.

On the Personhood Plus view, moral agency is not a necessary condition for having full and equal basic moral rights; but there is still room to argue it is a sufficient condition. In Chapter 6, I argue that Kant is right to hold that a being that is capable of treating others as ends in themselves—and willing to—cannot justly be denied the moral rights to life and liberty. This is the message of all those science fiction stories in which humans belatedly recognize the personhood of extraterrestrials, genetically engineered human be-

---

[78] John Harris offers one such intermediate definition of personhood, i.e. having the capacity to value one's own life. This capacity, he says, requires that a being 'be aware of itself as an independent centre of consciousness, existing over time with a future that it is capable of envisioning and wishing to experience': *The Value of Life: An Introduction to Medical Ethics* (London: Routledge, 1985), 18. This concept of personhood is more inclusive than Kant's in that it does not require moral agency, but less inclusive than Regan's concept of a subject-of-a-life, in that it requires a degree of self-awareness and conceptual sophistication that may not be possible for creatures that lack the capacity to use a human-style language. Thus, it probably does not apply to most non-human animals, with such possible exceptions as chimpanzees and other great apes (20–1); and it probably excludes many sentient human beings as well, such as young infants and some mentally disabled persons. Thus, while personhood in this intermediate sense is a plausible sufficient condition for strong moral status, it is not as plausible as a necessary condition for full moral status.

ings, or intelligent and self-aware robots, androids, or cyborgs.[79] It is also the insight that gives Kant's moral philosophy much of its lasting influence and appeal.

Nevertheless, Kant's theory fails to explain how it can be appropriate to ascribe strong moral rights to human beings who are not moral agents, even potentially. The plausible claim that the moral franchise must include all moral agents does not imply the implausible claim that it must exclude everyone else. If there were as yet no moral agents in the universe, then there would as yet be no moral obligations, and nothing would have moral status. Moral agents 'invent' moral status, by reasonably agreeing to accept specific moral obligations towards one another—and, often, towards other beings and things. No law of reason compels them to deny all moral status, or even the highest moral status, to entities that are not moral agents. On the contrary, they may have excellent reasons for according moral status to many such entities. These reasons will sometimes involve the roles that these entities play in the social and biological communities of which they are part. The relevance to moral status of social and ecosystemic relationships is the subject of the next chapter.

---

[79] Cyborgs are beings that are partly organic and partly mechanical.

# 5

## *The Relevance of Relationships*

The theories of moral status which we have considered thus far have two assumptions in common. First, each assumes that there is one and only one property which is (1) necessary for having any moral status, and (2) sufficient for having full and equal moral status. Albert Schweitzer nominates the property of being a living organism; Peter Singer opts for sentience, or the capacity to experience pleasure and pain; Immanuel Kant champions personhood, which he defines as the capacity for rational moral agency. And Tom Regan makes (or comes close to making) this claim for the property of being a subject-of-a-life. As we have seen, all of these uni-criterial theories are inadequate. None of these properties is necessary for having any moral status, and none is necessary and sufficient for having full moral status.

At the same time, each of these properties is, in my view, a sufficient basïs for a particular sort of moral status. As I argue in the next chapter, respecting life, avoiding cruelty to sentient beings, not harming subjects-of-a-life, and treating moral agents as ends in themselves, are all sound moral principles when properly interpreted. Yet none of these principles in isolation from the others yields a plausible account of moral status. This is a good reason for abandoning the assumption that moral status can be based entirely upon any one property.

A second assumption which these theories share is that the property which serves as the sole criterion of moral status must be an *intrinsic* property. An entity's intrinsic properties are those which it has, and which it is logically possible for it to have had even if it were the only thing in existence. By contrast, its relational properties are those which it has, but which it is not logically possible for it to have had were it the only thing in existence. Life, sentience, and the capacity for moral agency are in this sense intrinsic properties, whereas being a grandmother, or a recently naturalized citizen of Canada, are relational properties.[1]

This chapter examines two versions of the Relationships Only view. On either version of this view, an entity's moral status depends entirely upon certain of its relational properties; its intrinsic properties are irrelevant to what we owe it in the way of moral consideration. J. Baird Callicott holds that an entity's moral status depends upon its social and ecological relationships, i.e. its membership and role within a social or biological community.[2] Nel Noddings argues that the relationship of caring is the basis of all human moral obligations. In her view, we have moral obligations only towards beings for whom we are psychologically capable of caring, and who in turn have the capacity, at least potentially, to be aware of and responsive to our care.[3]

Each of these theories contains important insights; social and ecosystemic considerations can sometimes justify the ascription of stronger moral status to a group of entities than could be justified by the intrinsic properties of these entities. Nevertheless, neither version of the Relationships Only view provides an adequate account of moral status. Our obligations to living things, sentient beings, and moral agents are not entirely contingent upon the prior existence of social or ecological relationships between ourselves and them. Nor are these obligations entirely contingent upon our psychological capacity to care for such entities. There is, therefore, much to be said for the Relationships Plus view, which permits ascriptions of moral status to be justified on the basis of both intrinsic properties and relational ones.

## 5.1. *J. Baird Callicott's Relationships Only View*

Callicott is a philosophical interpreter and proponent of the environmental ethic pioneered by Aldo Leopold. On Leopold's theory, as

---

[1] Most intrinsic properties are relational in another sense. Every thing (except possibly the universe as a whole) has the intrinsic properties it has because of the causal processes that bring it into being, and those that act upon it during its existence. This does not vitiate the distinction between intrinsic and relational properties that I am making, which involves logical possibilities rather than empirical ones.

[2] Callicott, *In Defense of the Land Ethic*.          [3] Noddings, *Caring*.

Callicott expounds it, all of our moral obligations arise from the fact that we are members of communities. In Leopold's words,

All ethics so far evolved rest upon a single premise: that the individual is a member of a community of interdependent parts. His instincts prompt him to compete for his place in the community, but his ethics prompt him also to co-operate . . . The land ethic simply enlarges the boundaries of the community to include soils, waters, plants, and animals, or collectively: the land.[4]

As Callicott points out, Leopold was not a professional philosopher, and for that reason, 'the metaphysical and axiological implications of ecology are incompletely expressed in his literary legacy'.[5] Thus, there may be room for more than one interpretation of Leopold's moral philosophy. While I consider Callicott's interpretation to be essentially sound, I am concerned less with its complete consistency with Leopold's intentions than with the value of the theory of moral status that Callicott finds in Leopold's work.

### Humean/Darwinian Foundations

Callicott argues that Leopold's land ethic was inspired in part by Hume's moral philosophy. Hume argued that the primary foundation of morality is not reason, but sentiment. We are social creatures, equipped with an instinctive tendency to approve of attitudes and behaviours that serve the 'public utility', and to disapprove of those that harm it. Thus, it is natural for us to be pleased by such social virtues as 'friendship and gratitude, natural affection and public spirit, . . . a tender sympathy with others, and a generous concern for our kind and our species'.[6] Moral concepts and principles arise from this natural tendency to approve of that which serves the good of the human community. Reason enables us to serve the public good more effectively, e.g. by establishing principles of justice, legal rights and duties, and systems of legal enforcement. Through reason, we can extend our sympathies beyond the small community of family and friends within which they initially develop, to larger groups of human beings, and eventually to all of humanity.[7]

---

[4] Leopold, *A Sand County Almanac*, 239.
[5] *In Defense of the Land Ethic*, 5.
[6] Hume, *Enquiry Concerning the Principles of Morals*, 178.
[7] Ibid. 192.

Darwin also argued that human morality has an instinctive emotional foundation. His theory of the evolution of biological species through the natural selection of hereditary traits provides an explanation of how our distant ancestors must have come to have the social instincts that make morality possible. Human beings are mammals, and dependent upon parental care during an unusually long infancy and childhood. We are also primates that normally live within social groups larger than the 'nuclear' family. Under these conditions, our ancestors would have benefited from the development of co-operative—as well as competitive—social instincts. In Callicott's words,

the proto-moral sentiments of affection and sympathy . . . were naturally selected in mammals as a device to ensure reproductive success. The mammal mother in whom these sentiments were strong more successfully reared her offspring. For those species in which larger and more complex social organization led to even greater reproductive success, the filial affections and sympathies spilled over to other family members . . . Human beings evolved from highly social primates in a complex social matrix, and inherited highly refined and tender social sentiments and sympathies. With the acquisition of the power of speech and some capacity for abstraction, our ancestors began to codify the kinds of behavior concordant and discordant with their inherited communal-emotional bonds. They dubbed the former good and the latter evil. Ethics, thus, came into being.[8]

## The Land Ethic

To this Humean/Darwinian account of the psychological foundations of human morality, Leopold added the proposition that human beings naturally belong not only to *social* communities, but also to *biological* communities. Just as human beings are not naturally asocial beings who must somehow be persuaded to become social, so other living organisms are not biologically isolated individuals, thrown into the world to interact with one another as chance would have it. On the contrary, plant and animal species have co-evolved as functional parts of complexly ordered biological communities, or ecosystems. Biological communities include not only living organisms, but also such things as soil, water, and air.

---

[8] J. Baird Callicott, 'The Case Against Moral Pluralism', *Environmental Ethics*, 12, No. 2 (Summer 1990), 121.

Leopold describes a biological community as a pyramid structured by flows of energy:

Plants absorb energy from the sun. This energy flows through a circuit called the biota, which may be represented by a pyramid consisting of layers. The bottom layer is the soil. A plant layer rests on the soil, an insect layer on the plants, a bird and rodent layer on the insects, and so on up through various animal groups to the apex layer, which consists of the larger carnivores . . . Each successive layer depends on those below it for food and often for other services, and each in turn furnishes food and services to those above . . . Man shares an intermediate layer with the bears, [and] raccoons, . . . which eat both meat and vegetables.[9]

Biology and ecology teach us that we are akin to all terrestrial life, and wholly dependent upon the earth's ecosystems for our continued existence. 'The land ethic', Leopold says, 'simply enlarges the boundaries of the community to include soils, waters, plants, and animals, or collectively: the land.'[10] Just as it is appropriate to regard actions that are conducive to the good of the human community as morally good and those that are harmful to it as morally wrong, so it is appropriate to adopt the principle that 'A thing is right when it tends to preserve the integrity, stability, and beauty of the biotic community . . . [and] wrong when it tends otherwise.'[11] This principle, Leopold says, 'changes the role of *Homo sapiens* from conqueror of the land-community to plain member and citizen of it. It implies respect for his fellow-members, and also respect for the community as such.'[12]

## Biocentric Holism

Callicott argues that Leopold's land ethic differs from both utilitarian and deontological theories, in that the principles through which it ascribes moral status are holistic rather than individualistic.[13] This does not mean that the land ethic ascribes moral status only to species, ecosystems, or the biosphere as a whole. It means, rather, that our moral obligations to individual organisms and groups of organisms are not based upon their intrinsic properties. Rather, 'the good of the community as a whole . . . serves as a standard for the

[9] *A Sand County Almanac*, 252.    [10] Ibid. 239.
[11] Ibid. 262.    [12] Ibid. 240.
[13] *In Defense of the Land Ethic*, 11, 22.

assessment of the relative value and relative ordering of its constitutive parts'.[14] Although a small number of species would become extinct without human intervention, human activities have frequently brought about the extinction of far more species than natural processes would have done. Since natural biological diversity is vital to ecosystems, organisms of ecosystemically important species that are endangered by past or current human activities must be protected. Thus,

Animals of those species, which, like the honey bee, function in ways critically important to the economy of nature . . . would be granted a greater claim to moral attention than psychologically more complex and sensitive ones, say, rabbits and voles, which seem to be plentiful, globally distributed, reproductively efficient, and only routinely integrated into the natural economy.[15]

## The Biosocial Theory

This biocentric theory of moral status is unlikely to yield a strong status for human beings, who are plentiful, widely distributed, and increasingly destructive of the global biosphere. In 1980, Callicott boldly wrote:

The biospheric perspective does not exempt *Homo sapiens* from moral evaluation in relation to the well-being of the community of nature taken as a whole. The preciousness of individual deer, as of any other specimen, is inversely proportional to the population of the species. Environmentalists, however reluctantly and painfully, do not omit to apply the same logic to their own kind. As omnivores, the population of human beings should, perhaps, be roughly twice that of bears, allowing for differences in size.[16]

However, in more recent work Callicott argues that the land ethic does not require us to assess the moral worth of human beings *solely* in terms of their roles within the biological community. Leopold, he says, never expected the new environmental ethic to replace the older ethics that govern intrahuman relationships. Rather, he expected the land ethic to emerge as a natural addition to these older ethics. In Callicott's words,

[14] Ibid. 25.  [15] Ibid.
[16] J. Baird Callicott, 'Animal Liberation: A Triangular Affair', 27.

The biosocial development of morality does not grow in extent like an expanding balloon, leaving no trace of its previous boundaries, so much as like the circumference of a tree. Each emergent, and larger, social unit is layered over the more primitive and intimate ones.[17]

On this view, the land ethic is part of a more inclusive moral theory, which derives moral obligations from both social and biological relationships. Callicott calls this the *biosocial* theory. On the biosocial theory, 'How we ought and ought not to treat one another . . . is determined . . . by the nature and organization of communities.'[18] We are

members of nested communities each of which has a different structure and therefore different moral requirements. At the center is the immediate family . . . I have a duty not only to feed, clothe, and shelter my own children, [but also] . . . to bestow affection upon them. But to bestow a similar affection on the neighbors' kids is . . . not my duty . . . Similarly, I have obligations to my neighbors which I do not have to my less proximate fellow citizens . . . I have obligations to my fellow citizens which I do not have toward human beings in general *and* I have obligations to human beings in general which I do not have toward animals in general.[19]

Thus, on the biosocial theory, the structure of each community to which we belong determines the moral obligations that we have to co-members of the community; while the 'nesting' of communities—their arrangement into a pattern of concentric circles—provides the means of assigning relative weights to obligations arising from different communities. Generally speaking, Callicott says, 'the duties correlative to the inner social circles to which we belong eclipse those correlative to the rings farther from the heartwood when conflicts arise'.[20] Nevertheless, any expansion of the ethical balloon results in moral obligations to co-members of new (or newly recognized) communities, and may therefore 'demand choices which affect, in turn, the demands of the more interior social–ethical circles'.[21] Consequently, 'While the land ethic does not cancel human

---

[17] *In Defense of the Land Ethic*, 93; the tree-ring metaphor is that of Richard and Val Routley (now Richard Sylvan and Val Plumwood), in 'Human Chauvinism and Environmental Ethics', in D. Mannison, M. McRobbie, and R. Routley (eds.), *Environmental Philosophy* (Canberra, ACT: Department of Philosophy, Australian National University, 1980), 96–189.

[18] *In Defense of the Land Ethic*, 55.          [19] Ibid. 55–6.

[20] Ibid. 93–4.          [21] Ibid. 94.

morality, neither does it leave it unaffected.'[22] It does not, for instance, eliminate parents' obligation to care for their children; but it will sometimes oblige parents to deny children luxury products that are produced in ways that harm important ecosystems.

## Mixed Communities

Callicott's earlier exposition of the land ethic also has harsh implications for the moral status of domestic animals. Leopold, he notes, did not consider the treatment of battery chickens or feedlot steers to be a pressing moral issue.[23] On the contrary, Callicott says, 'Environmental ethics sets a very low priority on domestic animals as they very frequently contribute to the erosion of the integrity, stability, and beauty of the biotic communities into which they have been insinuated.'[24]

But domestic animals are not just members of our biological communities; they are also, in some instances, members of our social communities. Mary Midgley points out that, throughout human history, most 'human' social communities have also included some animals. She argues that domestic animals often have a legitimately distinctive moral status, because of their current and historical roles in our 'mixed' communities.[25] In his later work, Callicott adopts this suggestion. He argues that, since domestic animals of diverse species play diverse roles in our mixed communities, their moral status is correspondingly diverse:

Pets, for example, are . . . surrogate family members and merit treatment not owed either to less intimately related animals, for example to barnyard animals, *or*, for that matter, to less intimately related human beings . . . The animal-welfare ethic of the mixed community . . . would not censure using draft animals for work or even slaughtering animals for food so long as the keeping and using of such animals was not in violation . . . of a kind of evolved and unspoken social contract between man and beast.[26]

Callicott and Midgley agree that factory farming is morally objectionable not just because it causes suffering to animals, but because

---

[22] Ibid.  [23] Ibid. 16–17.

[24] Ibid. 37.

[25] Mary Midgley, *Animals and Why They Matter* (Athens, Ga.: University of Georgia Press, 1983), 112.

[26] *In Defense of the Land Ethic*, 56.

the practice of confining animals so severely that they are unable to engage in most of their natural behaviours violates an implicit and evolved contract between their kind and ours. It treats domestic animals as if they were inanimate objects, rather than members of our mixed social communities.[27] Wild animals, on the other hand, are not members of our social communities, and therefore they 'should not lie on the same spectrum of graded moral standing as family members, neighbors, fellow citizens, fellow human beings, pets, and other domestic animals'.[28] Wild animals are, however, parts of the biological community; consequently, we have moral obligations to them that 'may . . . be derived from an ecological description of nature'.[29]

The biosocial ethic requires that organisms of indigenous species be protected from human-caused extinction or decline. This is an obligation to them, to their species, and to the ecosystem as a whole—not merely to human beings who may be harmed by the loss of biological diversity. On the other hand, animals that are not native to the ecosystem, and not beneficial to it, sometimes must be removed for the good of the biological community. Even native animals, such as deer or rabbits, sometimes must be culled, in order to prevent their becoming too numerous—for instance, when previous human interventions have eliminated their natural predators.

## Practical Conclusions

On the biosocial theory, human beings are not morally obliged to be vegetarians. Forms of animal husbandry that are inimical to the health of the land are morally wrong, as are those that violate evolved and unspoken social contracts between humans and other animals. But on the question of diet, the land ethic recommends, 'not vegetables instead of animals, but organically as opposed to mechanico-chemically produced food'.[30] Hunting animals for food is not always morally objectionable. Some animal populations can withstand limited human predation, while others cannot—or cannot any longer. And some populations of non-indigenous animals may need to be eliminated entirely, in order to protect the biological community.

---

[27] *In Defense of the Land Ethic*, 55.　　　　[28] Ibid. 56.
[29] Ibid. 57.　　　　[30] Ibid. 36.

The biosocial theory implies that the reduction of human birth rates is a moral imperative. Because human moral rights must be respected, reductions in human birth rates must be achieved by voluntary means. Reducing the growth of the human population will not guarantee a healthy biosphere unless at the same time we adopt agricultural, industrial, land management, and waste disposal practices that are less ecologically destructive than many now in use. There are many facts—from the continuing loss of topsoil due to overgrazing and other unsound agricultural practices, to the onset of global warming due largely to the excessive burning of fossil fuels—that suggest that the earth's human population is already close to (and perhaps well above) the size that the biosphere can reliably support.[31]

## 5.2. Objections to Callicott's Relationships Only View

The biosocial theory has important virtues. It permits us to recognize moral obligations to plants and animals, and plant and animal species and populations, as well as to such inanimate elements of the natural world as rivers, seas, mountains, and marshes. These are obligations *towards* these various entities, born of the recognition of kinship, and of our membership in the biological community. This is a crucial advantage if, as I suspect, human beings who recognize moral obligations towards these elements of the natural world are more likely to find ways of protecting them over the course of many generations than are those who perceive them only as resources.[32]

It is also to the credit of the biosocial theory that it permits us to ascribe equal moral status to infants and young children who are not yet moral agents, and mentally disabled persons who may never be moral agents. Although the social roles of these individuals are often somewhat different from those of older and more able persons, they are nevertheless members of human social communities,

---

[31] For a good study of the limits to human population growth, see Lester R. Brown and Hal Kane, *Full House: Reassessing the Earth's Population Carrying Capacity* (New York: Norton, 1994).

[32] This is a utilitarian—or at least consequentialist—argument for the adoption of a non-utilitarian theory of moral status. The case for judging theories of moral status by such consequentialist considerations will be further explored in Chapter 6.

and entitled to the rights which that membership entails. In this respect, the biosocial theory is truer to moral convictions that most of us share than is Kant's deontological theory, which cannot readily explain how we can have moral obligations towards human beings who are incapable of moral agency.

A third strength of the biosocial theory is its pragmatism. It is a far more practical theory than those of Singer and Regan. These theories require us to expand the class of moral equals so far beyond the boundaries of our social communities that we are prohibited from doing what we often must do, for our own health and survival, or for the good of our social or biological communities. The biosocial theory recognizes that human and ecosystemic needs must sometimes take precedence over the needs of non-human individuals, be they microbes or mammals.

The most serious problems for the biosocial theory arise when we ask why we ought to base moral status *exclusively* upon social and ecological relationships. The advantage which Callicott claims for the biosocial theory is that of 'theoretical unity, coherency, and self-consistency'.[33] It is unsatisfactory, in his view, to hold that both social and biological relationships and such intrinsic properties as life, sentience, and moral agency, can legitimately serve as criteria of moral status. Such an eclectic approach, Callicott says, is incompatible with the essential goals of moral philosophy. There is, he says,

> both a rational philosophical demand and a human psychological need for a self-consistent and all-embracing moral theory. We are neither good philosophers nor whole persons if for one purpose we adopt utilitarianism, for another deontology, for a third animal liberation, for a fourth the land ethic, and for a fifth a life-principle or reverence-for-life ethic, and so on. Such ethical eclecticism is not only rationally intolerable, it is morally suspect—as it invites the suspicion of ad hoc rationalizations for merely expedient or self-serving actions.[34]

Although the biosocial theory utilizes a plurality of social and biological relationships as criteria of moral status, it is nevertheless a uni-criterial theory, in that it permits only such relational properties to serve as criteria of moral status. All of our moral obligations to other entities are held to spring from the structures of the communities to which both we and they belong. Thus, Callicott says, the

---

[33] *In Defense of the Land Ethic*, 50.     [34] Ibid. 264.

biosocial theory provides 'a framework for the adjudication of the very real conflicts between human welfare, animal welfare, and ecological integrity'.[35] In addition, he argues that it provides us with a coherent and unified world view, rather than forcing us to work with diverse moral principles that may be embedded within radically incompatible world views.

These advantages are smaller than they may at first appear. The biosocial theory provides no satisfactory principle for the resolution of conflicts between different *prima facie* moral obligations—either those arising from within a single community, or those arising from the different communities to which one person may belong. Moreover, it requires us to deny moral status to persons and other sentient beings that are not co-members of our social or biological communities. In this respect, it conflicts with moral judgements that most of us would make.

## The Illusion of Simplicity

Callicott credits to Mary Midgley the model of nested communities, each generating specific moral obligations, which become stronger as one moves closer to the centre of the circle.[36] But Midgley herself rejects the claim that moral obligations can be assigned appropriate relative weights by means of this model. Suppose, she says, that we try to arrange all of the communities to which we belong into a pattern of concentric circles, with the most intimate ones closest to the centre. We might place ourselves and our family members in the centre, followed by friends, professional colleagues, racial or ethnic group, socio-economic class, state or nation, humanity as a whole, animal members of the mixed community, the local ecosystem, and finally the terrestrial biosphere. If we do this, we will see at once

that the order of the circles is not at all certain . . . At each point we may want to reverse it, or be dissatisfied with either order. Further groupings constantly occur to us, and, at every stage, it seems that some groupings are more important for some purposes, some for others. The concentric arrangement will not work at all.[37]

Midgley is right; moral obligations cannot be given appropriate

[35] Ibid. 50–1.                                              [36] Ibid. 52.
[37] Midgley, *Animals and Why They Matter*, 28–9.

weightings through the method that Callicott suggests. Even if we could agree about the proper arrangement of the circles, we would still not know the relative strength of the moral obligations arising from different communities. For although some of our obligations to social intimates are stronger than any analogous obligations to socially distant individuals, there are other moral obligations that do not work in this way. For instance, our moral and legal obligation not to murder strangers is just as strong as our obligation not to murder friends or family members. As Peter Wenz points out,

We ordinarily think of negative human rights somewhat differently from positive human rights. In the case of negative human rights, we are less concerned with a person's placement on concentric circles . . . For example, people have a negative human right to freedom of religion. We do not ordinarily think that we have any more right to interfere with the religious practices of a stranger or a foreigner than of a friend or colleague. The same is true of people's freedom to live . . . If I kill someone, it is no defense to say, 'Well, she was a stranger' or 'He was a foreigner.'[38]

Callicott agrees that we must respect the basic moral rights of all human beings. But it is not clear how, on the biosocial theory, the obligation to respect the rights of strangers can override conflicting obligations generated within the inner circles. If murdering a stranger will help me feed my family, why should I refrain? The problem here is that we are given no method by which to identify counterexamples to the primary principle—that moral obligations arising close to the centre generally outweigh those arising farther out. This means that the practical problem-solving power that Callicott claims for the biosocial theory is largely illusory.

There are other ways in which moral uncertainty can arise within the biosocial theory. As Jim Cheney points out, neither the 'structure' of a community, nor any associated moral obligations, can be deduced from a purely descriptive account of the activities of its members. Rather,

the history of ethics parallels the attempts to provide ethically relevant 'descriptions' of the moral community. The lesson to be learned from that history is that descriptions of the moral community 'coevolve' with accounts of ethical obligation within the community. Once we have our description

---

[38] Peter Wenz, *Environmental Justice* (Albany, NY: State University of New York Press, 1988), 324.

in hand, it is true that ethical obligations can be derived from the account, but the description is not simply a given that is historically independent of the ethical theory derived from it.[39]

Not only may the structure of a community be differently understood at different periods of its history; persons who belong to the community at any given time may disagree about its structure. For instance, the beliefs that privileged persons hold may be different from those of persons closer to the bottom of the social heap. Even if we were to find that every member of the society held the same beliefs about its structure, and about the moral obligations that structure implies, we still would not know whether these beliefs were true. The society might not be structured in the way its members have been led to believe; or its structure may be clear enough, but fundamentally unjust. If the structure of the community is fundamentally unjust, then one would normally conclude that its members have no moral obligation to preserve that structure; slaves have no moral duty to obey their owners, even if the structure of the community requires their obedience.

These considerations undermine the claim that our moral theory will be simpler, more coherent, and more useful for the resolution of actual problems, if we treat moral status as solely a function of community relationships. On the contrary, our moral theory becomes *less* complicated in important respects when we recognize the equal relevance of certain intrinsic properties. If the fact that a being is sentient is enough to oblige us not to be cruel to it, then we need not study its role within the social or biological community before concluding that we ought not to kill it or cause it pain without good reason. Sometimes we need to understand specific social or biological relationships in order to know whether harming a sentient animal is justifiable—but not before concluding that justification is called for. Similarly, if we believe that all moral agents have basic moral rights, then we need not study a person's place (if any) in the social and ecological communities to which we ourselves belong, before concluding that we ought not to murder or torture that person.

[39] Jim Cheney, 'Callicott's "Metaphysics of Morals"', *Environmental Ethics*, 13, No. 4 (Winter 1991), 318–19.

## Extraterrestrials and Displaced Animals

Consider E.T., the endearing extraterrestrial in the Steven Spielberg film of that title. Accidentally stranded on Earth, E.T. has no pre-existing social relationship to any human being, and no natural role in any of the earth's biological communities. Nevertheless, most viewers sympathize with him, and with the children who protect him and help him to return home, rather than with the frightened adults who send armed squadrons to capture or destroy him. The children recognize E.T.'s gentle nature and make friends with him, while the grown-ups perceive only his strangeness, and would have killed him needlessly. Which group of human beings behaves more ethically?

Callicott has no patience with such science fiction scenarios. He argues that the immensity of interstellar space makes it unlikely that human beings will ever travel to other inhabited planets, or that aliens will ever visit us here. Moreover, if we do encounter extra-terrestrial organisms, they may not resemble any earthly plant or animal. Isn't it 'more than just a little fatuous', he asks, to seek to construct 'an ethic for the treatment of something we-know-not-what'?[40] The biosocial theory, he points out, does not require us to behave violently towards extraterrestrials; it simply has nothing to say about them.

This response is not entirely to the point. The philosophical pur-pose of thought experiments involving friendly aliens is not to sug-gest that we are likely to encounter such beings in the near future, but to test the hypothesis that all of our moral obligations to other persons are necessarily contingent upon the prior existence of social or biological relationships between ourselves and them. Friendly aliens are a metaphor for any group of persons with whom we have not yet established amicable relationships, but with whom such rela-tionships are possible. Audiences' sympathetic reactions to E.T. sug-gest that most people do not believe that the absence of prior relationships excuses ruthless aggression against an alien being that has shown no signs of hostility.

The biosocial theory is kinder to domestic animals than is the land ethic, considered in isolation. However, it denies moral status to terrestrial animals that are neither socially related to humans nor beneficial to the ecosystem. The enormous populations of intro-

---

[40] *In Defense of the Land Ethic*, 259.

duced rabbits in Australia and New Zealand are an example that has already been mentioned. Because the rabbits are neither members of human social communities, nor beneficial to the ecosystems to which they have been introduced, the biosocial theory implies that we can have no moral obligations towards them. But, while it may be essential to limit the number of rabbits, common sense suggests that they should not be killed in ways that entail severe or protracted suffering, if more humane methods are available. Moreover, if feasible means could be found to limit rabbit populations without killing rabbits (e.g. by dispersing contraceptives), that would be still better from a moral point of view.

These cases illustrate the inadequacy of the biosocial theory. While social and biotic relationships shape many of our moral obligations, they are not the sole determinants of moral status. Alien persons, human or otherwise, are not to be treated as mere means; and sentient beings are not to be needlessly killed or made to suffer—even if they do not belong to our social or biotic communities. Thus, this version of the Relationships Only view fails. But there is another version that may fare better. Nel Noddings's feminist ethic of care is worth examining, in part because it does a better job of accommodating common-sense judgements about the moral status of alien persons and non-indigenous animals.

### 5.3. *Nel Noddings's Ethic of Care*

Noddings holds that moral status is a function of the emotional relationship that she calls *caring*. It is this relationship, she says, that gives rise to all moral obligations. Our 'first and unending obligation is to meet the other as one-caring'.[41] Noddings regards caring as a human universal, in that all psychologically normal human beings are capable (at least potentially) of caring for other human beings.[42] The desire to be in caring relationships is, she holds, the original and enduring basis of all human morality.

In a caring relationship, the 'one-caring' is receptive to the feelings and needs of the 'cared-for', and is therefore spontaneously motivated to meet those needs. This is a 'feeling-receptive' mode,

---

[41] Noddings, *Caring*, 17.    [42] Ibid. 27–8.

although it does not always involve strong emotions.[43] Reason is in
constant use, determining the best means of meeting the needs of
those for whom we care, and setting priorities; but the motivation to
care is emotional and instinctive rather than rational. 'The relation
of natural caring' is, Noddings says, 'the human condition that we,
consciously or unconsciously, perceive as "good." It is that condition toward which we long and strive, and it is our longing for caring—to be in that special relation—that provides the motivation to
be moral.'[44]

### Femininity and the Rejection of Moral Principles

Noddings describes her moral theory as 'feminine'. To call this a
feminine theory, she says, is not to suggest that all women accept it,
or that all men reject it. Rather, a care-based ethic is 'feminine in the
deep classical sense—rooted in receptivity, relatedness, and responsiveness'.[45] Like Carol Gilligan, Noddings believes that women are
often alienated by the standard philosophical models of mature
moral reasoning. In deontological theories, and some forms of utilitarianism, actions are evaluated on the basis of rules and principles,
which in turn are ranked and ordered in the light of a supreme rule
or principle.[46] But this emphasis upon the ranking and ordering of
rules and principles is, Noddings says, 'the approach of the detached
one, of the father'.[47] Women, she says, do not lack the ability to formulate and rank moral principles; rather, they tend to see these
processes as peripheral to the solution of the moral problems that
they face. As ones-caring, women

> are not so much concerned with the rearrangement of priorities among
> principles; they are concerned . . . with maintaining and enhancing caring.
> They do not abstract away from the concrete situation those elements that
> allow formulation of deductive argument; rather, they remain in the situ-
> ation as sensitive, receptive, and responsible agents.[48]

---

[43] *Caring*, 34.          [44] Ibid. 5.          [45] Ibid. 2.

[46] The model of moral development that Noddings criticizes is Lawrence
Kohlberg's. On this model, mature moral reasoners employ a supreme principle of
justice very like that advocated by John Rawls. See Kohlberg's 'Stages in Moral
Development as a Basis for Moral Education', in C. M. Beck, B. S. Crittenden, and
E. V. Sullivan (eds.), *Moral Education: Interdisciplinary Approaches* (Toronto, Ont.:
Toronto University Press, 1971).

[47] *Caring*, 2.          [48] Ibid. 42.

Noddings advocates, therefore, what might be called a principled rejection of moral principles. The one-caring acts, 'not by a fixed rule, but by affection and regard'.[49] She is 'wary of rules and principles. She formulates and holds them loosely, tentatively, as economies of a sort, but she insists upon holding closely to the concrete'.[50] She will not value abstract principles above the needs of those for whom she cares. A woman, Noddings says, could not have written the Biblical account of Abraham and Isaac.[51] When Abraham's God demands that he ritually sacrifice his son Isaac, Abraham reluctantly prepares to obey what he regards as a higher law than that of family loyalty, although the command is rescinded at the last moment. A mother, Noddings says, would not have acted as Abraham did; nor would a mother-god have demanded what this father-god did:

> The mother in Abraham's position would respond to the fear and trust of her child—not the voice of abstraction. The Mother-as-God would not use a parent and child so fearfully . . . Here, says woman, is my child. I will not sacrifice him for God, or for the greatest good, or for these ten others. Let us find some other way.[52]

## Caring and Reciprocity

A caring relationship need not be fully symmetrical, and often it is not. Infants and young children cannot (yet) fully reciprocate the care that they receive. Nevertheless, Noddings holds, some eventual reciprocity is essential to an authentic caring relationship. The cared-for must contribute, at the very least, an awareness of the caring which is received: 'the perception by the cared-for of an attitude of caring on the part of the one-caring is partially constitutive of caring . . . Caring involves two parties: the one-caring and the cared-for. It is complete when it is fulfilled in both.'[53]

Like Callicott, Noddings uses the metaphor of concentric circles; but in her account the circles represent caring relationships, rather than social or biological communities. The relationships nearest the centre are based upon love; these generally give rise to the strongest obligations.[54] In the outer regions are our relationships to individuals for whom we have personal regard, and those whom we have not

---

[49] Ibid. 24.  [50] Ibid. 55.  [51] Ibid. 43.
[52] Ibid. 44.  [53] Ibid. 68.  [54] Ibid. 46.

met but for whom we are potentially willing to care. We are linked to many strangers through chains of personal relationships, and through formal and informal arrangements that establish wider communities of interest.

The ethic of care requires that proximate strangers be met with a caring attitude. This does not preclude vigorous self-defence when needed, since that can be essential to caring for oneself and others. Nor are we obliged to impoverish ourselves and our families for the sake of strangers. However, we must not fail to respond—within the limits of our other obligations—to the needs of each human being whom we meet, or by whom we are addressed. Conversely, Noddings says,

> Our obligation is limited and delimited by relation . . . We are not obliged to summon the 'I must' if there is no possibility of completion in the other. I am not obliged to care for starving children in Africa, because there is no way for this caring to be completed in the other unless I abandon the caring to which I am obligated.[55]

## Caring for Non-human Entities

Noddings argues that, because human beings vary greatly in their capacity to respond emotionally to animals, there is no universal moral obligation to care for animals. Persons who form affectionate relationships with animals come to have moral obligations towards them. On the other hand, persons who form no such relationships with animals are not thereby morally remiss. Because our affective responses to animals tend to be personal, and directed towards animals of particular species, the associated moral obligations are also personal and species-specific. For instance,

> If I have pleasant memories of caring for cats and having them respond to me, I cannot ethically drive a needy one away from my back door. A chain has been forged. A stranger-cat comes to me formally related to my pet. I have committed myself to respond to this creature. But what if the creature at the door is a rat? I would certainly not invite it in . . . Indeed, I might kill it with whatever effective means lay at hand. . . . the 'I must' arises (for me) with respect to cats, but I feel no such stirring in connection to rats.[56]

---

[55] *Caring*, 86.        [56] Ibid. 156.

Despite the variability of human emotional responses to animals, Noddings says, most human beings are able to 'receive' the pain of animals of a wide range of species. If an animal's pain signals are enough like ours, then we naturally respond to them. When an animal cries out in pain, 'We feel a sympathetic twinge . . . that arouses in us the induced feeling, "I must do something." '[57] We are therefore obliged not to inflict pain upon any animal without good reason. This obligation is not based upon the utilitarian principle, but upon the human capacity for empathic response:

insofar as we can receive the pain of a creature and detect its relief as we re- move the pain, we are both addressed and received. There is at least this much reciprocity in our contact and, therefore, at least this much obliga- tion—that we must not inflict pain without justification.[58]

Although she holds that some people have moral obligations to animals, Noddings says that these are never as strong as our obliga- tions to other human beings, because caring relationships between humans and animals are incomplete. Animals often respond to human care, but not in all of the ways necessary to complete the car- ing relationship. Noddings says that her cat, for instance,

is a responsive cared-for, but her responsiveness is restricted: she responds directly to my affection with a sort of feline affection . . . But she has no pro- jects to pursue. There is no intellectual or spiritual growth for me to nurture, and our relationship is stable. It does not possess the dynamic potential that characterizes my relationship with infants.[59]

One can also care for plants, things, and ideas; but Noddings says that here we have left the realm of the ethical for that of the aes- thetic. Unlike inanimate objects, plants can respond to care; but they cannot respond in the ways that create moral obligations. If one has undertaken to care for a plant, then one may feel as though one has moral obligations to it. But this is not 'the true ethical ought', since 'I cannot receive a plant as I can a human being, or even as I can certain animals, and the relation can never be doubly caring.'[60] Similarly, ideas or things may engross us and reward our attention by seeming to reveal themselves; but, Noddings says, 'we do not usually suppose that the thing or idea is itself somehow

[57] Ibid. 150.      [58] Ibid.      [59] Ibid. 156.
[60] Ibid. 160.

subjectively enhanced by our caring . . . there is . . . no affective reciprocity or manifestation of feeling for us as ones-caring'.[61]

## Practical Consequences

On Noddings's theory, our strongest moral obligations are to our fellow human beings. Because all of us are capable of caring for any human being, we have potential moral obligations towards all human beings. In contrast, our obligations towards animals are contingent upon our individual affective responses to them. Thus, becoming a vegetarian may be ethically obligatory for those whose emotional responses to animals are incompatible with meat eating, but it is not obligatory for those who are not so affected. We ought not to inflict pain upon animals without justification; but even that obligation is contingent upon our individual psychological capacity to receive the pain of animals of specific species.

This account precludes our having moral obligations to plants, species, and other non-sentient elements of the natural world. We have moral obligations respecting the protection of nature, but these are obligations to other human beings. Noddings says:

> If I care for human beings, I must not defoliate their forests, poison their soils, or destroy their crops. Similarly, I may wish to preserve the delicate desert from the damage caused by dirt-bikes but, in doing so, I am not behaving ethically toward the desert. Rather, I am supposing that the aesthetic appreciation I feel for the landscape may be shared by other persons, and I feel that I ought to preserve that possibility for them.[62]

## 5.4. Objections to Noddings's Relationships Only View

Noddings's caring-based theory of moral status is less vulnerable to counterexamples involving extraterrestrials and displaced animals than is Callicott's biosocial theory. On Noddings's account, a sentient being need not already be part of any of our communities for us to have moral obligations towards it; it need only be *possible* for us to care for it, and for it to respond appropriately. Thus, were we to meet extraterrestrials who appealed to our sympathies as much as

---

[61] *Caring*, 161.    [62] Ibid. 160.

E.T. does, then we would at least owe them humane treatment. And if, like E.T., they were appropriately responsive to our care and capable of caring for us in return, then we would have moral obligations to them much like those to proximate human strangers. Displaced terrestrial animals are also owed humane treatment, provided that their behaviours are enough like ours that we can receive their pain.

However, Noddings's theory has problems of its own. By making moral obligations contingent upon the agent's possession of specific empathic capacities, it appears to excuse persons who lack such capacities from all moral obligations. Such persons are, in effect, to be regarded as incapable of moral agency. Moreover, the rejection of moral rules and principles leaves us without moral guidance in cases where our empathic capacities fail us, or have no opportunity to come into play. These objections can be made from either a Kantian or utilitarian viewpoint. They can also be made from the standpoint of Callicott's biosocial theory, which says that our obligations are shaped by the structures of our social and biological communities, rather than by our individual emotional responses.

## Rational Egoists and Incurable Bigots

In Noddings's view, we can have moral obligations only to beings for which we are capable of caring, and which are capable of responding appropriately to our care. Thus, to support the common-sense conviction that we have some moral obligations to every human being whom we meet, she must hold that any human being is at least potentially capable of caring for any other human being. She says, 'the impulse to act in behalf of the present other is itself innate. It lies latent in each of us, awaiting gradual development in a succession of caring relations.'[63]

This an empirical claim, and not obviously true. The fact that human social instincts have evolved because of their survival value does not demonstrate that all human beings initially possess these instincts, still less that they will continue to possess them throughout their lives. Vision also has survival value, but there are persons who are born blind, and others who are permanently deprived of sight. There may also be persons who, though psychologically normal in other respects, have no capacity to care for other persons. On

---

[63] Ibid. 83.

Noddings's account, such persons could owe nothing to others, and thus could not be moral agents.

This conclusion is too strong. I do not know whether there are any pure egoists, that is, persons who can be motivated only by concern for their own interests. Such persons would probably not be good parents, friends, or lovers. But if they were able to observe basic moral constraints in their dealings with others—albeit on self-interested grounds—then it would be unreasonable to deny that they were moral agents. Although their moral agency might be flawed, that flaw would not render them incapable of moral agency. The mistake that Noddings makes here is the reverse of that which Kant makes in holding that actions can have no moral value if they are done because of feelings or emotions, rather than from respect for moral law. *Both* empathic concern for others, *and* the desire to follow sound principles, can often provide morally good reasons for action.

There are also persons whose ideological commitments or personal experiences make it impossible for them to care for certain human beings, e.g. those of a particular culture, sex, race, or religion. Noddings might say that we have obligations even towards human beings for whom we cannot care, because we could learn to care for them. But again, this is not obviously true. Perhaps in some persons the capacity to care for some portion of the human race is irreparably blocked. If so, then they may not be entirely to blame for this constriction of their emotional capacities; but it is implausible to suppose that the very depth of their bigotry relieves them of all moral obligations towards those for whom they cannot care.

## Rights, Rules, and the Limits of Caring

Noddings holds that human beings can receive the pain signals of animals of many species, and are therefore morally obliged not to inflict pain without justification. But it may not be true that all otherwise normal human beings can receive the pain of animals. Some may have had no opportunity to learn. Others may be unable or unwilling to learn, for example because of a philosophical or religious ideology that denies that animals can feel pain, or that their pain matters morally. If these persons are otherwise psychologically normal, then it is implausible to hold that they have no obligation to avoid needlessly inflicting pain upon animals. What might be for most of us an instinctive response, for them might require conscious thought. Nevertheless, it would not be unreasonable to ask them not to step on puppies and kittens. In making that request, we would be asking them to adopt a moral rule for which they could have no personal emotional basis; but that would not make the request inappropriate.

Rita Manning also defends a feminist ethic of care. Unlike Noddings, Manning argues that a feminist ethic requires some moral rules and principles—especially those establishing fundamental rights. Rights and rules, she argues, provide necessary guidance in cases 'where moral attention flags, for reasons which are beyond our control'.[64] They also 'provide a minimum below which no one should fall and beyond which behavior is morally condemned. Rules provide a minimum standard for morality. Rights provide a measure of protection for the helpless.'[65]

In Manning's view, such minimum standards enable us to extend our caring in important ways. A strong sense of minimum moral standards can facilitate collective action, e.g. to correct pervasive injustices, or to aid victims of distant disasters. Moral rights and rules can be used to deliberate about how best to care for others, especially when

we are not in direct contact with the objects of care, [and] our actions cannot be guided by the expressed and observed desires of those cared for . . . In these cases, we must make assumptions about their desires, and we can assume that they do not wish to fall below some minimum standard.[66]

Rules and rights can also facilitate the fair allocation of care, even in face-to-face situations. For example, in a hospital emergency room, the staff must not focus upon the needs of the first accident victim brought in, to the exclusion of later victims who may be more badly hurt. Finally, Manning says, the public recognition of rights and rules creates expectations in the cared-for to which the one-caring must be sensitive.

Merely adhering to the minimum standards established by the anti-cruelty principle, or by the principle that all human beings have moral rights, is not enough to make one a good person. In an ideal

---

[64] Rita Manning, *Speaking from the Heart: A Feminist Perspective on Ethics* (Lanham, Md.: Roman & Littlefield, 1992), 82.
[65] Ibid. 74.                                              [66] Ibid. 74–5.

world, we might be so strongly responsive to the needs of other beings that we would have no use for minimum moral standards. But the world is imperfect, and so are we. Sometimes we cannot care enough, even about people who are socially close to us—much less about plant or animal species that lack emotional appeal, or people whom we dislike. Respecting rights and rules is not a substitute for active caring, and 'we should not allow it to distance us from the objects of care'.[67] Yet, given our deficiencies as carers, the world would be worse without these minimum standards.

These points support the conclusion that, in giving due credit to the legitimate role of caring relationships in shaping our judgements of moral status, we need not deny moral status to things that we do not happen to (be able to) care for. Persons who lack the capacity to receive the pain of animals still have an obligation to avoid cruelty. Similarly, persons who can afford to help arguably have a moral obligation to co-operate with international efforts to aid starving children in Africa, even though most of them will never have the opportunity to care for any of these children in person.

## 5.5. *Conclusions*

Both intrinsic and relational properties play important roles in shaping our legitimate attributions of moral status. Our capacity to empathize with co-members of our social communities helps to both explain and justify many of the judgements that we commonly make about the moral status of human beings, and animals of certain species. Yet, in formulating concepts of moral status, we cannot always be bound by the limits of our empathetic capacities, or the borders of our social and biotic communities. Even those who are incapable of receiving an animal's pain can understand the ethical objections to the needless infliction of pain and suffering—even upon unattractive and ecologically harmful animals. With good moral education and luck, human moral agents can even learn to respect the moral rights of persons for whom they feel no empathy at all.

Social and biological relationships shape our moral obligations

[67] *Speaking from the Heart*, 82.

towards many entities, but not to the exclusion of moral principles based upon respect for life, sentience, and moral agency. A multi-criterial approach that integrates these diverse factors is called for. Sketching and defending such an approach is the task of the next chapter.

# 6

# *A Multi-Criterial Analysis of Moral Status*

This chapter presents an account that ties moral status both to certain intrinsic properties and to certain relational ones. Three key intrinsic properties—life, sentience, and moral agency—are directly relevant to moral status, each in a different way. I suggest three principles that express the general nature of that relevance. At the same time, our nature and circumstances, as individuals who exist within both social communities and terrestrial ecosystems, require us to make our judgements of moral status consistent with the demands of important social and ecological relationships. I suggest four principles that govern the way in which this is commonly and appropriately done. Arguments are given for each principle, but specific applications and examples are largely reserved for Chapters 8–10.

After stating and commenting on each of these principles, I discuss the advantages of this multi-criterial account, in comparison to the uni-criterial accounts that we have considered in the first five chapters; briefly explore some of the ways in which these diverse criteria are to be weighed and balanced; and comment on the important but limited role of cultural and personal differences in the justification of judgements of moral status.

## 6.1. *Seven Principles of Moral Status*

The principles which follow are meant to operate interactively. This means that the practical implications of each principle cannot be well understood except in the light of the others. Nevertheless, each principle usefully focuses our attention upon a property or set of properties that can appropriately be used as a criterion of moral status.

These principles are implicit elements of common-sense morality. This does not mean that everyone consciously uses them, but rather that most of the judgements about moral status that thoughtful people make, and can support with reasoned argument, can be defended by appealing to one or more of these principles. None of these principles is deducible from empirical facts, or from analytic truths about moral terms or concepts; yet each is defensible in common-sense ways.

**1. *The Respect for Life Principle:*** *Living organisms are not to be killed or otherwise harmed, without good reasons that do not violate principles 2–7.*

Like Schweitzer's ethic of Reverence for Life, the Respect for Life principle treats all harms done to living things as morally undesirable, other things being equal. But unlike that highly idealistic ethic, it imputes no wrongdoing to those who harm living things when there are morally sound reasons for doing so. To provide for human well-being, and that of the animals, plants, and ecosystems that are under our care, we are often obliged to engage in activities that harm living things. For instance, we cannot avoid causing the deaths of many common micro-organisms in the course of growing, harvesting, and preparing food, and keeping our bodies, our clothing, and our dwellings tolerably clean. Since these organisms generally have no significant claim to moral status other than that they are alive, and since the alternative would be to permit harm to organisms that have a stronger moral status than can be based upon mere organic life, we need feel no guilt in these cases.

The Respect for Life principle does not explain what counts as a sufficiently good reason for harming a living thing; nor could it, since the fact that something is alive tells us very little about its moral status. The strength of the reasons needed to justify harming any particular living thing depends upon additional factors specified in later principles: e.g. whether it is sentient, or a moral agent, or a member of a social community that includes human moral agents; whether it belongs to a species that has special importance to the ecosystem; and whether it is regarded by some people as sacred, or of special moral value.

That being the argument, it is reasonable to ask whether life is sufficient for any moral status at all. Might it not be better to restrict moral status to some subset of living things, e.g. those that can experience pleasure and pain? Both reason and empathy require us to recognize obligations to sentient beings. In interacting with these beings, we can apply the Golden Rule in a meaningful way, since sentient beings can suffer or enjoy, and thus can have preferences about what happens to them. But why should we accept obligations towards living things that cannot care what we do to them? The answer, in part, is that there are pragmatic reasons for recognizing moral obligations towards all living things.

Even from a strictly anthropocentric perspective, there are excellent reasons for avoiding the needless destruction of living things. Ecology teaches that the extirpation of even seemingly useless plant or animal species or populations can damage the ecosystems upon which we depend for our own existence. Furthermore, the loss of any plant or animal species may deprive us or future human beings of medical or other benefits that these organisms might have provided. Thus, concern for the present and future well-being of humanity is enough to recommend a cautious attitude towards the destruction of living things that could—with no appreciable loss to the quality of human lives—be left alone.

At first glance, this seems to be merely a reason for ascribing instrumental value to non-sentient organisms. But humanity may benefit more, in the long run, from according moral status to all living things. It makes a more than verbal difference whether we believe, on the one hand, that all living things have a claim to our consideration, however modest; or, on the other hand, that plants and other non-sentient life forms should be protected only when they have demonstrable value to human beings. If we believe that the needless destruction of living things is a wrong against them, not just a possible wrong against other human beings, then we will be more likely to search for ways to reduce the needless killing that we do, individually and collectively. We will not be permanently content with methods of agriculture, animal husbandry, fishing, manufacturing, mining, transportation, energy production, forestry, recreation, flood control, and waste disposal that cause the needless destruction of harmless plants and animals. Respect for life may, therefore, substantially improve humanity's chances of surviving and flourishing into the deep future. This is one lesson to be learned from the aboriginal Australian people's remarkable success in preserving the fragile ecosystems of that arid continent, throughout the tens of thousands of years prior to European settlement.

This is a pragmatic argument for regarding living things as worth protecting for their own sake. Such arguments cannot rationally compel us to respect all life. The facts of ecology provide no conclusive reason to respect *all* living things. For instance, many genetically engineered or artificially transplanted organisms make no positive contribution to the health of the biosphere. Ecology is an empirical science, and by itself it cannot prove that we have moral obligations towards even those organisms that we know to have special ecological importance; at most, it shows that it is in the interest of our own kind to accept such obligations.

Neither science nor pure reason can compel us to respect all life. For many people, the adoption of the Respect for Life principle seems to require something more akin to a spiritual conversion than to a logical deduction. Nevertheless, that principle is at least as sensible as those that require respect only for living things that pass some further test, such as sentience, ecological value, or the ability to inspire human affection. For one thing, the Respect for Life principle is easier to apply. It is often quite easy to ascertain that an entity is alive, but very difficult to determine its degree of sentience, or its ecological value. For example, many people doubt the sentience of spiders and insects, and most are unaware of the ecological roles of each of the many species of arthropod that they encounter; but few doubt that these creatures are alive. Ease of application is important, because a moral principle loses much of its value if it is excessively difficult to know whether or not it applies to the case at hand.

The Respect for Life principle also derives modest support from the teleological nature of life. Because living things are goal-directed systems that have a good of their own, they can be harmed, in that their goals can be thwarted. For this reason, we can often empathize—after a fashion—even with plants, and other organisms that appear to be wholly non-sentient. Living things are, therefore, logically and psychologically appropriate objects of a general moral obligation not to do harm without good reason. In this, they are unlike drops of rain, stones, and other non-living things. With a few possible exceptions,[1] inanimate objects cannot be treated in ways

---

[1] Complex teleologically organized machines constitute one apparent counterexample. However, if a machine were capable of the functions typical of organic life, or if it were sentient and/or self-aware, then it may be argued that it ought to be considered an artificial life form, rather than an inanimate object.

that defeat their natural goals, because they have no such goals. It is possible to 'empathize' with non-living things only to the extent that we imagine them to be alive or sentient (or both), or inhabited by living or sentient things. Because of the teleological nature of life, the Respect for Life principle can plausibly be applied not only to naturally evolved terrestrial organisms that are beneficial to the ecosystems of which they are part, but also to domesticated or genetically engineered organisms, transplanted organisms, and even extraterrestrial organisms—should we ever encounter any.

**2. The Anti-Cruelty Principle:** *Sentient beings are not to be killed or subjected to pain or suffering, unless there is no other feasible way of furthering goals that are (1) consistent with principles 3–7; and (2) important to human beings, or other entities that have a stronger moral status than can be based on sentience alone.*

Premature death is a harm to any living thing, because living things are internally organized to preserve—for a time—their own existence. But death is a greater harm to sentient than to non-sentient organisms. For a non-sentient organism, death terminates only a set of biological processes of which the organism itself was unaware. For sentient beings, it terminates an existence that may have been pleasurable. Sentient beings are also vulnerable to pain. Pain is an unpleasant experience, and one that all sentient beings strongly prefer to avoid, other things being equal. These are sound reasons for recognizing an obligation not to be cruel to sentient beings of any species.

### Empathy and the Rejection of Cruelty

If Hume and Darwin are right, our ancestors were capable of developing such concepts as cruelty and kindness only because they were already social beings, with an instinctive capacity to care about other members of their social communities. It may, therefore, be natural for human beings initially to apply the Anti-Cruelty principle only to human beings—and perhaps to non-human animals who are members of their social communities.[2] But even if this is so, it does

[2] It is also possible that the application of the Anti-Cruelty principle only to human or other members of our social communities is something that we learn as part of our acculturation. Children often empathize with animals that are reared for

not follow that we cannot rightly apply the Anti-Cruelty principle to sentient beings that are not members of our species, or our mixed social communities. As Hume puts it, 'General rules are often extended beyond the principle whence they first arise.'[3]

Whatever the original range of the human capacity for empathy, we now have good reasons to apply the Anti-Cruelty principle to all sentient beings. Logical consistency arguably requires that we do this. As Tom Nagel points out, we each regard our own pain as objectively bad, and hence as providing other persons with reasons to prevent or alleviate it. Thus, he says, consistency requires us to recognize that the pain of other persons is also objectively bad, and that we have objective reasons to prevent or alleviate it.[4] Bonnie Steinbock notes that, if Nagel is right, then

it would seem that the pain experienced by non-humans would also yield objective reasons for action. Pain is pain, no matter who feels it. So long as a being is sentient . . . it has an interest in not feeling pain, and its interest provides moral agents with prima facie reasons for acting.[5]

## Not All Beings are Equal

Although the Anti-Cruelty principle applies to all sentient beings, it does not require that we treat all sentient beings as our moral equals. While this is an inspiring moral ideal, it is not a principle that can be enforced upon human moral agents as a minimum requirement for morally acceptable behaviour. For it is often virtually impossible to avoid harming organisms that are probably sentient; yet the reasons that we have for deliberately or inadvertently harming sentient non-human beings are often insufficient to justify doing similar harms to sentient human beings.

If we were gods, having neither biological needs nor physical vulnerabilities, then we might be able to treat the interests of all sentient beings as equal in moral importance to our own. We could, at least,

---

meat, or with spiders, insects, and other animals that most adults perceive only as vermin.

[3] Hume, *Enquiry Concerning the Principles of Morals*, 207.

[4] Thomas Nagel, *The Possibility of Altruism* (Oxford: Oxford University Press, 1970).

[5] Bonnie Steinbock, *Life Before Birth: The Moral and Legal Status of Embryos and Fetuses* (New York: Oxford University Press, 1992), 24.

refrain from deliberately harming such beings, since we would never *need* to harm them. But because we are only human beings, we cannot accord full moral status to all sentient organisms. It is not human hubris, but human vulnerability and need that compels us sometimes to put the interests of human beings ahead of the interests of other animals. To meet important human needs, we must walk about outdoors, grow and harvest plant crops, and clean our homes from time to time; and these activities often, and unavoidably, cause harm to probably-sentient invertebrate animals.

Although the Anti-Cruelty principle does not require us to treat all sentient beings as our moral equals, it demands somewhat stronger justification for harming organisms that are sentient than is required in the case of many non-sentient organisms, whose only claim to moral status is that they are alive. Before we can with a clear conscience knowingly inflict death, pain, or suffering upon sentient beings, we need to be confident that the goals which we are serving are important, and that they cannot be served by means that cause less harm to sentient beings. We should, in general, be particularly reluctant to harm warm-blooded vertebrate animals (birds and mammals), because their capacity for pleasure and pain is more evident, and probably more highly developed, than that of most cold-blooded vertebrates (fish, reptiles, and amphibians) and most invertebrates. For instance, we should not condone the rearing of calves, pigs, chickens, or other sensitive vertebrate animals in quarters so crowded that they can scarcely move, unless we are sure that the important human interests served by these methods of animal husbandry could not be just about as well served in other ways.

## Cruel Practices vs. Cruel Persons

The cruelty of such practices as factory farming is not to be measured by the motives of those who earn their living in this way, or those who market, purchase, or consume their products. Few of these people intend to be cruel, and their involvement is not in itself a sign of a cruel disposition. As Carruthers points out, when human actions cause suffering to animals, 'almost any legitimate, non-trivial, motive is sufficient to make the action separable from a generally cruel or insensitive disposition'.[6]

<hr />

[6] Carruthers, *The Animals Issue*, 159.

But the moral character of agents is not the only important issue here. The Anti-Cruelty principle permits us to distinguish between the cruelty of persons and that of practices. Through ignorance, habit, custom, or inattention, people who are not cruel can become involved in practices that cause unnecessary pain and suffering. In such cases, their innocent intentions may absolve them from serious moral censure, but cannot render the practice immune from moral criticism. If no important human interests are served by the practice, or if the human interests served could be served about as well by means that do not subject sentient beings to so much harm, then the practice is presumptively a cruel one—even if the agents intend no cruelty, and are not (in other contexts) cruel persons.

## Why Not Require Kindness?

Kind persons may wonder why the obligation that we have to all sentient beings should be an obligation to avoid cruelty, rather than an obligation to be kind. Kindness is a great virtue—probably the greatest virtue. But if kindness is understood as active benevolence, then we are not morally obliged to be kind to all of the sentient beings that we encounter. Swatting a mosquito is not kind (to the mosquito), but neither is it cruel. Because we cannot persuade mosquitoes not to bite us; because mosquito repellents are neither always available nor always fully effective; and because mosquito bites are harmful and sometimes even lethal, we are fully entitled to swat mosquitoes. Even the use of chemical or biological insecticides is sometimes justified, given the danger to human life and health from malaria and other mosquito-borne illnesses, and the apparent relative environmental safety of some of the newer mosquito abatement products.[7]

## Sentience as a Matter of Degree

Although it is difficult to prove conclusively, it is likely that sentient organisms differ in their *degree* of sentience. They probably differ, if not in the intensity of the pains and pleasures that they experience,

---

[7] For instance, biological agents such as methoprene, a chemical that prevents mosquito larvae from maturing by mimicking an insect hormone; this chemical is thought to have little impact upon other organisms, and to biodegrade rapidly.

then in the variety and richness of those experiences. They probably differ also in the degree to which they are subjects-of-a-life, possessing such mental aptitudes as memory, anticipation of the future, thought, planning, and intentional action. These mental aptitudes require a high degree of sentience, and probably some degree of self-awareness. Thus, it is reasonable to believe that when subjects-of-a-life are deprived of life, health, or freedom, they lose more of what they value than do less mentally sophisticated beings.

Since most vertebrates appear to be more highly sentient than most invertebrates, harming vertebrate animals generally requires a stronger justification than does harming mites, snails, or other probably-sentient invertebrates. Moreover, birds and mammals generally appear to be somewhat more highly sentient than fish, reptiles, and amphibians, and more capable of the mental activities constitutive of subjecthood. Thus, the common presumption that it is morally worse to hurt animals that are warm and fuzzy than those that are cold and scaly may have a scientifically defensible basis.

**3. *The Agent's Rights Principle:*** *Moral agents have full and equal basic moral rights, including the rights to life and liberty.*

Many philosophers have argued that the capacity for moral agency logically entails the possession of full moral status. Kant argues that moral agents have full moral status because they are capable of using reason to discern and follow universal moral laws. Kant maintains that this capacity proves that moral agents are free of causal determination—not in the natural world, but in a transcendent noumenal world. Contemporary defenders of the Agent's Rights principle have presented arguments that do not require this dubious metaphysical claim. For instance, John Rawls argues that rational agents have equal rights to life and liberty because this is what they would choose, were they choosing behind a 'veil of ignorance'—i.e. without knowledge of their own identity or position in society.[8] And Alan Gewirth argues that, because life and liberty are fundamental preconditions for successful agency, each rational agent is necessarily committed not only to his or her own moral right to these goods, but also to the equal moral right of other rational agents to the same goods.[9]

[8] Rawls, *A Theory of Justice.*
[9] Alan Gewirth, *Reason and Morality* (Chicago, Ill.: University of Chicago Press, 1978).

These philosophical defences of the Agent's Rights principle are useful and enlightening. Moral claims are, among other things, claims 'about what rational agents should reasonably accept who share the aim of reaching free and unforced agreement'.[10] If we knew nothing about ourselves and our world except that we are rational moral agents, we might agree on few substantive moral principles; yet we could probably agree on a principle of respect for the life and liberty of all moral agents. At the same time, what we know of our species' social and emotional nature greatly strengthens the case for these rights. Thus, I want to stress some of the more pragmatic reasons for respecting the rights of moral agents, and demanding that they respect ours in return.

## The Pragmatic Case for Moral Rights

If human beings were psychologically similar to ants, termites, bees, or other social insects, then we would probably have no need for moral rights, since we would be naturally 'programmed' to fulfil our social roles without moral training or persuasion, and would have little tendency to act aggressively towards one another in ways that harm the community. But human beings are both highly social and highly individualistic in their thoughts, desires, and actions. We are neither social insects nor natural social isolates. As social beings, we need to trust and co-operate with one another. Yet our social instincts often fail to prevent resentment, duplicity, violence, and greed from undermining our social relationships, and our collective well-being.

Because we are both social beings who need to co-operate, and clever individuals who are frequently tempted to take what we want through deception or coercion, we badly need mutual understandings of our fundamental moral obligations to one another. Basic moral rights are socially enforced entitlements to such elementary goods as life and liberty. Without these moral entitlements, few of us can hope to live well. We are not equally strong, intelligent, virtuous, or beautiful; but we are equally in need of the physical security and trusting social relationships that are possible only where there is at least that minimum level of mutual respect. Without it, human lives

---

[10] *The Animals Issue*, 103.

may not be wholly solitary, but they are usually poorer, shorter, and nastier.

The Agent's Rights principle does not represent all that moral agents ought to do for one another. Like the Respect for Life and Anti-Cruelty principles, it provides a moral floor, not a moral ceiling. To violate a person's moral rights is not just to fall short of an ideal, but to do what should be morally condemned and socially prevented. Mutual respect for moral rights is a precondition for good social relationships amongst moral agents. For that reason, once present it becomes part of the background, and need not be what concerns human beings in most of their social relationships. Caring for other persons is not an alternative to mutual respect for moral rights; on the contrary, people find it a great deal easier to care for one another when there is that mutual respect.

## Why Moral Rights Do Not Presuppose Social Atomism

Moral rights are social creations, not phenomena that we discover through pure reason, or in the natural world—or a supernatural one. Philosophers such as John Locke, who describe basic moral rights as 'natural', i.e. as existing prior to human institutions, often claim that these rights are the gift of a deity, who wants us to respect them. But in the absence of such a benevolent deity, moral rights must be embodied in human attitudes, actions, and social institutions if they are to be operative.[11]

It is, therefore, a curious mistake to suppose that the concept of a moral right presupposes that human beings are 'social atoms'—creatures with no natural need or desire to associate with one another.[12] The truth is precisely the reverse: had we evolved as asocial beings, living in separate territories and meeting only to mate, then it would probably have been impossible for us to agree to respect one another's moral rights. Under those conditions, we would probably not have developed conventional languages capable of expressing moral concepts, and thus become capable of moral agency. Moreover, we would probably not have *needed* to become moral

---

[11] See Beth J. Singer, *Operative Rights* (Albany, NY: State University of New York Press, 1993).

[12] See Michael J. Sandel, *Liberalism and the Limits of Justice* (Cambridge: Cambridge University Press, 1982).

agents, since our natural isolationism would have kept us out of each other's way most of the time.

It is our social nature—together with the linguistic and cognitive abilities to which it has helped to give rise—that makes the recognition of moral rights both psychologically possible and morally necessary. Rights may belong to individuals; but only social communities can effectively implement them. Carl Wellman makes the point as follows:

The language of rights does presuppose some sort of individualism, for every [basic moral] right is possessed by some individual . . . But these individuals need not be social atoms—self-contained, independent and isolated persons. Indeed . . . any individual capable of possessing moral rights *cannot* be a social atom . . . Far from assuming the existence of atomic individuals, the assertion of any right presupposes a social nexus in which individuals interact.[13]

It is conceivable (though unlikely) that a moral agent could come into existence without the assistance of other moral agents. What is conceptually necessary is not that a moral agent already be involved in social relationships marked by mutual respect for moral rights, but that he or she be capable of entering into such relationships. As moral agents, we are capable of treating one another as moral equals; and because we can, we ought to, because our collective well-being depends upon it.

This pragmatic rationale for respecting the basic rights of moral agents does not imply that we are morally obliged to respect the rights of only those moral agents who are capable of harming us if we do not. Hume evidently believes that his pragmatic rationale for moral rights has that implication. He writes:

Were there a species of creatures intermingled with men, which, though rational, were possessed of such inferior strength, both of body and mind, that they were incapable of all resistance, and could never, upon the highest provocation, make us feel the effects of their resentment, the necessary consequence, I think, is that we should be bound by the laws of humanity to give gentle usage to these creatures, but should not, properly speaking, lie under any restraint of justice with regard to them, nor could they possess any right or property.[14]

---

[13] Carl Wellman, 'Doing Justice to Rights', *Hypatia*, 3, No. 3 (Winter 1989), 153–60.

[14] Hume, *Enquiry Concerning the Principles of Morals*, 190.

In this passage, Hume evidently departs from the spirit of his own analysis, in which human morality is founded upon the natural capacity for empathy. Moral common sense rejects the suggestion that persons may justly be denied basic moral or legal rights simply because they are powerless to make us feel the effects of their resentment. As Mary Midgley points out, the word 'justice' loses its normal meaning when defined in this way. 'In ordinary life', she says, 'we think that the duties of justice become *more* pressing, not less so, when we are dealing with the weak and inarticulate, who cannot argue back. It is the boundaries of prudence which depend on power, not those of justice.'[15]

But how is it possible to argue for moral rights by appealing to practical necessity, while at the same time holding that moral rights are to be respected even when that practical necessity is absent? The answer is that respect for the Agent's Rights principle has long-term social value, even though applying that principle in a given instance may or may not maximize happiness. Respect for moral rights generally serves the social good; yet an individual's moral rights to life and liberty do not evaporate whenever there is no proof that violating them will cause adverse consequences for other individuals. If they did, moral rights could not serve the social goals for which they are urgently required. The most vicious aggressors can always persuade themselves that their victims will not be missed, and the most cruel dictators will always claim to be serving the social good.

Just as we have pragmatic reasons for recognizing moral obligations to all living things, so we have what might be described as utilitarian reasons for adopting the non-utilitarian Agent's Rights principle. Moral rights are not absolute. Almost any moral right can justly be overridden in some circumstances. For instance, the right to life does not preclude violent self-defence when one has been wrongly attacked and there is no other way to escape serious harm. Similarly, the right to life implies a duty to assist, but it does not require us to provide other persons with whatever they need in order to sustain their lives. If I need one of your kidneys to survive, it does not follow that you are obliged to give me one, still less that I may take it by force. The precise content of any moral right can only be delineated through discussion and deliberation, in which all legiti-

---

[15] Mary Midgley, 'Duties Concerning Islands', in Peter Singer (ed.), *Ethics* (Oxford: Oxford University Press, 1994), 380.

mate interests receive equitable consideration. Nevertheless, basic moral rights cannot justly be overridden merely for the sake of an expected gain in the total amount of happiness. If they could, the lives and liberty of all but the most powerful individuals would be in constant jeopardy.

## Are Agents' Rights Species-Specific?

The Agent's Rights principle applies to all moral agents, whatever their species. There may be no non-human moral agents on this planet; but if we ever meet such beings, and if we can learn to communicate with them well enough to permit the mutual recognition of moral rights, then we will be morally obliged to treat them as our moral equals—and vice versa. Moreover, we will be morally obliged to do what we reasonably can to *learn* to communicate with them well enough to make mutual respect for basic moral rights possible. The same is true of any non-human terrestrial animals that may turn out to be moral agents.

There is at present no strong evidence that animals of any terrestrial species besides our own have a natural language suitable for the expression of moral concepts or principles. Many have social instincts and emotions that are akin to ours, and complex vocal, visual, olfactory, or other communication systems that might by analogy be called languages. But, while a social and communicative nature is probably a necessary condition for the evolution of moral agency, it is not a sufficient condition. Without a language *that is capable of representing moral concepts and principles*, real moral agency is not possible.

Nevertheless, it would be premature to conclude that there are no non-human moral agents on Earth. During the past three decades, a small number of chimpanzees, gorillas, and orang-utans have been taught to understand and use elements of simplified human sign languages. Some sceptics dismiss these apparent linguistic achievements as mere mimicry, or the result of animals responding to subtle cues given by humans—as in the case of Clever Hans, the trained horse that appeared to be doing arithmetic. But these hypotheses do not credibly explain the extensively documented ability of the chimpanzee Washoe, and other signing apes, not only to use linguistic symbols appropriately in a wide range of circumstances, but also to combine them in ways that give every appearance of expressing meaningful requests, observations, questions, and responses to questions directed towards them.[16] Carruthers points out that the sign languages that these apes employ have relatively little syntax or grammar.[17] This makes it unclear that their signed utterances can always be translated into well-formed English sentences; but it does not prove that these utterances have no linguistic meaning. Pidgin languages typically develop among human trading partners whose native tongues are mutually incomprehensible. These languages often lack verb tenses and other elements of grammar common to more developed languages; yet they are used effectively to conduct business, request aid, pass on information, and so on.

Some of the researchers who have worked with signing apes believe that there are apes who not only use language, but also employ moral concepts to guide their own behaviour and evaluate and influence the behaviour of others.[18] If they are right, then these apes have begun to be moral agents, and a good case can be made that they ought to have the same basic moral rights as other novice moral agents. From this, it would not follow that other apes of the same species are also moral agents. It would suggest, however, that the hypothesis ought to be taken seriously. Like humans, apes are highly intelligent social animals whose individual and collective well-being depends upon forming and sustaining complex networks of social relationship. It is therefore possible—though as yet unproven—that they have 'languages' of their own that are adequate for the expression of fundamental moral concepts. Perhaps we have failed to realize this simply because we do not understand their distinctive forms of communication as well as some of them understand some of ours.

Something similar might also be true of other large-brained mammals, such as cetaceans, seals, and elephants; and perhaps of some animals that are not exceptionally large-brained, such as dogs, cats, pigs, corvids (crows, ravens, jays, and magpies), and parrots. So

---

[16] Roger and Deborah Fouts describe Washoe's linguistic accomplishments in 'Chimpanzees' Use of Sign Language', in Cavalieri and Singer (eds.), *The Great Ape Project*, 28–41; also see Deborah Blum, *The Monkey Wars* (New York: Oxford University Press, 1994); and John Gribbon and Jeremy Cherfas, *The Monkey Puzzle* (Buffalo, NY: Prometheus Books, 1982).

[17] *The Animals Issue*, 140.

[18] See H. Lyn White Miles, 'Language and the Orang-Utan', in Cavalieri and Singer (eds.), *The Great Ape Project*, 53.

long as we know so little about the minds of these animals, we cannot entirely rule out this hypothesis. That it is not absurd is suggested by the fact that, within the belief systems of many aboriginal North and South American, African, and Australian peoples, some animals are regarded as persons, and as moral agents.[19] The Dyak people of Malaysia are said to have traditionally regarded orangutans as persons of a wise older race, who are capable of speaking to human beings, but generally choose not to.[20] These traditional belief systems may be the result, not of a naïve misunderstanding of the mental capacities of animals, but of generations of careful observation that have led to substantial success in learning ways of interacting with animals (including, at times, hunting them) that are conducive to the long-term well-being of both their species and ours. There is, of course, an important distinction between the achievement of ecologically sustainable modes of interaction with animals, and the mutual recognition of moral rights. However, these achievements may be sufficiently analogous that cultures in which some animals are regarded as fellow moral agents are closer to the truth than those moral theorists who explain the moral status of non-human animals solely in terms of their sentience.

Nevertheless, in the absence of unexpected communications breakthroughs, we will not always be able to treat even highly intelligent animals as moral equals. When an aggressive elephant repeatedly threatens the lives of tourists and rangers in a national park, or a lame tiger develops a taste for human flesh, there may be no feasible alternative to killing the animal. That alternative would be less acceptable in the case of a dangerous human; even those who believe in the death penalty for human criminals do not usually advocate summarily killing mentally incompetent persons who have become dangerous, or executing murderers without the formalities of arrest and trial.

---

[19] See J. Baird Callicott, *Earth's Insights: A Survey of Ecological Ethics from the Mediterranean Basin to the Australian Outback* (Berkeley and Los Angeles: University of California Press, 1994), 119–30, 172–84; also Callicott's 'Traditional American Indian and Western European Attitudes Towards Nature', reprinted in *In Defense of the Land Ethic* (Albany, NY: State University of New York Press, 1989), 177–203.

[20] T. L. Maple, *Orang-Utan Behavior* (New York: Van Nostrand Reinhold, 1980), 213; cited by H. Lyn White Miles, in 'Language and the Orang-Utan', 43.

**4.** *The Human Rights Principle: Within the limits of their own capacities and of principle 3, human beings who are capable of sentience but not of moral agency have the same moral rights as do moral agents.*

That all moral agents have full and equal basic moral rights does not imply that only moral agents have such rights. It is moral agents who shape and employ moral concepts, such as that of a moral right; and it is they who make rights operative, by establishing and maintaining social practices whereby respect for rights is taught and enforced. But the social, psychological, and biological realities of human existence require that basic rights not be restricted to human beings who are capable of moral agency.

It is true, of course, that young children and mentally disabled persons cannot always be accorded all of the liberties that more mature and mentally able human beings are entitled to have. For their protection and that of others, their liberty must sometimes be limited in ways that it would not be right to limit the liberty of competent adults who have committed no crime. Nevertheless, their interests carry the same moral weight as do those of other human beings.

The inadequacy of the view that only moral agents have full moral status becomes apparent once we consider how human beings *become* moral agents. While we can imagine a moral agent coming into existence without the help of any other moral agent, in reality human beings become moral agents only through a long period of dependence upon human beings who are moral agents already. During this period of dependency we learn language, and all of the other mental and behavioural capacities that make moral agency possible. In Annette Baier's words, 'A person is best seen as one who was long enough dependent upon other persons to acquire the essential arts of personhood. Persons essentially are second persons, who grow up with other persons.'[21]

For this reason, it is both impractical and emotionally abhorrent to deny full moral status to sentient human beings who have not yet achieved (or who have irreparably lost) the capacity for moral agency. If we want there to be human beings in the world in the fu-

---

[21] Annette Baier, *Postures of the Mind: Essays on Mind and Morals* (Minneapolis, Minn.: University of Minnesota Press, 1985), 84.

ture, and if we want them to have any chance to lead good lives, then we must at least value the lives and well-being of infants and young children. Fortunately, instinct, reason, and culture jointly ensure that most of us regard infants and young children as human beings to whom we can have obligations as binding as those we have to human beings who are moral agents.

## Infanticide and Human Rights

Throughout human history, especially in societies that have not been strongly influenced by the Judaeo-Christian tradition, some forms of infanticide have been more or less openly tolerated. Often, it has been considered the right of the parents, the family, or, in strongly patriarchal cultures, of the father alone, to decide which infants are to be reared and which are to be abandoned.[22] When the marriage system is patrilocal and patrilineal, it is female infants who are most likely to be abandoned. This is largely because daughters are expected to leave the community when they marry, while sons are expected to remain, continuing the paternal lineage and contributing to the parents' security in old age. Given the widespread occurrence of infanticide, how can we imagine that our social and emotional nature requires that infants have full moral status?

The answer is suggested by the fact that, in virtually all societies in which infanticide is openly practised, the decision is normally made soon after the infant's birth. Babies who have been held, washed, nursed, dressed, named, introduced to neighbours and relatives, or otherwise symbolically admitted into the social community, are unlikely to be abandoned, except in desperate circumstances. Permitting even early infanticide is an extreme measure by current Western standards, but one that in extreme conditions can be consistent with the Human Rights principle. When contraception and abortion are unavailable, and it is impossible successfully to rear all of the infants that are born, or all those that are severely abnormal, a tolerant attitude towards early infanticide is kinder and more just than the persecution of parents who choose it as the lesser evil.

[22] See, for instance, Maria W. Piers, *Infanticide* (New York: Norton, 1978); and Mary Anne Warren, *Gendercide: The Implications of Sex Selection* (Totowa, NJ: Rowman & Allanheld, 1985).

*Why Include the Mentally Disabled?*

The arguments for including mentally disabled human beings in the class of beings with full moral status may at first seem weaker than those for including infants, or adults who are temporarily disabled. Some disabled human beings never achieve moral agency, and some permanently lose it. Why should they be included in the moral community when, unlike most infants, they will never be able fully to reciprocate the consideration that is shown to them?

To be part of a social community in more than name, a being must be capable of sentience; a permanently unconscious organism has no capacity for social response. Thus, anencephalic infants, who will never be capable of conscious experience, cannot really be part of a social community, and neither can persons whose brains have been so severely damaged that no return to consciousness is even remotely possible. But with even a minimal level of sentience, a human being can often love and be loved. Empathy for disabled members of the human community, and for those who care for and about them, requires that they be accorded full moral status. Individual self-interest points in the same direction: because all of us are vulnerable to injury, illness, and other human frailties, we have self-interested reasons for supporting social practices that protect human beings who suffer from mental or physical disabilities. As in the case of infants, the rights of the disabled are sometimes limited by the society's genuine inability to provide for all of their needs. Nevertheless, their interests have the same moral weight as those of the mentally able.

**5. *The Ecological Principle:*** *Living things that are not moral agents, but that are important to the ecosystems of which they are part, have, within the limits of principles 1–4, a stronger moral status than could be based upon their intrinsic properties alone; ecologically important entities that are not themselves alive, such as species and habitats, may also legitimately be accorded a stronger moral status than their intrinsic properties would indicate.*

This principle requires us to accept stronger obligations towards some plants and animals than their intrinsic properties would indicate. The Respect for Life and Anti-Cruelty principles already accord moral status to these entities, and it is reasonable to accord them stronger status if their species are ecologically important, and endangered by human activities. The loss of a species through natural evolutionary processes is not always a tragedy, since the natural rate of extinction is usually very low, and other species are likely to emerge at a rate sufficient to prevent any permanent loss of biological diversity. But human-caused extinctions are occurring at a far greater rate, and these extinctions often leave ecosystems permanently devastated—at least on a human time scale. This is one reason for according an enhanced moral status to endangered animals and plants.

The Ecological Principle also permits us to recognize moral obligations towards water, air, plant and animal species, or other elements of the biosphere that are neither living organisms nor sentient beings. It does not, however, *require* us to ascribe moral status to these entities. It will, therefore, be rejected by those environmental ethicists who maintain that we have moral obligations even to the non-living parts of nature.[23] But I do not think that it is mandatory to accord moral status to entities that are neither sentient nor alive. Because such entities cannot be harmed in the ways that living things and sentient beings can, it is implausible to insist that our obligations regarding them must be understood as obligations towards them.

Nevertheless, we have good reasons to hold that earth, air, water, biological species, and natural ecosystems have a more than instrumental value. Human beings may be more inclined to protect these vulnerable elements of the natural world if they accept moral obligations towards them. If we believe that we owe nothing to these things, then we may be more willing to condone practices that threaten species or habitats that have not been shown to have much instrumental value. If, on the other hand, we recognize moral obligations to species, oceans, mountains, and rivers, then we may be less often tempted to agree to their destruction for the sake of jobs, profits, recreation, or other short-term goals.

To say that these elements of the natural world may legitimately be accorded moral status is not to be committed to the claim that they have inherent value, i.e. value that is entirely independent of the needs or desires of any living or sentient being. That claim is at best obscure, since a value that does not arise from the needs or desires

---

[23] For instance, Rolston, *Environmental Ethics*, 112–17.

of any valuer is scarcely a coherent notion. We may say, however, that these elements of the natural world should be protected not just because of what they might be good for, but also because of what they and we are.[24] They and we are part of the planetary biosphere, which began to exist over a billion years before our species appeared, and which may outlast us by as long if we do not destroy it. Like an organism, the biosphere seems to function teleologically, in ways that tend to maintain conditions tolerable to life.[25] Within its shelter, terrestrial life forms have evolved through 'a homeostatic "mountain climbing" against the current of entropy'.[26] There is nothing absurd in the recognition of moral obligations to non-living elements of the global biological community that sustains our existence. There is also nothing absurd in reserving moral status for living organisms—so long as we give adequate recognition to the need to protect species and habitats that are essential to the health of the biosphere. Nevertheless, if we wish humanity to survive and flourish into the distant future, we might be wise sometimes to accord moral status to plant and animal species, and other elements of the natural world that are not themselves living organisms.

**6.  *The Interspecific Principle: Within the limits of principles 1–5, non-human members of mixed social communities have a stronger moral status than could be based upon their intrinsic properties alone.***

The Interspecific principle requires us to accord an enhanced moral status to some animals on the basis of their social relationships to human beings; but it does not require that all captive or domesticated animals be accorded such an enhanced status. Nor does it require that the moral status of all domesticated or captive animals be the same. The Anti-Cruelty principle applies to all sentient animals. However, that principle establishes a moral floor, not a moral ceiling. It does not prohibit us from recognizing special obligations to animals that have social relationships with human beings.

Why is it morally appropriate to recognize stronger moral obligations towards animals that belong to our social communities than

---

[24]  See Callicott, 'On the Intrinsic Value of Nonhuman Species', 151.

[25]  See Lovelock, *The Ages of Gaia*.

[26]  The phrase is from Stanislaw Lem, *His Master's Voice*, trans. Michael Kandel (New York: Harcourt Brace Jovanovich, 1968), 162.

towards equally sentient animals that do not? Is this anything more than an anthropocentric prejudice? Of the theories that we have considered, only Callicott's biosocial theory and Noddings's ethics of care enable us to argue for an enhanced moral status for the animal members of our social communities. Callicott's argument for this is that moral status is a function of co-membership in a community; and that co-membership in a social community confers a stronger moral status than does co-membership in a biological community. Noddings's argument is that caring relationships are the wellspring of morality, and must be respected. When we enter into caring relationships with animals, we rightly feel that we have stronger moral obligations to them than to most other animals. Noddings notes:

Farm people have a saying: 'If you are going to eat it, don't name it.' This is doubly wise. It is not only that it takes a certain stoicism to go on eating 'Goldie' or 'Henrietta' but [that] naming a creature and eating it seem symptomatic of betrayal. By naming it, we confer a special status upon it and, if we would be ethical, we must then honor that status.[27]

Callicott and Noddings present sound reasons for protecting the animal members of our social communities. But are these moral reasons, or merely prudential ones? Do we really owe more to animals that have social relationships to human beings than to equally sentient animals that do not? Or do we merely have self-interested reasons for being nicer to animals that we or other human beings care about? I would argue that there are quasi-Kantian reasons for preferring the first answer. When humans and animals enter into relationships of mutual trust and affection, something akin to a promise is made. Although most animals are not full-fledged moral agents, in their relationships with human beings they often display many of the social virtues that we admire in one another, such as affection, loyalty, courage, patience, kindness, and good humour. Thus, they are sometimes enough *like* moral agents for it to be reasonable to accord them almost the same status.

The moral status that is ascribed to animals, even by animal rights advocates, is usually somewhat weaker than that of human beings. Even Tom Regan argues that in the lifeboat case—where either a human or an animal must be thrown overboard in order to

---

[27] Noddings, *Caring*, 157.

save a larger number of human lives—we ought to prefer the sacrifice of an animal to that of a human being.[28] At the same time, the moral status of animals is often strong enough to override narrowly utilitarian considerations. For instance, I do not think that it would be right for me to abandon my two adult cats, even if it were the case (as it is not) that I would get so much pleasure from replacing them with new kittens as to increase the total amount of happiness in the universe. To do this would be to betray a trust, and to commit something very like an injustice.

**7. The Transitivity of Respect Principle:** *Within the limits of principles 1–6, and to the extent that is feasible and morally permissible, moral agents should respect one another's attributions of moral status.*

This principle does not require us to *accept* other people's attributions of moral status—at least, not without good reason. We are entitled to reject attributions of moral status that are irrational, disrespectful of life, cruel, incompatible with the moral rights of human or non-human beings, or inimical to the health of social or biotic communities. Nevertheless, the Transitivity of Respect principle requires that we give fair hearing to other people's reasons for ascribing to certain entities either a stronger or a weaker moral status than we think appropriate. It also requires that, to the extent that is feasible and morally acceptable, we must seek to avoid harming entities to which other persons ascribe a high moral status.

The Bible provides an illustration of why the failure to follow the Transitivity of Respect principle is morally objectionable. The story is told to King David of a rich man and a poor man:

the poor man had nothing, except one little ewe lamb which he had bought and nourished; and it grew up together with him and his children . . . and it was like a daughter to him. (2 Sam. 12: 3)

When told that the rich man took and killed the lamb belonging to the poor man, in order to prepare a feast for his guests, the king declares that 'he shall restore fourfold for the lamb, because he did this thing and because he had no pity' (2 Sam. 12: 6). The king's anger is easy to share, not only because the rich man stole from one who was poor, but because the lamb was 'like a daughter' to the poor man.

---

[28] Tom Regan, *The Case for Animal Rights*, 185–6.

Thus, the rich man's action was more cruel, and more disrespectful of the poor man, than a simple act of theft.

The Transitivity of Respect principle permits us to accord moral status to some entities that would have little or none on the basis of the first six principles. For instance, objects or places that are considered sacred by some people might not qualify for moral status either on the basis of (what we take to be) their intrinsic properties, or on the basis of any special ecological value. Nevertheless, protecting these things can be obligatory. Uluru (a stone formation which is sacred to Australian aboriginal people) and Shiprock (a stone formation which is sacred to the Navajo people of Southwestern North America) are sites that play such an important role in the spiritual life of some people that to damage them or intrude upon them without permission is deeply disrespectful of these people.

It may be possible adequately to protect such sacred objects and places without supposing that we owe anything to them. Respect for the ethical or religious beliefs of other people need not mean adopting those beliefs, or even regarding them as reasonable. But respecting people is difficult if one does not also, to some degree, respect those things or beings to which they accord strong moral status. Respect is, in this sense, transitive.

Respecting other people's ascriptions of moral status is part of respecting persons, part of caring for and about them. Noddings expresses the spirit of the Transitivity of Respect principle in the following passage:

It may well be that you care deeply for some plant, animal or environment in which I have no interest. My carelessness may shock and offend you. Now my obligation as one-caring is to listen, to receive you in all your indignation . . . What matters to you is of interest and concern to me. We do not draw the line . . ., choose sides, and confront each other across it. Rather, . . . we allow ourselves to feel what the other feels, and then we reason together.[29]

Having reasoned together, we may still disagree, for instance about the moral status of human embryos or the use of animals in biomedical research. In some cases, the disagreement may be so sharp, and the common ground so meagre, that no compromise can satisfy both sides. We have no guarantee that the world views of the

---

[29] *Caring*, 161.

contestants will not turn out to be so different that they will never be able to agree in their ascriptions of moral status. But respect on each side for sincere beliefs on the other will greatly increase the odds that a consensus will eventually emerge.

## 6.2. *The Virtues of the Multi-Criterial Account*

The preceding chapters have shown that none of the uni-criterial theories of moral status can deal adequately with the full range of problem cases. A multi-criterial account comprising only principles 1 through 3 would be more consistent with common sense than any of the uni-criterial theories. It would permit us to distinguish between what we owe to living but non-sentient organisms, what we owe to sentient beings that are not moral agents, and what we owe to fellow moral agents. But so long as only intrinsic properties are permitted to serve as criteria of moral status, the account will clash with some core common-sense beliefs. For instance, it will imply that sentient human beings who are not moral agents have a moral status more like that of non-human animals than that of moral agents. It will also prohibit us from recognizing special obligations towards plants or animals of endangered species, or towards the animal members of our social communities. And, finally, it leaves no room for moral status based upon respect for the religious or spiritual beliefs of other people.

Principles 4–7 permit—and in some cases require—the use of relational properties as criteria of moral status. These might be described as corrective principles, whereby the oversimplified judgements of moral status that we might otherwise make on the basis of principles 1–3 are adjusted to the realities of human existence, and the functioning of terrestrial ecosystems. It would, however, be just as plausible to argue that the relationship-based principles are historically and psychologically primary, while intrinsic-property-based principles are brought into play at a later historical or developmental stage, to correct deficiencies in the original relationship-based principles. Rather than seeking to determine which type of principle is more ancient, or more psychologically primitive, I would suggest that considerations of both sorts are always relevant to questions about moral status.

Each of these seven principles must be understood in conjunction with the others. Thus, principles 1–3 must be interpreted and applied in the light of specific circumstances, including any relevant social or ecological relationships. Only the context can reveal whether an act that harms a living organism is morally objectionable, or whether an act that causes pain or death to a sentient being is cruel. Similarly, principles 4–7 must be applied consistently with the first three principles. We may not deny full moral status to moral agents on the grounds that we have no social relationships to them, or that we consider them harmful to the ecosystem, or that our culture or religion does not recognize their equal rights to life and liberty. Nor may we condone practices that needlessly harm sentient beings, even those that are neither socially related to us nor ecologically important.

### 6.3. *Balancing Multiple Criteria*

To abandon the dream of finding a single necessary and sufficient condition for having moral status is not to abandon the attempt to reason clearly about the subject. Simplicity is not the only virtue of a moral theory. It is also important that a theory be capable of handling all of the most puzzling and problematic cases, and of doing so in ways that are consistent with the intractable realities of human life. Because we have moral obligations towards a variety of things and for a variety of reasons, it is predictable that no simple formula will capture all of these obligations. In making this point, Mary Midgley provides the following list of entities to which we may reasonably be held sometimes to have moral obligations:

1. The dead
2. Posterity
3. Children
4. The senile
5. The temporarily insane
6. The permanently insane
7. Defectives, ranging down to human 'vegetables'
8. Embryos, human and otherwise
9. Sentient animals
10. Nonsentient animals
11. Plants of all kinds
12. Artefacts, including works of art

13. Inanimate but structured objects—crystals, rivers, rocks, etc.
14. Unchosen groups of all kinds, including families or species
15. Ecosystems, landscapes, warrens, cities, etc.
16. Countries
17. The biosphere.[30]

All of these entities may plausibly be argued to have moral status on the basis of one or more of the principles just presented. (Art objects and other human artefacts are perhaps the least obvious candidates for moral status; but they, like natural objects, may be held sacred by some people, and may thus sometimes be protected by the Transitivity of Respect principle.) Although the seven principles leave room for disagreement about the moral status of at least some of these entities, they nevertheless suggest a decision procedure for cases that we find puzzling. In deliberating about our moral obligations to entities of a given sort, we need to consider all of the reasons that might lead rational persons to accord these entities moral status. This consideration begins (but should not end) with an analysis of the harms that may be done to these entities if we do not accord them moral status, and of the likely effects of moral or legal constraints upon moral agents and the beings and things that they care about.

It will not do to say that, since entities of these sorts are incapable of moral agency, it is never possible for moral agents to have obligations towards them. Nevertheless, what we say about the moral status of such entities must be consistent with respect for the basic rights of moral agents. We must not, for instance, ascribe to the dead a moral status that is incompatible with the lives, liberty, and well-being of living persons. If traditional funerary practices have been found to cause the transmission of a lethal virus, as happened not long ago in Papua New Guinea, that is a sound reason for concluding that no one owes it to the dead to continue those practices.

At the same time, the boundaries of human rights must be delineated in ways consistent with the health of social and biological communities. The extension of strong protections to human posterity, children, and senile, insane, or mentally impaired persons is a social need that our social instincts and emotions will not let us forget.

[30] Midgley, 'Duties Concerning Islands', 381–2.

Our capacity for empathy with non-human beings, and even with non-sentient organisms, prohibits the cruel treatment of any sentient being, or the needless destruction of any life form—even a plant or microbe. Works of art and other human artefacts, along with such natural objects as crystals and unusual rock formations, may be protected for their aesthetic, historical, or cultural value; but to do this is not necessarily to grant them moral status. We may, however, sometimes reasonably decide to grant such status, for instance out of respect for the spiritual or religious beliefs of a particular group of people. Species, ecosystems, and the biosphere can reasonably be accorded moral status, and organisms of species that are endangered or especially important to the ecosystem ought to be accorded a stronger status than their intrinsic properties would indicate. Finally, families, cities, and countries are communities to which members may have moral obligations, based upon respect for co-members of the community, and upon morally justified institutional arrangements.

## 6.4. *The Limited Role of Cultural and Personal Relativity*

The multi-criterial account leaves room for some legitimate cultural and personal variations in judgements of moral status. However, it is incompatible with both (1) the ethical relativist view, i.e. that moral truth is entirely determined by what is accepted by a majority of people within a given culture or group; and (2) the ethical subjectivist view, i.e. that moral truth is entirely a matter of individual opinion. Individuals can be mistaken in their judgements of moral status, and so can cultural and religious traditions. The principles I have proposed are not universally accepted; yet each is a viable candidate for general acceptance among reasonable people who share the aim of reaching an uncoerced consensus.

There is, nevertheless, an important grain of truth in both the cultural relativist and the subjectivist views. We need to be cautious in evaluating judgements about moral status made by people whose cultures are unfamiliar to us, because judgements that initially strike us as odd or even perverse may make excellent sense, once the context is better understood. The term 'sacred cow' is used in the West to refer to something that is accorded more respect than is appropriate. Yet the refusal of many Indian people to kill cattle is not only an important religious tenet, but arguably also an economically and ecologically sound policy.

Individuals within the same society may also make different judgements of moral status. If the ethical subjectivist view were true, any judgement that any person made about moral status would be true *for that person*. The multi-criterial account disallows that extreme form of subjectivism, while allowing individuals sometimes to differ legitimately in their judgements of moral status. For instance, moral obligations towards particular animals depend in part upon human social relationships with those animals, which are not the same in all cases, or for all human beings. If I am fond of cats, then it is not absurd for me to feel obliged to feed the stray cat at my door, even though not all persons would be similarly obliged. If my neighbours abhor cats, they are entitled to ignore the passing stray—but not to shoot it for target practice. The Anti-Cruelty principle applies, regardless of our individual attitudes or emotional responses.

## 6.5. Conclusions

In making judgements about moral status, we must balance a number of considerations. That something is a living organism is a *prima facie* reason for not harming it, but one that is easily overridden when it has no other claim to moral status. Pathogenic microbes may normally be destroyed without guilt. That an organism is sentient provides a reason not to kill it or cause it pain, unless an important human or ecological need is at stake. That it is a moral agent is enough to establish that it has basic moral rights—whatever its race, sex, age, species, or planetary origin. That it is a sentient human being and a member of a human social community is also sufficient to establish that it has basic rights. Social or ecological relationships can enhance moral status, but may not depress the status of any entity below that specified in the Respect for Life, Anti-Cruelty, Agent's Rights, and Human Rights principles. Similarly, religious or spiritual beliefs can enhance the moral status of particular entities, but not in ways that are incompatible with these principles.

Each of the uni-criterial theories fails, not because it selects a criterion of moral status that has no validity, but because no single criterion can represent all of the relevant considerations. Only a multi-criterial account of moral status can incorporate the sound ethical considerations that underlie each of the uni-criterial accounts, while avoiding the distortions of moral common sense that result from the attempt to make all valid judgements about moral status follow from a single principle.

# PART II

## *Selected Applications*

# 7

## *Applying the Principles*

The multi-criterial account explains why many common-sense judgements about moral status are more reasonable than they appear from the vantage-point of any of the uni-criterial theories. It explains, for instance, why it is appropriate to accord full moral status to infants and other sentient human beings who are not moral agents, while denying it to most non-human animals—including many whose mental capacities are more impressive than those of a human infant. It does this by giving due weight to the fact that many sentient human beings who are not moral agents are nevertheless members of human social communities. Thus, it is important to the well-being of the community, and in conformance with our natural social sentiments, that their interests be accorded the same importance as those of moral agents. In contrast, most animals are not members of our social communities, and we do not have that reason for according them full moral status.

The multi-criterial account also explains why it is sometimes reasonable to accord a stronger moral status to some animals than to others that are probably just as highly sentient. Some animals are members of our mixed social communities, and have established trusting and affectionate relationships with human beings. Others belong to species that are endangered by human activities, and vital to the integrity, stability, and beauty of the ecosystems of which they are part. Still others may reasonably be accorded an enhanced moral status out of respect for their special religious or spiritual importance to some people. Each of these factors can justify the recognition of stronger moral obligations towards animals of certain species than could be based solely upon their intrinsic properties.

But a theory of moral status must not only agree reasonably well with moral judgements about which there is a strong consensus; it must also help to illuminate issues that are more contentious. In the following chapters I comment on three controversial topics in applied ethics: euthanasia, abortion, and human uses of animals. My purpose is not to present completely supported solutions to these complex problems, but to illustrate the ways in which the principles presented in Chapter 6 can contribute to these discussions. Moral principles expressed in abstract terms are inevitably subject to multiple interpretations. (Think, for instance, of the lack of agreement among those in the Judaeo-Christian tradition about whether the Sixth Commandment, 'Thou shalt not kill', is meant to prohibit capital punishment, suicide, abortion, violent self-defence, or military war.) These chapters will at least help to clarify some of the ambiguities in the principles that I have formulated.

## 7.1. *Review of the Principles*

Because the principles presented in Chapter 6 will be frequently referred to in the next three chapters, it will be useful to list them at the outset. Notice that the first three principles refer to nested classes of entities: living organisms, sentient beings, and moral agents. Beings of each class have some moral status based upon their intrinsic properties. Organic life confers only a modest moral status; sentience confers a stronger moral status; and moral agency is sufficient (but not necessary) for full moral status. The fourth principle expands the community of moral equals to include sentient human beings who are not moral agents. Finally, the last three principles require the acceptance of special obligations to plants and animals of ecosystemically important species, and animal members of our social communities; and permit the acceptance of obligations to some non-living things that have ecosystemic importance, or that have special religious or spiritual value to some people.

### 1. *The Respect for Life Principle*
Living organisms are not to be killed or otherwise harmed, without good reasons that do not violate principles 2–7.

### 2. *The Anti-Cruelty Principle*
Sentient beings are not to be killed or subjected to pain or suffering, unless there is no other feasible way of furthering goals that are

(1) consistent with principles 3–7; and (2) important to human beings, or other entities that have a stronger moral status than could be based upon sentience alone.

### 3. *The Agent's Rights Principle*

Moral agents have full and equal basic moral rights, including the rights to life and liberty.

### 4. *The Human Rights Principle*

Within the limits of their own capacities and of principle 3, human beings who are capable of sentience but not of moral agency have the same moral rights as do moral agents.

### 5. *The Ecological Principle*

Living things that are not moral agents, but that are important to the ecosystems of which they are part, have, within the limits of principles 1–4, a stronger moral status than could be based upon their intrinsic properties alone; ecologically important entities that are not themselves alive, such as species and habitats, may legitimately be accorded a stronger moral status than their intrinsic properties would indicate.

### 6. *The Interspecific Principle*

Within the limits of principles 1–5, non-human members of mixed social communities have a stronger moral status than could be based upon their intrinsic properties alone.

### 7. *The Transitivity of Respect Principle*

Within the limits of principles 1–6, and to the extent that is feasible and morally permissible, moral agents should respect one another's attributions of moral status.

## 7.2. *Preview of Chapters 8, 9, and 10*

The moral questions raised by euthanasia, abortion, and human uses of animals force us to clarify both what it means to have the rights to life and liberty, and to whom those rights should be ascribed. Each of these issues has complexities that cannot be well addressed on any of the uni-criterial theories. Chapter 8 deals with questions surrounding some controversial forms of euthanasia. Some of these questions involve the boundaries of the right to life. For instance, should persons who are permanently comatose, or infants who will never become sentient, have the same moral and legal right to life as other human beings? Other questions involve the content of the rights to life and liberty, and the relative weight of these rights when they appear to be in conflict. Does one, for instance, violate an obligation to oneself by deciding to hasten one's own death when illness or injury lead one to judge that continued life is no longer a benefit? How much may others legitimately do to assist in carrying out such a decision? How much, if anything, may they do in the absence of a fully voluntary request from the afflicted individual?

In Chapter 9, I consider the morality of abortion. Here too, questions arise concerning who or what has the right to life, and about what having rights to life and liberty entails. When, in the course of its development, does a human individual begin to have a right to life equal to that of older human beings? Should the line be drawn at conception, at birth, or at some point between? Should it sometimes be drawn shortly after birth? Are early abortions morally different from late abortions, or are all voluntary abortions equally justifiable—or unjustifiable?

Finally, in Chapter 10 I consider questions involving the moral status of animals. Do non-human animals have moral rights? Are we morally obliged to abandon some practices that have long been widely accepted, such as hunting animals, rearing them for food and other consumptive uses, or employing them as 'guinea pigs' in commercial, scientific, or medical research? If not all such uses of animals are objectionable, then how can we distinguish those that are?

# 8

## *Euthanasia and the Moral Status of Human Beings*

The term 'euthanasia' derives from Greek words meaning 'a good death'. It normally refers to the act of intentionally causing or helping to bring about the death of another being, based upon a reasonable judgement that, under the circumstances, death is in that being's best interest. In most cases, the basis for this judgement is an extremely painful and/or severely disabling illness or injury that cannot be cured or alleviated, and that is thought to make continued life a harm rather than a benefit to the individual.

Euthanasia for animals that are dying in pain or disastrously and permanently disabled is not usually controversial. Indeed, when a captive or domestic animal in such a plight is not humanely 'put to sleep', we are likely to suspect a violation of the Anti-Cruelty principle. But when the being in such a plight is human, mercy killing is rendered morally problematic by the strong rights to life and self-determination that human beings have. Thus, my discussion will focus upon the human cases, which are more controversial.

Disagreements about euthanasia involve both the boundaries of the right to life—to whom it should be extended—and its content. Euthanasia opponents argue that the right to life forbids deliberately hastening the death of innocent human beings, even at their urgent request, and in what is thought to be their interest. They fear that any social toleration of euthanasia will undermine the moral status of all human beings. Their concern is that, if the right to life is withdrawn from persons whose lives are considered no longer worth living, it may later be withdrawn from many whose lives obviously *are* worth living.

In contrast, many people see no contradiction between the human right to life and certain carefully circumscribed forms of euthanasia. The freedom to hasten one's death when continued life has become unbearable is arguably itself an important human right. It may also be argued that, when a human patient is close to death, and clearly incapable of making a reasoned decision about how best to die, those who care for the patient should be permitted—within limits—to make that decision on the patient's behalf.

The chapter begins by distinguishing several forms of euthanasia. I argue that the human right to life is consistent in some cases with a decision to hasten or not to delay one's own death, or that of another human being. I also argue that there are cases in which the moral right to life does not fully obtain, because the individual has suffered either whole-brain death or irreversible brain damage that precludes any future return to consciousness. In these cases, the Transitivity of Respect principle assumes a more central role in shaping our moral obligations.

## 8.1. *Types of Euthanasia*

Before confronting these issues, we need to define some of the terms that bioethicists have used to distinguish between diverse forms of euthanasia. First, an act of euthanasia may be characterized as either *active* or *passive*. It is considered active if death is deliberately caused through such direct means as administering a lethal injection. It is considered passive if death is deliberately hastened by the omission of actions that might have prolonged life, such as performing cardiopulmonary resuscitation when cardiac arrest occurs, or administering antibiotics to combat acute infection.

An act of euthanasia may also be characterized as *voluntary* or *non-voluntary*. It is voluntary if done in response to the uncoerced request of a mentally competent adult who is aware of the relevant facts, and has arrived at a reasoned decision. It is non-voluntary if the individual is so severely mentally or physically disabled as to be clearly unable to express a reasoned preference about the alternatives, and others therefore decide on the basis of what they reasonably take to be in the individual's best interest.

It is important to stress there is no third category of *involuntary* euthanasia, i.e. that which is done against the will of the individual. It is virtually never reasonable to believe that it is in a person's interest to be killed or allowed to die against their will. Moreover, even if it were reasonable to believe this in a particular case, it would still be a violation of the right to life to kill a person who does not wish to be killed, or needlessly to let such a person die. The right to life protects individuals from being killed or allowed to die *against their will*, when they have done nothing that could reasonably be thought to justify such violence, or such neglect. Killing a person who wants not to be killed is not euthanasia, but murder, or some other form of wrongful homicide. For a health professional deliberately to let a patient die by withholding readily available treatment that the patient clearly wants, is at least malpractice, and might sometimes be prosecuted as criminal homicide.

Assisted suicide can sometimes be classified as a form of voluntary euthanasia. A person facing a painful death may ask a friend, family member, or health care provider to assist in obtaining a means of committing suicide. If the individual then voluntarily performs the action which is the proximate cause of their own death, e.g. by taking pills, then this is a case of assisted suicide. If the assistant acts with the reasonable hope and intention of helping the person to die well (or in the 'least worst' way), then what the assistant does is a form of euthanasia.

## 8.2. *Voluntary Passive Euthanasia*

Voluntary passive euthanasia is unique among these forms of euthanasia in that in most jurisdictions it is legal under some circumstances. Mentally competent adults normally have the legal right to reject any proposed medical treatment, even if they are likely to die without it, and even if they refuse because they do not want their lives prolonged. There is, in this sense, a legal right to voluntary passive euthanasia. The right to refuse medical treatment is not always respected in practice, and some courts have recognized exceptions to it.[1] Yet few ethicists now argue that medical treatment should be

---

[1] See Keith Burton, 'A Chronicle: Dax's Case As It Happened', in John D. Arras and Bonnie Steinbock (eds.), *Ethical Issues in Modern Medicine* (Mountain View, Calif.: Mayfield, 1989), 195–9. Some courts have recognized exceptions to the right to refuse treatment, e.g. in cases where adult Jehovah's Witnesses have refused blood transfusion, and in which pregnant women have refused Caesarean sections. See Ruth Macklin, 'Consent, Coercion, and Conflicts of Rights', in Thomas A. Mappes and Jane S. Zembaty (eds.), *Biomedical Ethics* (New York: McGraw-Hill, 1991), 330–6; and Nancy Rhoden, 'Cesareans and Samaritans', in Tom L. Beauchamp and LeRoy

routinely inflicted upon competent adults who have made an informed and voluntary decision to refuse it.

The primary basis for this consensus can be found in the right to liberty that the Agent's Rights principle accords to moral agents. The authority to control what is done to one's body is a vital part of the right to liberty. To inflict medical treatment upon a mentally competent and unwilling adult, even with benevolent intentions, is to treat a person as a mere means. The laws of most nations reflect this moral judgement; in the absence of special circumstances, the imposition of unwanted medical treatment upon a mentally competent adult patient is usually classified as a criminal assault.

There are, of course, cases in which medical treatment may legally be provided in the absence of fully voluntary consent by the patient. Children may legally be treated without their consent, since (with some exceptions) the law gives the right to consent to their medical treatment not to them, but to their parents or guardians. Even mentally competent adults may be treated without their consent in emergency situations, where immediate treatment is urgently needed and the individual is incapable of either voluntary consent or voluntary refusal. For example, injured persons who are unconscious, semi-conscious, or too shocked to think clearly, may be given emergency care without their explicit consent. In such cases, the provision of medical treatment is consistent with the patient's right to liberty; most of us strongly prefer to be treated should we be in this situation, since the alternative is that we may die or be injured by non-treatment.

### 8.3. *Voluntary Active Euthanasia and Assisted Suicide*

While voluntary passive euthanasia is widely recognized as a legitimate option for persons who are close to death, voluntary active euthanasia is almost always classified as wrongful homicide. One exception is the Northern Territory, the Australian state that in 1995 passed legislation permitting voluntary active euthanasia in certain cases, thereby becoming the first jurisdiction in the world to do so. At the time of writing, this statute has just come into effect, al-

Walters (eds.), *Contemporary Issues in Bioethics* (Belmont, Calif.: Wadsworth, 1994), 337–42.

though there are legal challenges pending. The other is the Netherlands. There, active euthanasia remains technically illegal, but it is not prosecuted when voluntary and in conformity with legal and professional guidelines.

Assisting a person to commit suicide is also a criminal act in most jurisdictions, although it is unusual for charges to be brought when the agent is a licensed physician, acting in compliance with the wishes of a competent adult patient. In Oregon, a proposition to permit physician-assisted suicide in certain cases of terminal illness has passed the electorate, and been held constitutional by the Ninth Circuit Court of Appeals. However, the state of Oregon has challenged this ruling, and implementation of the law has been deferred until the case can be heard by the United States Supreme Court.

Although the law usually treats voluntary active euthanasia as criminal homicide, it differs in important ways from more typical homicides. Voluntary euthanasia is by definition in accord with the will of the individual, and usually done from compassionate motives. In more typical homicides, the victim does not want to be killed, and there is no reason to believe that death is in the victim's interest. Few doubt that killing a person who does not want to be killed—and who has done absolutely nothing to deserve it—violates that person's right to life. But when a person who is approaching death (but still able to think clearly) chooses to hasten death for reasons they believe to be sound, then it is not clearly wrong for others to help in implementing that decision.

Human beings facing death or extreme disability sometimes reasonably judge that hastening death will be a benefit to them, and possibly to others as well. Terminal illness—especially some forms of cancer—can produce extreme pain that cannot be alleviated, except by heavy sedation that keeps the individual in a virtually comatose state. When continued treatment would be very costly, this can be an additional reason for judging that one's life is no longer a net benefit. Another prospect that many persons reasonably regard as worse than death is that of progressive and irreversible mental and/or physical incapacitation which will increasingly destroy their agency, independence, and dignity.[2] In such cases, suicide or active

---

[2] For a discussion of this point, see R. B. Brandt, 'The Morality and Rationality of Suicide', in Mappes and Zembaty (eds.), *Biomedical Ethics*, 319–25.

euthanasia may be the only way to escape a fate that is reasonably regarded as intolerable.

Those who hold that deliberate self-destruction is always wrong sometimes say that our lives belong to a god, and thus are not ours to take. This argument has little appeal to those who do not believe in the god in question, or who do not agree that a morally good god would prohibit suicide in all cases. Immanuel Kant's arguments against suicide are meant to be independent of such religious premises. He holds that suicide violates the Categorical Imperative, because it is self-contradictory to will that rational beings use their freedom to bring about their own annihilation. In his view, self-destruction is inherently incompatible with human worth and dignity.[3] Since he defines suicide as any intentional act of self-destruction, he would probably have regarded voluntary active euthanasia as a form of suicide, and raised similar objections to it.

These objections are unpersuasive. Suicide may be morally culpable in some cases, e.g. when it leaves young children financially destitute. But this is not true in all cases. The right to life which the Agent's Rights principle accords to moral agents is designed to benefit them and their social communities. Thus, when life is no longer a benefit to oneself or others, suicide is not plausibly construed as a violation of the Agent's Rights principle. It cannot reasonably be viewed as a denial of human dignity when so many thoughtful persons consider it essential to their own peace of mind. The right to life serves to protect individuals against violence, neglect, and other actions or omissions *on the part of others* that may *needlessly* shorten their lives. Thus, it may be argued that the right to life justifies intervening to prevent suicide when there is no reason to believe that life is not a benefit to the suicidal individual. But the right to life does not entail a duty to live when life is not a benefit. Consequently, laws and mores that permit assisted suicide or voluntary active euthanasia in such cases do not violate the right to life that the Agent's Rights principle accords to moral agents.

A more troubling argument against legalizing either assisted suicide or voluntary active euthanasia is that permissive laws are likely to lead to many wrongful deaths. Relatives desirous of sparing the family fortune, or acquiring it sooner, might manipulate, deceive, or coerce a sick person into accepting an early death. Hospital or

---

[3]  Kant, *Lectures on Ethics*, 147–54.

nursing-home personnel might use improper methods to induce in-
digent patients to accept death when their lives are still worth living,
because caring for them is unprofitable. People who cannot deliberate rationally because of depression, dementia, or the effects of
medication may request death when it is in their interest to live, and
no one nearby may be perceptive enough to realize that these requests are not fully voluntary. Some people might simply be murdered, and their deaths disguised as assisted suicide or voluntary
active euthanasia.

To avoid such abuses, legislation permitting assisted suicide or
voluntary active euthanasia needs to be carefully drafted. In the
Netherlands, physicians may administer active euthanasia without
fear of legal prosecution under circumstances that include: (1) a diagnosis of terminal illness that has been confirmed by at least one
other physician; and/or (2) a diagnosis of intractable pain and suffering, with no prospect for improvement; and (3) a rational, voluntary, and consistently repeated request on the part of an informed
and competent patient.[4] There is little or no evidence that the toleration of voluntary active euthanasia in the Netherlands has resulted
in patients being killed against their express will. However, some
observers claim that undue pressures are sometimes exerted by
physicians or family members to obtain consent from confused
or ambivalent patients.[5] If this concern is discovered to be well
founded, stricter regulation of the practice may be called for.

Some critics of Dutch policy have also claimed that voluntary active euthanasia has led to non-voluntary active euthanasia—the
killing of persons who are mentally incompetent, and can neither
voluntarily consent nor voluntarily refuse.[6] Other observers doubt
that voluntary active euthanasia has had this consequence.
Whichever report is correct, it is important to ask whether the occurrence of non-voluntary active euthanasia would necessarily indicate a wrongful weakening of the right to life. If voluntary active
euthanasia is sometimes compatible with the right to life, might not
non-voluntary active euthanasia also sometimes be reconcilable

---

[4] *The Lancet*, 343 (25 June 1994), 1630.

[5] Richard Fenigsen, 'A Case Against Dutch Euthanasia', in Beauchamp and
Walters (eds.), *Contemporary Issues in Bioethics*, 500–6.

[6] See Henk A. M. J. ten Have and Jos V. M. Welie, 'Euthanasia: Normal Medical
Practice?', *Hastings Center Report*, 22, No. 2 (Mar.–Apr. 1992), 35.

with that right? Before addressing that question, it will be helpful to consider the case of non-voluntary passive euthanasia.

### 8.4. *Non-voluntary Passive Euthanasia*

The right of competent adults to refuse in advance specific life-prolonging treatments is (incompletely) protected in the United States by federal and state legislation. Individuals may make 'living wills', specifying treatments which they wish omitted—or not omitted—should they be terminally ill and mentally incapacitated. They also have the option of signing a durable power of attorney, or otherwise legally empowering another person to make medical decisions for them should those circumstances obtain. Where valid advance directives exist, a decision to withhold life-prolonging treatment may be considered voluntary in an extended sense, since it is in accord with the desires and interests of the individual as that individual foresaw them while still mentally competent. Having the opportunity to influence one's fate in such circumstances is sufficiently important to most persons, and sufficiently compatible with the rights of others, that it may be regarded as a legitimate part of the right to liberty.

If, on the other hand, the individual is a young child or an older human being who has never been mentally competent, then voluntary euthanasia is not an option, even in this extended sense. The Human Rights principle ascribes the right to life to all sentient human beings, within the limits of respect for the rights of moral agents. In the case of the mentally competent, the absence of a fully voluntary request entails that any form of euthanasia would be a violation of the right to life. However, in the case of a mentally incompetent individual, it is not clear that the absence of a voluntary request always has that implication.

I would argue that the Human Rights principle does not rule out non-voluntary passive euthanasia in every case. A decision by parents and physicians not to pursue an aggressive course of medical therapy for an infant born with multiple congenital malformations, or not to begin another course of chemotherapy for a young child in the final stages of leukaemia, may be justifiable even on the presumption that the child has full moral status. When the only probable result of more intensive medical treatment is a longer period of suffering prior to an inevitable death, many caring parents consider it their obligation to the child not to consent to that treatment; and many bioethicists agree with them.[7]

The legal right of parents to veto medical treatment in such cases is often limited by the rights of the child, and those of other involved persons or institutions. Other parties may, for instance, be entitled to petition a court to find that the parents' decision is not in the child's best interests, and to authorize the treatment without parental consent. However, in the absence of such court action, the parents' decision not to pursue further treatment that might prolong the child's life may be legally sound. It may also be consistent with the child's human rights. If a proposed treatment would cause suffering, and if it would not extend life for long, or would extend life only by inflicting upon the child a miserable existence, then it is reasonable to judge that it is against the child's best interest, and therefore not required by the Human Rights principle.

## 8.5.  *Non-voluntary Active Euthanasia*

What should be done when a person who is no longer mentally competent is close to death, and a natural death predictably will be prolonged and miserable, yet there are no advance directives or other indications of what the person would have wished done? In this situation, compassionate persons sometimes judge that a painless death brought about by injecting a lethal dose of morphine is better for the dying individual than a painful death by natural causes.[8] In such cases, non-voluntary active euthanasia can be advocated without contradicting the Human Rights principle.

[7] See Robert F. Weir, *Selective Nontreatment of Handicapped Newborns: Moral Dilemmas in Neonatal Medicine* (New York: Oxford University Press, 1984); John Arras, 'Toward an Ethic of Ambiguity', in Arras and Steinbock (eds.), *Ethical Issues in Modern Medicine*; and Nancy K. Rhoden, 'Treating Baby Doe: The Ethics of Uncertainty', in Beauchamp and Walters (eds.), *Contemporary Issues in Bioethics*, 419–30.

[8] James Rachels argues for this view in 'Active and Passive Euthanasia', in Mappes and Zembaty (eds.), *Biomedical Ethics*, 374–81; also see Helga Kuhse and Peter Singer, *Should the Baby Live? The Problem of Handicapped Infants* (Oxford: Oxford University Press, 1981); and Helga Kuhse, *The Sanctity of Life Doctrine in Medicine: A Critique* (Oxford: Oxford University Press, 1987).

Nevertheless, non-voluntary active euthanasia is unlikely to be legalized in many jurisdictions in the near future. The resistance to legalization stems in part from the fact that, in the absence of voluntary consent—even where such consent is clearly impossible—the analogy with murder or execution is too close for comfort. There is also a reasonable concern that if some human beings are legally empowered to kill others for benevolent reasons, tragic mistakes will be made, and lives will be ended that might have gone better than expected. As John Robertson points out, it is easy to be mistaken about another human being's quality of life; we may illicitly import our own values, assuming that a life that we would find intolerable must also be intolerable to the individual whose life it is.[9] However, against this danger we must weigh the likelihood that some lives really are intolerable for those who live them, and that prolonging those lives can be an unintentional cruelty.

Although the Human Rights principle does not preclude non-voluntary active euthanasia in all cases, it is understandable that the risk of error may be seen as too great to justify legalization. But in some cases the risk of error is small, i.e. cases in which a clearly incompetent patient is clearly dying, and clearly suffering from pain that drugs do not alleviate. While there are moral risks in permitting physicians or family members openly to carry out active euthanasia in such cases, there are also moral risks in not permitting them to do so. When mercy killing is prohibited in all cases, some deaths are needlessly painful and protracted, and some compassionate persons feel compelled to circumvent the law in order to provide those they care for with a less painful death than nature would have provided. This is not an issue that can be decided simply by further analysis of the Human Rights principle. It also turns upon the empirical question of whether human beings can ever correctly discern that death is the best option for an individual who lacks the capacity to choose it. I believe that, in some cases, they can.

---

[9] John Robertson, 'Involuntary Euthanasia of Defective Newborns', in John Arras and Nancy Rhoden (eds.), *Ethical Issues in Modern Medicine* (Mountain View, Calif.: Mayfield, 1989), 220–30. (Robertson uses the term '*in*voluntary euthanasia' to refer to what I call '*non*-voluntary euthanasia'.)

## 8.6. *Euthanasia and Permanently Non-sentient Humans*

Some human infants are born with no capacity for consciousness, and no potential to develop that capacity. Other human beings permanently lose the capacity to have conscious experiences, due to massive injury to parts of the brain essential to the occurrence of consciousness. Such individuals cannot experience pleasure or pain, or any other conscious mental state.

The Human Rights principle applies only to human beings who are capable of sentience. Nevertheless, permanently unconscious human individuals have a stronger moral status than do most non-sentient organisms. The moral status of permanently unconscious individuals is based largely upon the Transitivity of Respect principle. A person who will never regain consciousness may still be loved and perceived as a member of the family. Similarly, a baby born without a brain that is sufficiently complete and intact to permit the occurrence of conscious experiences may nevertheless be perceived as a son or daughter. Thus, permanently unconscious individuals often have a stronger moral status than could be derived solely from the Respect for Life principle. That principle is relevant; but the Transitivity of Respect principle often requires a stronger moral status than could be based upon organic life alone.

Anencephaly is perhaps the most common developmental abnormality that can cause an infant permanently to lack the capacity for consciousness. In anencephalic infants most of the brain fails to form, making any form of conscious experience a permanent impossibility, and ensuring an early death, even with intensive medical care. Such an infant can experience nothing—not even the most rudimentary sensations. Its condition is, in this respect, analogous to that of a person who has been rendered permanently unconscious by catastrophic injury. Such a child can derive no experiential benefit from continued life. However, it does not follow that there can never be a moral obligation to prolong the life of such a child.

Although an infant who is incapable of conscious experience can experience no benefit from continued life, other persons often have legitimate interests in prolonging the infant's life. The parents may want the child to be well cared for during its short existence, even though it will not be aware of that caring. They may distrust the diagnosis—sometimes rightly so. Or they may retain an unrealistic hope for an improvement in the child's condition, and need time to comprehend the reality. Some parents wish the infant to be kept alive long enough for recipients to be found for its donatable organs, which may save the lives of other children, who *will* be able to benefit from continued life. The Transitivity of Respect principle requires that, when possible, these wishes should be respected.

However, the Transitivity of Respect principle does not require that parents' wishes always be respected in such cases. It would be unfair to sentient patients to deprive them of needed care in order to provide expensive care for a patient who will never experience any benefit from it. The right to life arguably includes the right to receive medical care when it is needed, and when it can be provided without violating other rights. But when life-prolonging care for a permanently unconscious patient can be provided only at the expense of care needed by sentient human beings, it is reasonable for health care providers to set limits that would not be morally appropriate in the case of a patient who is sentient, or who may someday return to sentience.

One case in which a human individual cannot have a full-fledged right to life is that in which whole-brain death has occurred. (This condition is different from persistent vegetative state, which will be discussed next.) A person whose entire brain has permanently ceased to function will never regain consciousness, and will rapidly lose all biological functions without mechanical life support—and usually within a few days or weeks even with it. For these reasons, most jurisdictions throughout the world recognize whole-brain death as a sufficient condition for declaring the person legally dead. This recognition is essential if life support procedures are to be discontinued without legal liability, or organs taken for transplantation.

The classification as dead of individuals who have suffered the permanent loss of the functioning of the entire brain is more than a legal fiction. Whole-brain death means not only that consciousness has been irreparably lost, but that the organism as a whole has permanently ceased to function as an organism. Some physiological functions may be artificially maintained for a while; but without a functioning central nervous system this is only a simulation of life.[10]

---

[10] This is a point made by Charles M. Culver and Bernard Gert, in 'The Definition and Criterion of Death', 388–9.

To terminate life support in such cases is only marginally a form of euthanasia, since death has in essence already occurred. Nor is it a violation of the Human Rights principle. Since death is irreversible, those who have already died can no longer have a right to life.[11]

Nevertheless, terminating life support when whole-brain death has occurred can sometimes violate the Transitivity of Respect principle. If the involved members of the individual's family still regard the individual as alive, and make it clear that they want life support continued, and if the continuation of life support would not significantly deprive living patients of needed care, then the Transitivity of Respect principle suggests that the family's wishes should be respected.

Whole-brain death must be distinguished from what is often called 'persistent vegetative state'. Individuals who have sustained severe damage to the cerebral cortex or other parts of the brain may remain alive, yet be incapable of ever regaining the capacity for conscious experience. Such individuals may exhibit 'spontaneous, involuntary movements such as yawns or facial grimaces',[12] and their eyes may sometimes be open; but consciousness is thought to be entirely absent. Despite some near-miraculous recoveries by persons who had been wrongly diagnosed as permanently vegetative, it is sometimes clear that the damage to the brain is too extensive to permit the return of consciousness.

Some bioethicists have argued that human beings who are persistently vegetative, but not whole-brain dead, should be regarded as dead, since without the capacity for consciousness they can no longer benefit in any significant way from continued life.[13] But the claim that such individuals are dead is highly counterintuitive, since 'death' normally refers to the end of biological life, not just the end of consciousness. Persons in a persistent vegetative state are biologically alive; they are often capable of breathing without assis-

---

[11] Death is the *permanent* cessation of the biological life of the organism. Persons who suffer cardiac arrest, but are successfully resuscitated, are sometimes said to have died and been brought back to life; but this is more accurately described as a case in which death almost occurs, but is prevented by timely intervention.

[12] President's Commission for the Study of Ethical Problems in Medicine, *Defining Death*, in Mappes and Zembaty (eds.), *Biomedical Ethics*, 390.

[13] See Robert Veach, 'Whole Brain, Neocortical, and Higher Brain Related Concepts of Death', in Arras and Rhoden (eds.), *Ethical Issues in Modern Medicine*, 148–56.

tance, and with nursing care, artificial feeding, and antibiotics to combat pulmonary and other infections, they sometimes survive for many years.

It is true, however, that persons who are permanently unconscious cannot benefit—in any way that (still) matters to them—from continued life. Thus, there is room to doubt that they have the same right to life as those who are still capable of sentience. Nevertheless, while life lasts, the moral right to self-determination remains operative, in that the individual's prior wishes carry considerable moral weight. If the individual previously expressed preferences about being kept alive yet permanently unconscious, then the right to liberty that the Agent's Rights principle accords to moral agents argues for compliance with those preferences.

The Transitivity of Respect principle is also relevant here. Family members, friends, or caretakers may have good reasons for believing that the person would not have wanted to be kept alive in a permanently vegetative condition, and that respect for the person requires that this not be done. Alternatively, they may want the individual kept alive, either because of their own moral or religious convictions, or those of the individual. They may distrust the diagnosis, and hope for an eventual recovery—and in a few cases, they will turn out to be right. In a world of infinite resources, such wishes would always have to be respected, so long as they were consistent with the prior wishes of the individual. In the real world, it is not always possible to provide all human individuals with all of the medical and nursing care that they or their families would have wanted. An existence permanently devoid of conscious experience has no continuing value for the individual. Thus, when the resources necessary to maintain that existence could help others, it is possible to justify the withholding of expensive medical care in a case where the diagnosis of permanent unconsciousness is clearly correct—though not in the case of a conscious patient, or an unconscious one who may eventually return to consciousness.

## 8.7. *Conclusions*

The moral problems surrounding the diverse forms of euthanasia require for their solution a plurality of principles of moral status.

The Agent's Rights principle supports the right of moral agents to hasten their own death, and of others to help them do this, when there are reasonable and morally legitimate grounds for such a choice. But to give a plausible account of our obligations towards sentient human beings who are incapable of making voluntary decisions regarding their own care, we need to appeal to the Human Rights principle; and to account for our obligations towards human beings who are permanently unconscious, we need to make use of the Transitivity of Respect principle.

Reflecting on these forms of euthanasia leads to the recognition that the right to life that all sentient human beings have does not entail an obligation never to cause the death of an innocent human being. Causing the death of another sentient human being is *usually* wrong—and suicide is very often a mistake—because, for most persons most of the time, continued life is clearly an enormous benefit, and death would clearly be an unqualified disaster. But there are cases in which persons who are approaching death reasonably judge that hastening that process is the best option available to them, in the light of their ethical, spiritual, or other values, and in the absence of less grim alternatives. There are also cases in which those who are responsible for the care of a mentally incompetent individual who is suffering from a painful and terminal illness, or who has been rendered permanently unconscious by massive and irreparable brain damage, reasonably judge that further prolongation of life will be harmful, or at least in no way beneficial, to that individual. The categorical prohibition of passive or active euthanasia in such cases can result in needless suffering, or in the long-term maintenance of permanently unconscious human beings who would not have wanted to be maintained in this way.

The moral status of human individuals who never have been and never can be sentient is governed by the Transitivity of Respect principle rather than by the Human Rights principle. This is because, while sentient or once-sentient human beings may have (had) strong preferences about their own future, the never-conscious individual has no such preferences, and can experience no benefit from life. Consequently, their moral status is largely determined by the emotional, familial, and other relationships that others have to them, and by the moral judgements that are reasonably made in the light of those relationships.

Yet to be addressed is the moral status of human individuals that have never yet been sentient, but that may have the potential to become sentient in the future. Questions about the moral status of these individuals lie at the heart of the abortion issue, which is the subject of the next chapter.

# 9

## Abortion and Human Rights

The morality of abortion is often discussed as though it were entirely a matter of the correct moral status to ascribe to the human foetus. Conservative abortion opponents maintain that, once a human ovum has been fertilized, the conceptus is a human being with the same right to life as any other. From this, they conclude that the intentional termination of a human pregnancy is a form of homicide, and thus generally impermissible. Some would permit abortion when the pregnancy was caused by rape or incest, or when the woman would otherwise die; others would permit no such exceptions.[1] Moderates argue that a foetus does not have an equal right to life until it has passed some developmental milestone, such as the first occurrence of detectable brain activity,[2] the emergence of sentience,[3] or viability—the capacity to survive if born immediately. In their view, abortion is morally permissible before that stage, but not thereafter—except perhaps under special circumstances, such as when the pregnancy threatens the woman's life or health, or the foetus is severely abnormal. And liberals argue that it is only at birth, or possibly somewhat later, that a human individual begins to have a strong right to life; and that therefore abortion can be morally permissible even in the later stages of pregnancy.[4]

There are two weaknesses inherent in approaches to the ethics of abortion that focus exclusively upon the nature of the foetus, and the moral status this is thought to imply. In the first place, the moral status of embryos and foetuses cannot be determined solely through

[1] John Noonan, 'An Almost Absolute Value in Human History', in Joel Feinberg (ed.), *The Problem of Abortion* (Belmont, Calif.: Wadsworth, 1984), 9–14.

[2] See Baruch Brody, *Abortion and the Sanctity of Human Life* (Cambridge, Mass.: MIT Press, 1975).

[3] See Sumner, *Abortion and Moral Theory*, and Steinbock, *Life Before Birth*.

[4] See Tooley, *Abortion and Infanticide*; and Mary Anne Warren, 'On the Moral and Legal Status of Abortion', *The Monist*, 57, No. 1 (Jan. 1973), 43–61.

a consideration of their intrinsic properties, as most of the uni-criterial approaches require. Their unique relational properties are also relevant; in particular, their location within and complete physiological dependence upon the body of a human being who is (usually) both sentient and a moral agent. These relational properties have to be considered in determining the moral status that may reasonably be ascribed to foetuses.

The second, and closely related, problem with the exclusively foetus-centred approaches to the ethics of abortion is that the moral status of foetuses is not all that is relevant to the moral permissibility of abortion. The moral status of women is also at stake, as is the ability of the human species to maintain population levels that can be sustained, and that will not deprive posterity of the resources necessary for good lives. But, while the discussion cannot end with the intrinsic properties of foetuses, it is useful to begin there, since it is these properties that are most often thought to confer upon foetuses a moral status that precludes abortion—and since on any account these properties are important.

## 9.1. *Life, Biological Humanity, and Sentience*

In the industrialized world, the large majority of abortions take place in the first ten weeks of pregnancy.[5] Foetuses at this stage are obviously not moral agents, and thus are not accorded full moral status by the Agent's Rights principle. Nor, at this early stage, are they capable of sentience; thus neither the Anti-Cruelty principle nor the Human Rights principle apply. They are, however, alive, and thus have moral status based upon the Respect for Life principle. Since they are regarded by some people as having full moral status, they may gain some moral status through the Transitivity of Respect principle. However, unless they have full moral status for some other reason, the status that they can be accorded on the basis of the Transitivity of Respect principle is limited by the moral rights that

---

[5] In the United States, the figure is roughly 88 per cent; see Grimes, 'Second Trimester Abortions in the United States', *Family Planning Perspectives*, 16 (1984), 260, cited by Nan D. Hunter, 'Time Limits on Abortion', in Sherrill Cohen and Nadine Taub (eds.), *Reproductive Laws for the 1990s* (Clifton, NJ: Humana Press, 1989), 149.

women enjoy under the Agent's Rights principle. The question, then, is whether there is any independent reason to accord full moral status to zygotes, embryos, and foetuses.

Those who regard all abortions as wrongful homicides often maintain that science has proven that human life begins when a human ovum is fertilized. The successful combination of the DNA contained within the spermatozoon with that contained in the nucleus of the unfertilized ovum provides the newly fertilized ovum, or zygote, with a complete human genotype—the genetic 'blueprint' that will guide its further development into an embryo, foetus, and infant. This fact is said to demonstrate that even the one-celled zygote is already a human being with full moral status. On this view, the Human Rights principle ought to apply not just to sentient human beings, but also to the conceptus from fertilization onwards. A foetus is innocent, in that it has done nothing to deserve to be killed. Thus, it is concluded, abortion is a form of murder.

One problem with the argument that the newly fertilized ovum is a human being with equal rights *because it is alive and biologically human,* is that the ovum does not begin to be alive and biologically human only when it is fertilized. Human ova are initially formed in the ovaries of female foetuses; thus, those that are fertilized have already been alive for a number of years. Nor does the ovum become biologically human only when it is fertilized; it has been a biologically human cell throughout its previous years of life. True, it is a haploid cell, containing in its nucleus twenty-four chromosomes, rather than the forty-eight that most (diploid) human cells possess; but this is entirely normal for a human gamete (a sperm or ovum), and does not call into question its biological species.

Perhaps what begins with fertilization is not biologically human life as such, but rather the life of a specific human individual. The argument for this claim is that, once the complete human genome is present, so in essence is the new human being—the same individual that will be born, grow up, and eventually die. But this claim can also be disputed on empirical grounds. It is not clear that the zygote is the same organism or proto-organism as the embryo that may later develop from it. During the first few days of its existence, the conceptus subdivides into a set of virtually identical cells, each of which is 'totipotent'—capable of giving rise to an embryo. Spontaneous division of the conceptus during this period can lead to the birth of genetically identical twins or triplets. Moreover, it is thought that two originally distinct zygotes sometimes merge, giving rise to a single and otherwise normal embryo. These facts lead some bioethicists to conclude that there is no individuated human organism prior to about fourteen days after fertilization, when the 'primitive streak' that will become the spinal cord of the embryo begins to form.[6]

On my account, not much follows from the biological aliveness of the zygote, or from whether or not it is numerically identical to the embryo that may develop from it. The Respect for Life principle accords only a modest moral status to living things that have no other claim to moral status. The reasons for which women choose abortion often involve vital human needs, such as the welfare of existing children, and the protection of their own lives and health, and of the livelihood upon which they and their families depend. These needs are sufficiently compelling to justify the destruction of a living thing that is not yet sentient and not yet a member of a human social community. Woman's rights under the Agent's Rights principle must be permitted to override the modest protection provided to the pre-sentient foetus by the Respect for Life principle, just as in many other cases in which agents can protect themselves, or those for whom they are responsible, only by engaging in activities that cause harm to non-sentient living organisms. Women's rights to life and liberty must also be permitted to override the respect for the pre-sentient foetus that is demanded by the Transitivity of Respect principle, since the moral implications of this principle are limited by the basic rights of moral agents.

Nor does much about the moral status of first-trimester foetuses follow from their biological humanity, or from their status as individuated organisms. Membership in the human species is highly relevant to the moral status of an individual who is already sentient, or who once was sentient and may someday return to sentience. However, prior to the initial occurrence of conscious experience, there is no being that suffers and enjoys, and thus has needs and interests that matter to it.

The information that we now possess does not enable us to date with accuracy the emergence of the capacity for sentience. Few

---

[6] For example, Norman M. Ford, *When Did I Begin? Conception of the Human Individual in History, Philosophy and Science* (Cambridge: Cambridge University Press, 1988).

neurophysiologists have addressed the question, which is in part a conceptual one. But, although no one knows exactly when human sentience begins, it is fairly certain that first-trimester and early second-trimester foetuses are not yet sentient, since neither their sense organs nor the parts of their central nervous systems that are necessary for the processing of sensory information are sufficiently developed. It is also likely that by some point in the third trimester normal foetuses begin to have some capacity for sentience.[7] Once born, most infants quickly begin to exhibit very clear behavioural evidence of sentience.

Some abortion opponents dispute the claim that first-trimester foetuses are not yet sentient. One anti-abortion film purports to show an ultrasound image of a twelve-week foetus writhing in pain as it is about to be aborted. But, as Bonnie Steinbock points out,

even if the film was not doctored, such movements are not by themselves evidence of pain. A mimosa plant shrinks from touch, but no one claims that the mimosa plant feels pain. The reason is that the plant lacks the nervous system necessary for the experience of pain. Similarly, the fetal nervous system at 12 weeks is not sufficiently developed to carry and transmit pain messages.[8]

If the first-trimester human foetus is not sentient, then it does not come under the protection of the Anti-Cruelty principle. That principle protects beings that are capable of experiencing pleasure and pain, and hence whose lives can have value to them. Moreover, because it is not sentient, the early foetus does not come under the protection of the Human Rights principle. That principle protects human individuals who are already capable of sentience, and who have not permanently lost that capacity.

## 9.2. *Foetal Potential*

But why should we not extend the Human Rights principle such that it applies to presentient zygotes, embryos, and foetuses, as well as to

---

[7] See J. A. Burgess and S. A. Tawia, 'When Did You First Begin to Feel It?—Locating the Beginning of Human Consciousness', *Bioethics*, 10, No. 1 (Jan. 1996), 1–26.

[8] Steinbock, *Life Before Birth*, 58.

already-sentient human beings? Why should not the *potential* sentience of the foetus entail the same full and equal moral status as the actual sentience of the older human individual?[9] And how can we exclude presentient individuals without also excluding older human beings who are asleep, unconscious, or temporarily comatose, whose sentience is also (it is argued) merely potential?

The answer to the second question is straightforward. Human infants, children, and adults who are temporarily unconscious are protected by the Human Rights principle because they have not lost the capacity for sentience; they are simply not exercising it at present, or not at present able to exercise it. Thus, the interests they have in their own futures, and the obligations that moral agents have towards them by virtue of those interests, remain. No one's sentience, moral agency, or membership in the human community is placed in doubt by an afternoon nap, or even an extended coma from which they can reasonably be expected eventually to emerge.

The claim that the potential of the presentient foetus to become a human being is enough to give it full moral status is subject to a *reductio* argument. The problem is that the unfertilized ovum also has the potential to develop into a human being, under the right circumstances. The incorporation of genetic material from a human spermatozoon is only one of many processes and events that are necessary for the ovum's further development—some of which occur before, and some after fertilization. Thus, it is odd to suppose that, while the fertilized ovum has the potential for further development, the unfertilized ovum has no such potential. This assumption may be a reflection of the Aristotelian view that both the soul and the physical form of the foetus are derived entirely from the *pneuma* in the paternal semen, making the male the only true parent.[10] Even if unfertilized ova have no developmental potential by themselves, they surely have that potential in combination with the genetic material that could be provided by almost any fertile human male. Thus, the view that potential human beings should never deliber-

---

[9] For philosophical defences of this claim, see Don Marquis, 'Why Abortion is Immoral', *Journal of Philosophy*, 76, No. 4 (Apr. 1989), 183–202; and Jim Stone, 'Why Potentiality Matters', *Canadian Journal of Philosophy*, 17, No. 4 (Dec. 1987), 815–30. For a critique, see John Bigelow and Robert Pargetter, 'Morality, Potential Persons and Abortion', *American Philosophical Quarterly*, 25, No. 2 (1988), 173–82.

[10] Aristotle, *Generation of Animals*, trans. A. L. Peck (Cambridge, Mass.: Harvard University Press, 1948), 191; 739b23–30.

ately be prevented from becoming actual ones implies that not only is abortion morally wrong, but so is the use of contraception. Indeed, if this view is correct, then it is also wrong avoidably to abstain from heterosexual intercourse during periods of probable fertility—at least for women, and perhaps also for men.[11]

The usual response to this objection is to deny that an unfertilized ovum is a potential human being. It may be argued, for instance, that because an ovum lacks a complete genotype, it is not identical to the human being that develops from it.[12] But, as we have seen, there are also reasons to doubt that a fertilized ovum is identical with the human being that develops from it. In any case, the identity debate seems irrelevant to whether ova or zygotes are potential human beings. If an entity may develop into a human being, then surely it is a potential human being—even if the developmental process would alter it so greatly that we might reasonably wonder whether it has remained the selfsame entity.

A more direct objection to the claim that potential human beings have the same moral status as actual ones is that the pragmatic reasons for extending full moral status to human beings who have already been born are largely inapplicable to presentient foetuses. Excluding infants and other sentient and already-born human beings from full moral status would clash with aspects of our social and emotional nature that we rightly value. Infants are members of the human social world, as are sentient human beings who have mental disabilities. Thus, the denial of their moral status might threaten the psychological foundations of human morality. But denying full moral status to presentient foetuses does not contravene our natural social instincts in the same way. In Peter Carruthers's words,

It is natural to be struck by the suffering of senile old people or babies, in a way that both supports and is supported by assigning direct rights to these groups. It is not so natural for us to respond similarly to a foetus, however, especially in the early stages, unless we already have prior moral beliefs about its status. A rule withholding moral rights from foetuses, and hence permitting at least early abortions, may therefore be quite easily defended against abuse.[13]

---

[11] Sumner makes this point, in *Abortion and Moral Theory*, 104.
[12] Stone, 'Why Potentiality Matters', 816.
[13] Carruthers, *The Animals Issue*, 117.

It is true that many people are capable of being moved by verbal or photographic representations of what they believe to be suffering on the part of human foetuses—even those in the earliest stages of development. The Transitivity of Respect principle requires that this empathic response be respected, to the extent that is feasible and consistent with other sound moral principles. Persons who feel empathy for first-trimester foetuses are entitled not to harm them, and to seek in non-coercive ways to persuade others not to harm them. However, they cannot reasonably demand that others share their belief that first-trimester foetuses are already sentient, or insist that others must accept the moral conclusions that might follow if this belief were true.

### 9.3. *Abortion and Reproductive Freedom*

If the intrinsic properties of presentient foetuses do not entail that they must be accorded a strong moral status, then why is abortion such a sharply contested issue? The abortion issue has been almost as divisive of American society as slavery was in the last century. Indeed, the current situation resembles a state of civil war. Women's health care clinics have been besieged by anti-abortion protesters; many clinics have been the targets of bomb or arson attacks; and doctors and clinic workers have been threatened, and sometimes murdered. This is remarkable since, in the past, abortion has rarely inspired so much conflict. The Roman Catholic Church has always rejected it as incompatible with the natural procreative purpose of heterosexual intercourse. But not until 1869 did the Church officially take the position that even early abortion is a crime comparable to homicide. Early abortion was outlawed in the United States, and much of the Western world, only in the second half of the nineteenth century.[14]

One reason that abortion is controversial now is that it has become a symbol of contemporary cultural and political struggles over sexual morality and the social roles of women. Kristen Luker has documented the differing world views of Americans who favour

---

[14] James C. Mohr, *Abortion in America: The Origins and Evolution of National Policy* (New York: Oxford University Press, 1978).

legal abortion and those who oppose it.[15] Abortion opponents tend to believe that women are psychologically very different from men, and must have different social roles. Abortion is seen as a threat to women's familial roles, because it frees them to engage in heterosexual intercourse without the risk of unwanted motherhood. For this reason, abortion opponents tend to oppose sex education in schools and easy access to contraceptives, especially for young or single women. In contrast, those who support a right to abortion are likely to believe that men and women are psychologically similar (though not identical in all respects), and entitled to similar opportunities; and that women must have access to contraception and abortion if they are to fulfil their human potential. Abortion rights supporters are also likely to believe that all women—and men—should have access to the means (short of celibacy) of avoiding unwanted pregnancies and sexually transmitted diseases. Thus, they are likely to favour early and adequate sex education, and universal access to contraception.

It might be supposed that a mutually satisfactory compromise between these conflicting world views could be reached through the Transitivity of Respect principle. If each side respected the judgements about the moral status of women and foetuses that those on the other side make, then each would be free to act on their own beliefs, while respecting the right of the others to do likewise. But the Transitivity of Respect principle requires us to respect other people's ascriptions of moral status only to the extent that this is feasible, and consistent with other basic moral principles. Respecting the right of women to make their own decisions about abortion is perfectly feasible. However, that policy is inconsistent with the other side's understanding of the Human Rights principle. From the pro-choice perspective, women who believe that abortion is morally wrong are entitled to decline to abort their own pregnancies. But those who oppose the right to choose abortion cannot be expected to be equally tolerant of women who seek abortions and physicians who perform them, since they believe that abortion is an egregious violation of the foetus's right to life. Thus, the Transitivity of Respect principle provides no solution to the impasse.

[15] Kristen Luker, *Abortion and the Politics of Motherhood* (Berkeley and Los Angeles: University of California Press, 1984), 159–85.

The Agent's Rights principle is more central to the ethics of abortion. Unlike presentient foetuses, women are moral agents, with the rights to life, liberty, and the responsible exercise of moral agency. These rights are undermined when women are denied the freedom to decide whether and when to have children, and how many of them to have. Reproductive freedom is an essential part of women's right to liberty. It is vital to both liberty and responsible moral agency that we be free to protect our health, to plan and shape our lives, and to act upon what we reasonably take to be our moral obligations to ourselves and other human beings. As Beverly Wildung Harrison puts it, 'what socially elite women have come to expect for themselves—the capacity to shape their procreative power rather than to live at the caprice of biological accident—is, in fact, a social good that all women require'.[16]

So vital is this social good that wherever safe, legal, and affordable abortion is unavailable, many women risk death, permanent physical injury, social disgrace, and legal prosecution, in order to end unwanted pregnancies. In much of the Third World, illegal and improperly performed abortions remain a leading cause of death among women of childbearing age.[17] As Betsy Hartmann points out,

In Latin America, where abortion is outlawed in most countries because of opposition from the Catholic church, one fifth to one half of all maternal deaths are due to illegal abortion, and scarce hospital beds are filled with victims. In Bolivia, complications from illegal abortions account for over 60 percent of the country's obstetrical and gynecological expenses. Seeking to limit their pregnancies, women . . . are also risking their lives.[18]

These are powerful arguments for universal access to safe and legal abortion. The importance to women and their families of women's access to safe abortion is so great that even if early abor-

---

[16] Beverly Wildung Harrison, *Our Right to Choose: Toward a New Ethic of Abortion* (Boston, Mass.: Beacon Press, 1983), 3.

[17] World Health Organization, Division of Family Health, *Reproductive Health: A Key to a Brighter Future* (Geneva: WHO, 1992).

[18] Betsy Hartmann, *Reproductive Rights and Wrongs: The Global Politics of Population Control and Contraceptive Choice* (New York: Harper & Row, 1987), 47. The estimate of mortality rates is from the World Health Organization, *Health and the Status of Women* (Geneva: WHO, 1984); the Bolivian figure is from Kathleen Newland, *The Sisterhood of Man* (New York: Norton, 1979), 171.

tion were the killing of a sentient being, the moral problems would not automatically be resolved. But the first-trimester foetus is not yet sentient. Nor is it a member of the human social community, in the ways that it normally would be once it is born. It may, of course, be greatly valued by the prospective parents and other involved persons. This means that the Transitivity of Respect principle often applies, giving the foetus a stronger moral status than could be based upon its intrinsic properties alone. But the value of a presentient foetus is contingent upon the social context, and upon the woman's willingness and ability to carry and give birth to it. Rosalind Petchesky makes the point as follows:

because the fetus is not a subjectivity . . . we cannot recognize it as a person. We can only recognize its value in a context of relationships with others, defined by *their* subjectivity. For loving 'expectant parents,' an unwanted abortion is an event occasioning mourning and a deep sense of loss because of the social context of longings, care, and expectations that envelope the pregnancy. The scarcity of children available for adoption to infertile couples, or the desires of a potential father or grandparent for a child, may be other circumstances that endow the fetus with value. But those [reasons for valuing the foetus] are . . . extrinsic and utilitarian . . . and cannot be used to argue that the fetus has value in and of itself.[19]

The Transitivity of Respect principle does not override the basic rights of moral agents. Because the early human foetus is not yet sentient, it is unreasonable to seek to protect it through the imposition of severe harms—up to and including death—upon women who are unwillingly pregnant. The inclusion of infants within the scope of the Human Rights principle requires no severe contraction of women's rights to life and liberty, since an infant's physical separateness usually makes it possible for others to care for it should the mother be unable or unwilling to. In contrast, the inclusion of presentient foetuses within the scope of the Human Rights principle constricts women's freedom in ways that severely threaten their liberty and well-being, as well as their ability to exercise moral agency. In Petchesky's words, 'If things can be done to my body and its processes over which I have no control, this undermines my sense of integrity as a responsible human being and my ability to act respon-

[19] Rosalind Pollack Petchesky, *Abortion and Woman's Choice: The State, Sexuality and Reproductive Freedom* (New York: Longman, 1984), 344–5.

sibly in regard to others.'[20] If foetuses were sentient beings from
conception, then perhaps this loss of liberty and physical integrity
would be one that women could reasonably be asked to bear, at least
if they have become pregnant through their own voluntary activities.
But first-trimester and (in all probability) early second-trimester foetuses are not yet sentient; and they are not yet members of the
human community in the ways that infants usually are. This makes
it difficult to argue that their moral status is strong enough to justify
overriding women's most basic rights.

### 9.4. *The Indirect Significance of Viability*

Viability is the capacity of a foetus to survive—perhaps with medical assistance—should it be born immediately. In its 1973 *Roe* v.
*Wade* decision, which legalized abortion in the United States, the
Supreme Court established foetal viability—then estimated to occur
between twenty-four and twenty-eight weeks—as the point after
which states may prohibit abortions that are not deemed necessary
to protect the life or health of the woman. More recent decisions
have permitted state legislatures to assume that viability may occur
as early as twenty weeks.[21] However, the basic *Roe* doctrine, that the
right to abortion may not be denied prior to viability, has been consistently upheld. This doctrine represents a compromise between the
most conservative and the most liberal views, and one that many
abortion rights supporters consider reasonably satisfactory.[22]

As previously mentioned, the great majority of abortions in the
industrialized world are done in the first trimester; very few occur
after the twentieth week of pregnancy, and still fewer after the
twenty-fourth week.[23] Second-trimester abortions are often the re-

[20] *Abortion and Woman's Choice*, 379.

[21] Notably the 1989 case of *Webster* v. *Reproductive Health Services*.

[22] Other aspects of US abortion law are less compatible with universal access to
abortion; e.g. states are permitted to refuse to pay for abortions for women on
Medicaid, to require parental notification and consent for abortions for minors, to
mandate a waiting period before an abortion, and to require physicians to provide
women with 'information' that is intended to dissuade them from choosing abortion.

[23] Abortions after 20 weeks are reported to be 1 per cent of the total in the
United States, and those after 24 weeks, 0.01 per cent. See Henshaw, Binkin, Blaine
and Smith, 'A Portrait of American Women Who Obtain Abortions', *Family
Planning Perspectives*, 17 (1985), 91, cited by Hunter in 'Time Limits on Abortion',
130.

sult of difficulty in obtaining an earlier abortion, e.g. in the case of many teenage women, and many women who live in rural areas and find it difficult to travel to the towns or cities in which abortion services are available. In some cases, second-trimester abortions are done because diagnostic tests have revealed serious abnormalities in the foetus; the introduction of tests that can safely be done earlier in pregnancy may eventually make this reason for second-trimester abortion uncommon.

Third-trimester abortions are rarely done unless the foetus is found to have conditions incompatible with survival, such as anencephaly.[24] This would almost certainly continue to be true even if late abortion carried no risk of legal liability. Even second-trimester abortions are considerably more physically traumatic, and often more emotionally difficult for the woman and her family, as well as for nurses and physicians. For this reason, few women would willingly delay an abortion until the third trimester, and few physicians would perform a third-trimester abortion in the absence of disastrous foetal abnormalities. When standard contemporary medical technology is available, and the foetus is viable, there is rarely a medical need for third-trimester abortion; should a medical emergency occur that requires that the pregnancy be ended, there are usually options—such as Caesarean section or induced labour—that will allow the infant a chance of survival.

Late abortion differs morally from early abortion in several respects. First, the late-gestation foetus looks more like an infant, which makes it natural for us to want to accord it a more similar moral status. Jane English argues that this similarity in appearance is morally important, because a functional morality requires a certain 'coherence of attitudes'. She says:

Our psychological constitution makes it the case that for our ethical theory to work, it must prohibit certain treatment of non-persons which are significantly personlike. If our moral rules allowed people to treat some personlike non-persons in ways we do not want people treated, this would undermine the system of sympathies and attitudes that makes the ethical system work . . . A fetus one week before birth is so much like a newborn

---

[24] Nan Hunter reports that staff from the Centers for Disease Control investigated all reports of post-24-week abortions in Georgia from 1979 and 1980 and found only three confirmed cases, of which two involved anencephalic foetuses; these three cases constituted 0.004 per cent of abortions performed ('Time Limits on Abortion', 149).

baby in our psychological space that we cannot allow any cavalier treatment of the former while expecting full sympathy and nurturative support for the latter.[25]

The similarity between infants and viable foetuses is more than a matter of appearance. The period of development during which viability becomes increasingly probable is also the period during which the foetus is increasingly likely to have a capacity for sentience. A viable foetus may no longer be merely a living thing that has the potential to become sentient; it may already be an incipiently sentient being. Its possible sentience brings the Anti-Cruelty principle into play, establishing a claim to protection from the needless infliction of pain or death. Should it be medically necessary to abort a foetus that may be sentient, the Anti-Cruelty principle requires that no procedure be used that is likely to subject it to serious pain, if medical alternatives exist, and if these alternatives will not be more dangerous to the woman's life, health, or future fertility. But the moral status of the late-gestation foetus does not derive entirely from the Anti-Cruelty principle. It gains additional moral status through the Transitivity of Respect principle, because of the feelings it naturally evokes, and because it is likely soon to be a member of the human social community. Moreover, because it is a possibly-sentient *human* being, it arguably gains a claim to the rights accorded by the Human Rights principle. (I will say more about this in the next section.) It is largely for these reasons that today, when with adequate medical care the abortion of a viable foetus is rarely necessary to protect maternal life and health, there are relatively few such abortions.

There is, however, a potentially serious problem in the use of viability as the cut-off point for abortion, absent medical necessity. The concept of viability contains an important ambiguity. On one interpretation, a viable foetus is one that has reached the stage of late gestation and that, if born, would have some chance of surviving *without highly intensive medical care*. On another interpretation, 'viability' refers to the possibility of survival outside the womb *with the best medical care currently in existence*. At present, the distinction between these interpretations is largely academic, since infants

[25] Jane English, 'Abortion and the Concept of a Person', in Feinberg (ed.), *The Problem of Abortion*, 158.

born under twenty-two weeks gestational age almost never survive, and there is no immediate prospect for survival at earlier ages. However, if viability were interpreted in the second way, then the invention of an 'artificial womb' capable of sustaining foetuses born at earlier gestational ages would imply a contraction of the period during which abortion is permissible. Moreover, on that interpretation of viability, the invention of a device that could support the normal development of a human conceptus from fertilization to 'birth' would mean that abortion is never permissible. Thus, if viability is used to define the point after which medically unnecessary abortion is to be discouraged or forbidden, then it is important that it be defined as a stage of foetal development, i.e. that which is often reached by the start of the third trimester, rather than in relationship to the current state of medical technology. For it is only in the developmental sense that viability has evident moral significance.[26]

## 9.5. *The Moral Significance of Birth*

If foetuses begin to be sentient at some point during late gestation, then this is the point at which they begin to come under the protection of the Human Rights principle. However, there is wisdom in the Common Law doctrine, which treats as legal persons with an equal right to life only those human beings that are born alive. Foetuses cannot be given all of the same legal rights and protections as infants without undermining women's most fundamental legal and moral rights. The unique physiological relationship between a pregnant woman and the foetus she carries makes her its primary guardian and defender. It is she who must watch her diet, consider taking vitamin supplements, exercise appropriately, try to avoid exposure to alcohol and other teratogenic substances, and finally labour to give birth. Because the pregnancy occurs within her body, anything that another person does for or to the foetus must be done for or to her.

Thus, while a possibly-sentient foetus may have moral rights under the Human Rights principle, caution must be used in em-

---

[26] This is a point made by Nancy K. Rhoden, in 'Trimesters and Technology: Revamping *Roe v. Wade*', in Arras and Rhoden (eds.), *Ethical Issues in Modern Medicine*, 303–10.

powering the state—or any other institution or individual—coercively to enforce those rights against the woman who carries it. Because of the foetus's location and its physiological dependence upon the woman's body, it is not always possible for both to be accorded full moral rights. In some cases, the Agent's Rights principle must override the rights to which a sentient foetus would otherwise be entitled. It is, for instance, socially counterproductive and morally unsound to impose civil or criminal penalties upon women who are suspected of harming their foetuses, e.g. by using alcohol or other potentially harmful drugs while pregnant, or failing to follow other sound medical advice. Inadequate attention to one's health during pregnancy is not directly analogous to the violent physical abuse of a child, as some bioethicists have contended.[27] Subjecting women's personal health care habits to punitive legal scrutiny severely undermines their rights to privacy and autonomy. Thus, even if some net utilitarian benefit could be achieved through such a policy, it would still be ruled out by the Agent's Rights principle. However, such a punitive policy is unlikely to produce any net benefit. Treating pregnant women who have drug or alcohol problems as criminals is unlikely to help them or their children, and it deters many from seeking needed medical care during pregnancy. In the United States (at least), it also has an unjust differential impact upon women of disadvantaged racial and ethnic groups. Poor women of colour constitute the majority of those who are criminally prosecuted for foetal abuse, or subjected to the loss of custody of the child, because traces of illegal drugs are found in their bodies or in the newborn—even though the use of illegal drugs is probably no more prevalent among these women than among wealthy or middle-class white women.[28]

The legal right of mentally competent persons to refuse unwanted medical interventions has sometimes been set aside in the

---

[27] See John Robertson, 'The Right to Procreate and In Utero Fetal Therapy', in Arras and Rhoden (eds.), *Ethical Issues in Modern Medicine*, 321–8.

[28] A Florida study found that, while drug traces were found as often in the urine of white and black babies, only black mothers were referred to the prosecutors's office or child welfare authorities. Ira J. Chasoff, 'The Prevalence of Illicit Drug Use during Pregnancy and Discrepancies in Reporting in Pinellas County, Florida', *New England Journal of Medicine*, 344 (1990), 1202, cited by John Robertson, *Children of Choice: Freedom and the New Reproductive Technologies* (Princeton, NJ: Princeton University Press, 1994), 184.

case of pregnant women. In the United States, the 1980s saw a number of court-ordered Caesarean sections performed upon mentally competent women who did not want to undergo this surgical intervention. Some bioethicists argue that such involuntary surgeries can be justified by the probable medical benefits to the infant, and sometimes to the woman herself. Some hold that pregnant women who plan to give birth should be legally required to undergo *in utero* surgery, or other invasive medical treatments, should their physicians judge that these treatments would be beneficial to their foetuses.[29] Ironically, it is now widely agreed that many of the Caesarean births performed in the United States provide little or no medical benefit to either mother or infant. Moreover, the coercive invasion of one person's body for the medical benefit of another has never been legally sanctioned in a case in which the second individual has already been born. A person cannot legally be compelled to donate an organ to another person, even if the latter will die without it. In the 1978 case of *McFall* v. *Shimp*, a Pennsylvania court ruled that a man who was suffering from aplastic anaemia, and whose best hope of recovery was a bone marrow transplant, could not compel his cousin to provide the bone marrow, even though the cousin was the only person thought to have sufficiently compatible tissue. The court held that to require such an invasion of one person's body for the medical benefit of another person 'would change every concept and principle upon which our society is founded'.[30] The right to bodily integrity is a presupposition of all other basic rights. In the court's words, 'For a society . . . to sink its teeth into the jugular vein . . . of one of its members and suck from it sustenance for *another* member, is revolting to our hard-wrought concepts of jurisprudence . . . [and] would raise the specter of the swastika and the Inquisition.'[31]

Birth is morally important, in part because it results in the physical separateness of the infant and the mother. Birth ends the unique biological unity that makes the coercive enforcement of equal rights for foetuses perilous to women's rights to life and liberty. Birth is also important because an infant soon becomes part of the human

[29] Robertson, 'The Right to Procreate and In Utero Fetal Therapy'.

[30] *McFall* v. *Shimp*, No. 78-17711 (CP Allegheny City, Penn., 26 July 1978), cited by Lawrence J. Nelson and Nancy Milliken, 'Compelled Medical Treatment of Pregnant Women: Life, Liberty, and the Law in Court', in Mappes and Zembaty (eds.), *Biomedical Ethics*, 476.

[31] *McFall* v. *Shimp*, cited in Steinbock, *Life Before Birth*, 152–3.

social world, in ways that are not possible while it is still in the womb. Social relationships amongst human beings provide a basis for the extension of full moral status, not just to human moral agents, but to other sentient human beings as well. In Loren Lomasky's words,

birth constitutes a quantum leap forward in the process of establishing social bonds . . . Consider a typical infant just a few hours after its birth. Although this is little time in which to enter into contact with other members of one's world, it has already become part of a surprisingly large number of social relationships. It has been handled, fed, and medically cared for by several people . . . It has been given a name . . . Grandparents, aunts, uncles, siblings and cousins have been notified of their new status, social service agencies stand ready to provide assistance, and an income tax exemption has been established.[32]

On any theory that permits only intrinsic properties to serve as criteria of moral status, the infant's fundamental rights cannot legitimately be influenced either by its entry into the human social world, or by the physical separateness that it gains through being born. It either has the morally important intrinsic property or properties, or it does not; no relational property can alter its moral status. But on the multi-criterial account, these relational properties play a legitimate role in determining what rights an infant may reasonably be accorded. Birth enables the infant to be cared for as a known and socially responsive individual. It also ends the infant's complete and necessary dependence upon the woman's body, thus removing the potential conflict between her moral rights and the infant's rights under the Human Rights principle, and bringing the latter principle fully into play for the first time. For these reasons, birth is still the most appropriate point at which to begin fully to enforce the moral rights that the Human Rights principle accords to sentient human beings.

Some philosophers argue than an infant cannot have a strong right to life until it is capable, not only of sentience, but of more sophisticated mental states or activities. Michael Tooley argues that a being cannot have a strong right to life unless it can have an interest in its own survival. He maintains that a being cannot have such an

---

[32] Loren E. Lomasky, 'Being a Person—Does It Matter?', in Feinberg (ed.), *The Problem of Abortion*, 172.

interest unless it possesses 'at some time, the concept of a continuing self, or subject of experiences and other mental states'.[33] Without such a concept, he says, a being cannot desire the continuation of its own existence as a subject of conscious experiences, and thus cannot have an interest in its own survival. Since it is unlikely that a newborn has a concept of itself as a subject of conscious experiences, Tooley concludes that the newborn cannot have a strong right to life.

Tooley is making an important point. Because a newborn infant is not sufficiently self-aware consciously to wish for continued life, its death is probably not so great a loss, to it, as the death of an older human being usually is. This observation might lead us to question the common assumption that there are no circumstances in which early infanticide can be justified. However, it is a mistake to suppose that a newborn's lack of self-awareness implies that it cannot reasonably be accorded a strong right to life. I argued in Chapter 3 that, although sentient beings that are not self-aware probably cannot value their lives as much as self-aware beings can, the lives of non-self-aware beings may nevertheless have value for them, since they may experience their existence as (on the whole) pleasurable. If this argument is sound, then newborn infants may already have an interest in continued life, even though they are probably unable consciously to wish for their own survival.

The more important point, however, is that on the multi-criterial account, the moral status of infants does not depend entirely upon their mental capacities. It is also relevant that most infants are members of human social communities—or capable of soon becoming so, with no violation of anyone else's basic rights. So long as there are people who are willing and able to care for children who are orphaned or abandoned, there is no compelling reason not to accord newborns the same right to life as older human beings have. The newborn's lack of well-established social relationships provides a plausible moral rationale for the toleration of early infanticide only when the circumstances are genuinely desperate: for instance, when food is scarce, contraception and abortion are unavailable, and attempting to rear all of the infants that are born would endanger the lives of older children.

---

[33] Michael Tooley, 'In Defense of Abortion and Infanticide', in Feinberg (ed.), *The Problem of Abortion*, 132.

## 9.6.  *Reproductive Freedom and the Fate of the Earth*

After decades during which it has been unfashionable to call attention to the continuing expansion of the global human population, there is now a growing recognition of the need to stabilize our numbers at a level that can be sustained without destroying the Earth's remaining natural ecosystems, or totally precluding the restoration of important ecosystems that have already been damaged. The coercive population control policies that a few nations have pursued have been widely condemned as violations of human rights. While there may be no universal human right to have as many children as desired, only the most dire emergency—worse than any so far— could possibly justify a state policy of controlling population through involuntary sterilization, contraception, or abortion. These are severe infringements of the right to bodily integrity. Furthermore, the loss of the right to reproduce is an extremely serious one for many people. Although John Robertson tends to overstate the point by making the right to reproduce very nearly absolute, he explains the importance of this right very well:

being deprived of the ability to reproduce prevents one from an experience that is [often] central to individual identity and meaning in life. Although the desire to reproduce is in part socially constructed, at the most basic level transmission of one's genes through reproduction is an animal or species urge closely linked to the sex drive. In connecting us with nature and future generations, reproduction gives solace in the face of death . . . Its denial— through infertility or governmental restriction—is [sometimes] experienced as a great loss, even if one has already had children.[34]

If we do not wish to compel future generations to implement coercive birth control policies, we have no option but to support voluntary birth control. Stabilizing human populations at sustainable levels usually does not require state coercion. In most of the industrialized world, birth rates have already been greatly reduced (in some cases, to below the replacement level), often without any deliberate state pressure in that direction—and sometimes despite strong state pressure in the other direction. State pressure to maintain high birth rates has sometimes taken the form of anti-abortion

---

[34] Robertson, *Children of Choice*, 24.

legislation, as in Romania prior to the fall of the Ceausescu government. Yet even where abortion is prohibited, economic development is usually accompanied by lower birth rates. Unless the benefits are confined to those at the top, economic development usually encourages lower birth rates, by reducing infant mortality and enabling parents to feel secure with fewer children. It also tends to provide women with improved opportunities for education and economic advancement—especially if they are able to postpone parenthood and limit the number of children that they have. People in the poorest countries often lack these incentives to have fewer children. But even in the poorest countries, the availability of contraception and abortion contributes significantly to the reduction of birth rates. The nations that are currently most endangered by rapid population growth—e.g. many in Africa and South America—are those in which contraceptives are expensive and difficult for many people to obtain, and abortion is illegal and unsafe.

As Paul and Anne Ehrlich like to point out, all causes are lost causes without voluntary population control.[35] As human populations expand, pressures on ecosystems increase. Larger populations mean more grazing by domesticated animals, more cultivation of previously uncultivated land, more damming of rivers for power and irrigation, more cutting of timber and scrub for firewood and building materials, and more contamination of air, land, and water by industrial, agricultural, and human waste products. Nor is this entirely a new phenomenon. All of the continents of the Earth, except Antarctica and perhaps Australia, contain remnants of civilizations that vanished after exhausting the fertility of the land. Today, however, we are in danger of destroying not only local resources but global ones—such as the ozone layer that protects terrestrial life from excessive ultraviolet radiation, and the relatively stable global climate that makes it possible to grow enough food to sustain a human population as large as that which now exists.

The largest single factor in a people's ability to limit its population to sustainable levels is the freedom of women: not only the freedom to have children when they wish to, but the freedom to obtain an education, to make an adequate living, and to take part in the cultural and political life of the society. If heterosexual intercourse

---

[35] Ehrlich and Ehrlich, *The Population Explosion*, 23.

were a minor part of human life, if it were easy for any woman or girl to avoid, and if avoiding it did not often entail adverse personal consequences, then reproductive freedom might not so desperately require universal access to contraception and abortion. If contraceptives were entirely safe and effective, and available to all, then abortion would be less frequently needed—although medically dangerous pregnancies and those caused by incest and rape would prevent the need from being eliminated entirely. As it is, access to both contraception and abortion remains essential to reproductive freedom; and reproductive freedom is essential to voluntary human population limitation, and hence to the fate of the Earth. In Mary Gordon's words,

We must be realistic about the impact on society of millions of unwanted children in an overpopulated world. Most of the time, human beings do not have sex because they want to make babies . . . Thinking about abortion . . . forces us to take moral positions as adults who understand the complexities of the world and the realities of human suffering, and to make decisions based on how people actually live and choose.[36]


## 9.7. *Conclusions*

Because women are both moral agents and sentient human beings, while first-trimester and probably second-trimester foetuses are neither, the Agent's Rights principle supports women's right to terminate dangerous or unwanted pregnancies at any stage prior to the third trimester. Moreover, although the foetus gains in moral status as it becomes increasingly likely to be capable of sentience, until it has been born it cannot be accorded a fully equal moral and legal status without endangering women's basic rights to life and liberty.

Nevertheless, viable and possibly-sentient foetuses are very close to the point where they will have equal moral status, and most people regard them as already having a strong moral status. Even second-trimester foetuses can look enough like infants to make the thought of abortion troubling. For this reason, and for the sake of women's physical health, it is highly desirable that early abortion be

[36] Mary Gordon, *Good Boys and Dead Girls, and Other Essays* (New York: Penguin Books, 1991), 147.

readily available to all women. If safe early abortion is available to all women, including those who are legal minors, then a case can be made for a social policy that seeks to avoid late second-trimester or third-trimester abortion, except in cases of medical need or severe foetal abnormality. Unfortunately, early abortion is not readily available to all women, even where abortion is legal; and in much of the world abortion is still illegal or beyond the economic reach of many women. Moreover, even in the case of late abortion, the final decision is best left in the hands of the woman and her medical advisers, since it is they who are best able to judge the severity of the medical need, or the likelihood that an abnormal foetus will have a reasonable chance to live a good life if it is brought to term.

# 10

## *Animal Rights and Human Limitations*

The moral problems raised by human uses of animals are usually thought not to be as important—or as conceptually difficult—as those raised by abortion. But in some ways the issues about animals are more difficult. Unlike human foetuses, many non-human animals are highly sentient, and many are subjects-of-a-life. Many appeal to human sympathies through their beauty, intelligence, and expressive behaviours. Some are members of our mixed social communities. Some belong to species that are extinct in most of their original habitats and threatened with extinction in the few that remain. Theories that recognize only the intrinsic properties of an entity as valid criteria of its moral status do not permit these social and ecological considerations to influence what we owe to animals of diverse species; only the mental or behavioural capacities of individual animals can be relevant. On the multi-criterial account, the capacities of individual animals are relevant, but so are their social and ecological relationships.

### 10.1. *Are All Animals Equal?*

The primary obstacle to according equal moral status to all sentient animals is the fact that, to the best of our knowledge, most non-human terrestrial animals are not moral agents. True, many are highly social, and many possess social instincts and abilities that tend to limit intraspecific aggression to forms that are usually not lethal. As Konrad Lorenz observed, carnivorous animals of the same species do not, as a rule, continually kill one another in disputes over food, sex, or territory, even though they may be physically capable of doing so. Often, potentially lethal assaults against conspecifics are inhibited by instinctive behaviours, such as ritualized gestures of submission or appeasement.[1] Intelligent and highly social animals—e.g. many birds and mammals—can enjoy relationships of mutual trust, affection, and loyalty. But this is not conclusive evidence of moral agency in the full sense. To be a moral agent is to be able to supplement or contravene the promptings of instinct, guiding one's behaviour by reasoning from moral concepts and principles. This ability requires a language, spoken or otherwise, that is adequate to the expression of moral concepts; and it is reasonable to believe that most animals do not have such languages. Thus, while animals of many species may be subjects-of-a-life—capable of emotion, memory, reason, and intentional action—most are probably not moral agents.

If this is true, then most animals do not have equal moral status on the basis of the Agent's Rights principle. The primary justification for this distinction is that inescapable practical realities make it impossible always to treat non-human animals as moral equals. We cannot always accord animals moral rights that are equal in strength and content to our own, because we cannot hope that they in turn will respect our rights, making possible the peaceful resolution of any conflicts that arise between their needs and important human or ecological needs.

To say this is not to say that non-human animals have no moral status. The Respect for Life principle requires that moral agents recognize an obligation to all living things, never to harm them without morally defensible reasons. Sentient beings gain additional moral status through the Anti-Cruelty principle, which requires that we take care not to inflict suffering or death upon sentient beings, unless there is no other feasible and morally legitimate way to further important human or ecological needs.

The Anti-Cruelty principle has two important corollaries. The more highly sentient a being is, the more future pleasure it is likely to lose if killed, and the more pain it may suffer if injured. Thus, one corollary is that the more highly sentient a being is, the more care moral agents should take to avoid needlessly killing or injuring it. Similarly, the more capable an animal is of the mental activities that make a being a subject-of-a-life, the more future-oriented desires it

---

[1] Konrad Lorenz, *On Aggression*, trans. Marjorie Kerr Wilson (New York: Harcourt, Brace, & World, 1963).

is apt to have, and therefore the more it is likely to lose if deprived of life, health, or freedom. Thus, another corollary is that moral agents should take special care to avoid needlessly visiting such harms upon animals that are probably subjects-of-a-life. Yet neither the fact that a being is highly sentient, nor that it is probably a subject-of-a-life, is sufficient to oblige moral agents always to accord it full moral status, since neither is sufficient to establish the conditions for moral reciprocity.

Some animals have, besides the moral status afforded by the Respect for Life and Anti-Cruelty principles, additional status derived from the Interspecific, Ecological, or Transitivity of Respect principles. On the Interspecific principle, we have stronger moral obligations towards animals that are members of our mixed social communities than towards equally sentient animals that do not have social relationships with human beings. On the Ecological principle, we are required to accept special obligations towards animals of species that are endangered by human activities, and important to the integrity of the ecosystems of which they are part. And on the Transitivity of Respect principle, we are obliged to respect—to the extent that is feasible and consistent with other sound moral principles—the special moral status that some people accord to certain animals, for personal, ecological, religious, or other reasons.

The great apes—chimpanzees, gorillas, and orang-utans—are one group of animals that qualify for strong moral status on all of these grounds. They are highly sentient and exceptionally intelligent subjects-of-a-life; they often form close social relationships with human beings; human intervention has rendered their species extinct or endangered in virtually all of their original habitats; and they have a special appeal to many human beings, because of their clear and close consanguinity. Rhinoceroses, on the other hand, are probably less intelligent, and certainly less sociable, but even more in danger of human-caused extinction. The need to preserve the remaining rhinoceros species of Africa, Asia, and Indonesia, and to maintain populations that are genetically viable, justifies the expenditure of considerable effort to protect each individual.

## 10.2.  *Do Animals Have Moral Rights?*

All sentient animals are entitled to protection against cruelty, and some are entitled to a level of protection that may amount in practice to something close to full moral status. But it does not immediately follow that all sentient animals, or all those that are subjects-of-a-life, have moral rights. The term 'rights' has so many uses in moral and legal discourse that semantic analysis cannot definitively answer the question of whether animals that have moral status also have moral rights, or which moral rights they have. Nevertheless, as I argued in Chapter 4, it is a central feature of the concept of a moral right that to have moral rights is not just to have interests that are worthy of moral consideration; it is to have interests that moral agents are obliged to respect even at substantial cost to themselves or to their social or biological communities. Moral rights can justly be overridden in some circumstances; but neither the goal of producing a net increase in happiness, nor that of protecting the health of the ecosystem, is sufficient to justify serious violations of basic moral rights.

What does this feature of the concept of a moral right imply about the moral rights of animals? On the one hand, it shows that those who believe that we ought to accept stronger moral obligations towards animals have substantive reasons for claiming that animals have moral rights. Speaking of rights brings to the fore the idea that our obligations respecting the treatment of animals are often obligations to the animals themselves, not merely to human beings who might indirectly be harmed by the inhumane treatment of animals. Moreover, to speak of moral rights is to imply that the principles in question are not just moral ideals—appropriate standards for saints, but optional for those who do not aspire to sainthood. If animals have moral rights, then moral agents are entitled to call one another to account for transgressing against those rights; and if moral suasion and informal social pressures fail, then they are entitled to seek to enact laws and regulations protecting animals from further violations of their rights.

On the other hand, this feature of the concept of a moral right shows that it is awkward to speak of the moral rights of animals, since most of the rights that we can reasonably accord to animals are contingent upon circumstances in ways that the rights of moral agents (and sentient human beings that are not moral agents) are not. The strength of a moral agent's right to life is not a function of the rarity of its biological species, or of the impact of that species upon the integrity, stability, and beauty of the biological community; but the strength of an animal's right to life is sometimes dependent upon such ecological considerations. A moral agent's basic rights may not justly be overridden simply because there are important human interests that cannot be as well served in any other way; but an animal's moral rights may sometimes appropriately be overridden for that reason.

The contingency of animal 'rights' upon social and ecological circumstances may be the strongest argument against the use of the term in this context. If animals were able to participate in the shaping and enforcement of moral rights, they would probably not agree to making their rights contingent upon important human and ecological needs. But most animals are not moral agents—or, if they are, then we have not yet discovered how to communicate with them well enough to make mutual respect for rights possible. Human beings are vulnerable organisms with physical needs. Consequently, we must sometimes place our own good above the good of other animals—such as the mice, rats, and cockroaches that seek to inhabit our homes, or the ticks, spiders, and mosquitoes that would like to dine on us. This suggests that, while some animals have strong moral status, not all sentient animals have moral rights, in the usual sense of the term.

And yet, as Mary Midgley points out, it will not do simply to deny that animals have moral rights, and let it go at that. For there is a strong tendency in ordinary speech to express virtually all moral claims upon us in terms of moral rights. This tendency is so pervasive that the denial that animals have rights is likely to be taken to mean that nothing that human beings do to animals is of any direct moral significance. As Midgley points out,

to say that 'animals do not have rights' does not sound like a remark about the meaning of the word *rights* but one about animals—namely, the remark that one need not really consider them. Subsequently saying that they have some other vague thing instead will not get rid of this effect.[2]

We face, then, a choice between saying either (1) that all sentient

---

[2] Mary Midgley, *Animals and Why They Matter*, 63.

animals—or, alternatively, all that are subjects-of-a-life—have moral rights, but these rights are usually weaker than those of moral agents and sentient human beings that are not moral agents; or, (2) that non-human animals that are not moral agents do not have moral rights, although we have moral obligations towards them. I doubt that a great deal depends upon which of these two philosophically defensible options we elect. Perhaps the best compromise is to accord strong moral status—including some moral rights—to those non-human animals that display exceptional sensitivity and intelligence, or whose species are endangered due to human activities, while declining to ascribe moral rights to all sentient animals, or all animals that may be subjects-of-a-life.

This compromise permits us to employ a sliding scale of moral status, recognizing stronger moral obligations towards flying foxes and baboons than towards scorpions and tadpoles, and still stronger obligations towards fellow moral agents—human or otherwise—and sentient human beings that are not moral agents. The more highly sentient an animal is, and the more likely it is to be a subject-of-a-life, the stronger the reasons that are needed to justify harming it. But only in the case of such highly sensitive and mentally sophisticated animals as cetaceans, apes, and elephants, is it plausible to hold that it is virtually never morally permissible to treat them in ways that would violate their moral rights if they were human beings.

## 10.3. *Should All Humans Be Vegetarians?*

Tom Regan's deontological Animal Rights view implies that the moral rights which the Human Rights principle accords to sentient human beings should also be accorded to non-human subjects-of-a-life. On this view, the moral right to life that these animals possess is no weaker than that of human beings. Consequently, no moral agent can be justified in eating a creature that was a subject-of-a-life—unless, perhaps, it died of natural causes, or was killed by a natural predator that was not acting on behalf of moral agents.

In contrast, Peter Singer's equal consideration principle implies that killing animals for meat may sometimes be morally justified, for instance when there are no adequate alternative food sources, and the animals are not made to suffer needlessly. However, Singer argues, persons who have access to other types of food have a moral obligation not to eat meat, or other products that are produced in ways that cause suffering to sentient animals. For, he says, the pleasure that some people gain from eating meat does not outweigh the pain and suffering that are inflicted upon animals in order to supply that pleasure. This argument does not depend upon the ascription of moral rights to animals, but upon the premiss that the total amount of happiness—that of humans and non-humans combined—will be increased if most humans stop eating meat.

Singer's view of the morality of meat eating is more respectful of human needs than is Regan's; however, it is still somewhat too strong. It is not clear that all human beings are obliged not to eat animal products except when other food sources are unavailable or inadequate to sustain life. There may be human beings who have such important nutritional, cultural, or religious interests in eating meat, or in hunting or rearing animals for food, that to compel them to refrain would be to violate their moral rights.

One way to see that a universal ban upon the use of meat and other animal products cannot easily be reconciled with human moral rights is to consider peoples whose long-established modes of subsistence involve hunting or rearing animals for meat and other consumptive uses, and who cannot now find satisfactory substitutes without surrendering valued cultural traditions. For instance, the Inuits and other indigenous peoples of the Arctic claim the right to continue limited hunting of whales of species that are otherwise protected against human predation. Hunting these animals not only brings needed food and revenue, but also links them to the practices and beliefs of their ancestors. Despite the exceptional intelligence and sensitivity of all cetaceans, it is not obvious that indigenous peoples are morally obliged to give up hunting them entirely, unless it is clear that only a total ban on hunting will afford the affected species a chance to survive and recover. As indigenous people frequently point out, it is not their traditional hunting practices that have initially put these species at risk of extinction.

A second example is provided by the Masai of East Africa, many of whom retain a mode of subsistence based primarily upon the herding of cattle. Milk, meat, and blood from their own animals form the core of the traditional Masai diet, and many Masai believe—perhaps with good reason—that the grain-based diets of their agricultural neighbours are disastrous to Masai health and vigour. A third example is rural Australia, where the economy is still based in large part upon rearing sheep and cattle. In many parts of both Africa and Australia, excessive grazing by domestic herbivores is eroding soil, eradicating native plants in much of their former range, and displacing native animals. Nevertheless, it would be unreasonable to insist upon the immediate cessation of all grazing of domestic animals, since there are at present no adequate alternative modes of subsistence for much of the human population. A better strategy is to pursue research and education aimed at reducing the ecological harms done by domestic animals, and to develop economic alternatives that will permit grazing to be phased out in the more fragile areas.

These examples show that a vegetarian diet is not a standard that can now be imposed upon all human beings without violating the moral rights of some people. But it might still be argued that people who have access to vegetable foods, and whose cultures and economies are not fundamentally based upon hunting or animal husbandry, have a moral obligation to adopt a vegetarian diet. The Anti-Cruelty principle prohibits the infliction of pain or death upon sentient beings, unless there are important and morally permissible goals that cannot be furthered in other ways; and it may be argued that, so long as other foods are available, there are no important human needs or interests that can be served only by eating meat.

There are also some moral arguments for vegetarianism that are not based upon the wrongness of killing animals or making them suffer. Singer argues that we owe it to undernourished human beings to stop eating meat, thereby permitting more plant crops to be grown exclusively for human consumption. One problem with this argument is that there is no reason to believe that if affluent people stopped eating meat, more grain and other vegetable foods would become available to poor people. If farmers were suddenly unable to sell grain for the production of livestock, then, other things being equal, the price of grain would be apt to fall. However, it would be unlikely to remain at a level that would make grain affordable to the poorest nations and individuals. Instead, the governments of grain-exporting nations would be likely to implement price support measures, such as subsidizing farmers who plant fewer acres, or funding the development of new processes for the conversion of grain into fuel for automobiles, and other inedible products. If grain prices remained low, farmers would have no choice but to grow less grain, until prices returned to levels that made it sufficiently profitable.

For this reason, there is no guarantee that the more people give up eating meat, the more nutritional benefits will accrue to the roughly twenty per cent of the world's human population who are inadequately nourished. Nevertheless, converting to vegetarianism may contribute to that goal, especially if it helps to inspire more people to become vegetarians in the future.[3]

It may also be argued, on the basis of the Ecological principle, that we owe it to the non-human world to become vegetarians. If very few people ate meat, it would be possible to reduce the damage done to uncultivated land by the grazing of domesticated herbivores; and it might also be possible to reduce the amount of land kept under cultivation, making more room for habitats that support a diversity of indigenous plants and animals.

These are important reasons for non-vegetarians who can find alternative food sources to *reduce* their consumption of meat. But these arguments do not add up to a proof that most human beings are morally obliged to be strict vegetarians. Not all animal products are produced in ways that are inhumane or destructive of the ecosystem. If animals have reasonably good lives and are not killed inhumanely, then it is not clear that the Anti-Cruelty principle has been violated. (I will say more about this in the next section.) If cattle are grazed on land that is unsuitable for cultivation, or fed agricultural by-products that human beings cannot eat (e.g. silage made from corn stalks), then raising cattle need not result in any net reduction in the human food supply. Not all grazing by domestic animals does serious damage to the land; this is largely a function of the aridity of some land, and the number of animals grazed. In some areas, grazing by cattle can even be beneficial to the ecosystem, keeping non-native grasses short enough to allow native herbs to grow.[4]

Moreover, it is not as clear as many vegetarians believe that all human beings can be just as healthy on a strictly vegetarian diet as

---

[3] For a good response to this argument, see Michael W. Martin, 'A Critique of Moral Vegetarianism', *Reason Papers*, No. 3 (Fall 1976), 33–6.

[4] For example, the California Native Plant Society has concluded that the grazing of cattle in the Point Reyes National Seashore is essential to the survival of a number of rare plants found there, which would otherwise be crowded out by the imported annual grasses that have largely replaced the native perennial grasses.

on one that includes some meat, fish, eggs, or dairy products. If some human beings need animal products in order to enjoy good health, then to prohibit these products may violate rights to which they are entitled under the Agent's Rights and Human Rights principles. The absence of normal health can greatly reduce the value of the nominal rights to life and liberty. Kathryn Paxton George has collected a great deal of epidemiological evidence that some groups of people are more nutritionally at risk on strictly vegetarian (or vegan) diets than others. She concludes:

Although most men between the ages of twenty and fifty in industrialized countries can choose to be vegetarians without significant risk, the same cannot be said for other people identifiable by characteristics over which they have no control: infants, children, adolescents, gestating and lactating women, some elderly people, and many people living in cultural and environmental circumstances that are not dependent on industrialized agriculture and high-tech society. That nutritional needs differ with stages of life and between the sexes is well documented in the medical and nutritional literature; vegan diets present greater risk than lacto-ovovegetarian diets, but even these latter diets pose risks for some groups.[5]

George argues that, because some people have a greater need for a diet that includes animal products, proclaiming vegetarianism as a universal moral obligation discriminates unfairly against these people. Even if their nutritional needs are regarded as a valid *excuse* for eating meat, an unfair burden is placed upon them; they are, in effect, stigmatized as physiologically incapable of doing the morally right thing. This sets up 'the conditions of unwarranted guilt and lowered self-esteem'.[6] It may also have an unjustly discriminatory impact upon women, children, and the elderly, since children, elderly persons, and women who are pregnant or lactating are among the groups that appear to be most vulnerable to the nutritional deficiencies associated with a strictly vegetarian diet.

These points are well taken. If not all people can be optimally nourished on a vegetarian diet, then it is unreasonable to treat vegetarianism as a moral requirement. A more reasonable approach, and one that is probably more likely to succeed, is to advocate considerably less meat in the diet than is standard in many industrial-

---

[5] Kathryn Paxton George, 'Should Feminists Be Vegetarians?', *Signs: Journal of Women in Culture and Society*, 19, No. 1 (Winter 1994).
[6] Ibid. 425.

ized nations. A low-meat diet, if generally adopted, would yield most of the environmental and societal benefits of strict vegetarianism, without the associated health risks for some groups of people. A diet lower in animal fat and protein would, in fact, be highly beneficial to the health of many Westerners, whose diets often include more of these than is nutritionally optimal. The excessive consumption of fatty meat and dairy products is thought to play a major role in causing obesity, strokes, coronary artery disease, adult-onset diabetes, colon cancer, and other human illnesses.

### 10.4. *Obligations to Captive and Domestic Animals*

To keep animals in captivity is to undertake responsibility for their welfare. Even if they are destined for the dinner table, the infliction of needless pain or suffering is a violation of the Anti-Cruelty principle. Some painful or uncomfortable processes are essential for the animals' own well-being; e.g. vaccinating them against contagious illnesses, or dipping them in disinfectant to prevent parasitic infections. Other painful processes benefit only human interests; e.g. castrating cattle to improve their taste and docility, or docking the ears and tails of dogs to match the standard of the breed. The Anti-Cruelty principle requires that only human interests that are objectively important, and unable to be served in other ways, be used to justify the infliction of serious pain upon highly sentient beings.

The Anti-Cruelty principle also requires that we pay attention to kept animals' overall quality of life. Those who keep animals are morally obliged to do what they reasonably can to provide them with conditions that permit them to live reasonably well, enjoying the pleasures that are natural for members of their species. Confining kept animals is often necessary, both for their own welfare and because leaving them unconfined may be dangerous, illegal, or impractical. However, they should at the very least be free to move around, stretch, and exercise. If their social nature demands it, they should have some form of companionship. If their minds and senses demand stimulation, they should not be kept in small and featureless quarters that cause them to go mad from boredom. Since important human interests can usually be served without subjecting kept animals to conditions that make them miserable, sick, or deranged, the Anti-Cruelty principle demands that this minimum standard be met in virtually all cases.

The Interspecific principle requires us to accept stronger moral obligations to animal members of mixed communities, especially those that have trusting and affectionate relationships with human beings. As Kant recognizes, these animals are not to be killed or abandoned whenever they cease to be useful. What Kant mistakenly denies is that we owe it *to them* not to lightly betray their affection, trust, and loyalty. To be sure, we also owe it to other human beings not to needlessly harm animals that they care about; but even if we do not share their feelings, the Transitivity of Respect principle requires us to respect the creatures with whom they have social relationships.

Some people argue that we have no moral obligation to provide animals that are bred for human uses with conditions that permit them to live well, since if humans had not bred these animals then they would never have existed. Even a short and boring life is arguably better than no life at all. Thus, it is argued, so long as these animals do not suffer so much that it would have been better for them never to have existed, we have not violated any moral obligations towards them. The flaw in this argument is that knowingly to cause unnecessary suffering is cruel, regardless of how the victim came into existence. If the infliction of unnecessary suffering could be justified by the fact that the victim's existence was the result of some prior act by the perpetrator, then parents could not wrong their children by abusing them, so long as the children did not suffer so much that it would have been better for them never to have been born. The creation of a new being, far from entailing an exemption from the Anti-Cruelty principle, frequently obliges the creator to protect the new being, and try to ensure that it has a chance to live a good life. The Anti-Cruelty principle protects not only domestic animals, but also genetically engineered animals, and any sentient robots, androids, or computers that human beings may some day manufacture.

Killing domestic, feral, or wild animals in order to meet important human or ecological needs is not a violation of the Anti-Cruelty principle, provided that it is done humanely. But keeping animals in excessively cramped or crowded conditions, without room to move about and exercise, can depress their overall quality of life far below what we could readily afford to provide. Some animals, such as the great whales, may always be deeply discontent in confinement. If so, this is a strong argument against keeping them in zoos or amusement parks, where their captivity serves few human needs that could not be served in other ways. (There is, however, a case to be made for keeping a few whales in temporary captivity, so that people who cannot view them in their natural habitats can have the opportunity to see them, and perhaps be inspired to work for the protection of all whales.) Other animals, such as guppies and gold-fish, seem to be reasonably content in captivity, because it is fairly easy to provide them with quarters that are spacious enough for them to pursue most of the activities that they naturally enjoy. Experience and careful observation are needed to learn what members of a particular species need, in order to live well in captivity or domestication.

But what about cases in which captive or domestic animals cannot be kept in conditions that enable them to lead good lives? What if research that may lead to a cure for a devastating human illness requires that sensitive and highly social animals be kept in isolation, infected with a miserably painful disease, and eventually killed? What if the only way to protect an avian species such as the California condor from extinction is to capture the last free individuals, thereby consigning them to a life that they are unlikely to enjoy? When highly sentient animals are made to suffer for human or ecological ends, those ends need to be scrutinized, and alternative means sought. But there are cases in which these needs override the obligations that we would normally have to individual animals. Even if the condors are unhappy in cages, this is a smaller tragedy than the extinction of their entire species, and thus morally defensible. Of course, not all extinctions are equally tragic. Few will mourn the demise of the last smallpox germ; and extinctions that are not caused by human intervention are arguably not tragic either, since they are an inevitable part of the process of evolution. But the California condor is an especially splendid animal, the largest soaring bird in North America and the top scavenger in pre-European California; its permanent loss would diminish the beauty and integrity of the land community.

If suffering is inflicted on animals because of important human or ecological needs that cannot otherwise be met, and if everything feasible is done to minimize that suffering, then the Anti-Cruelty principle has not been violated. In this important respect, the moral status accorded to animals by that principle is weaker than that which the Agent's Rights and Human Rights principles accord to moral agents, and to human moral patients, respectively. It is, however, strong enough to preclude many practices that are now widespread, such as rearing highly sentient animals under conditions of excessive crowding and confinement.

## 10.5. *The Moral Obligations of Hunters*

Another practice that is difficult to reconcile with the Anti-Cruelty principle is that of hunting and killing highly sentient animals for sport. Hunting is sometimes justified, for instance when it is an essential part of an ecologically sustainable mode of subsistence. It is also justified when it is the only way to control introduced animals that are harmful to indigenous plant or animal species, or indigenous animals that have been deprived of their natural predators. But hunting that serves neither human subsistence nor ecological integrity is more difficult to justify.

Yet the human interests served by non-subsistence hunting are not always trivial. Some hunters say that the experience is important to their spiritual and psychological well-being. For many, hunting is the primary way in which they have learned to enjoy the wilderness, and to feel part of it. For others, it represents an element of their culture that they think it important to retain, even if their subsistence does not depend upon it. Hunting or fishing, like collecting mushrooms or mussels, is for many a relaxing way to obtain food that is much enjoyed.

These personal reasons for non-subsistence hunting show that the human interests involved may be somewhat more substantial than mere amusement. These interests cannot excuse practices that cause needless suffering, such as using leg-hold traps, or leaving wounded animals to wander off and die slowly. Nor do such human interests justify forms of hunting and fishing that are destructive of indigenous species or their habitats. Yet the values that some people find in hunting may be great enough to justify some ecologically sustainable forms of non-subsistence hunting.

Sport hunting clearly falls short of the moral ideal of never harming any sentient being without the compulsion of necessity.

Unlike the right to choose abortion, the right to engage in sport hunting is not essential to the life and liberty of a large proportion of human moral agents. Consequently, since some people ascribe to animals a moral status that precludes hunting, the Transitivity of Respect Principle militates against such sport. Yet, because many people find in hunting a way to fill important needs, and because most animals are not reasonably considered the moral equals of sentient human beings, it is not clear that opponents of sport hunting are always entitled to use legal coercion to prevent it; ecologically responsible regulation is frequently a more reasonable goal. If sport hunting is done in ways that are not cruel, that do not damage species or ecosystems, and that do not endanger human beings or animal members of mixed communities, then it need not fall below the minimum moral standard.

### 10.6. *The Myth of Human Superiority*

To argue that human beings have a stronger moral status than most terrestrial animals is not to presuppose that members of the human species have an inherent value that is superior to that of other animals. Our ascriptions of moral status need not be based upon the assumption that the natural world contains hierarchies of inherent value, existing apart from the reasonable judgements of any moral agent; and it is better that they not be. It is our own needs, as vulnerable organisms, that require us to distinguish between what we owe to one another and what we owe to most other animals—not the value that the universe places upon us.

   The belief that human beings are inherently superior to all other terrestrial life forms is dramatically expressed in the medieval Christian image of the Great Chain of Being. In this metaphysical model, God is the most perfect being, and has the greatest inherent worth. Below him, the 'hierarchical order continues down through various levels of angels and archangels, then to humans, followed by animals and plants (which are themselves arranged hierarchically), and ends with mere matter at the bottom'.[7] God and the angels are spiritual beings, and immortal; animals and plants are material, and mortal; and humans occupy an intermediate position, possessing

---

[7] Taylor, *Respect for Nature*, 139.

mortal bodies but immortal souls. As the highest order of being in the natural world, humans are the natural masters of all other earthly life, responsible to God for wise stewardship of the land and animals, but owing nothing to any non-human part of the natural world.

The residue of this medieval model survives today in the common assumption that human moral rights are rooted in the superiority of our kind to all other animal species. Yet once we understand the pragmatic arguments for human moral rights, and the way in which these are grounded in our natural capacity for empathy, we no longer need to appeal to the myth that humans are superior to all other living things in order to make sense of our special moral obligations to sentient human beings.

Of course, human beings are superior to other terrestrial animals in some domains. As sophisticated language users, we can create complex conceptual models, teach them to one another, and improve on them through the generations. Our nimble hands and brains enable us to invent increasingly powerful technologies. But our refined powers of speech, reason, and invention—invaluable as they are for us—do not prove that we are stronger or more beautiful than tigers, or that our unaided powers of vision and flight are greater than those of eagles. We are *collectively* more powerful—and more destructive—than other terrestrial animals; but however much we may value that power, it does not make us more valuable to the universe. Visiting aliens might be no more impressed by humans than by armadillos or army ants; each species has unique adaptations and abilities. Realizing this, we may learn to think of our fellow earthlings, 'not [as] underlings . . . [but as] *other nations*, caught with ourselves in the net of life and time, fellow prisoners of the splendour and travail of the earth'.[8]

## 10.7. *Conclusions*

The moral status of non-human animals depends in part upon their sentience and mental sophistication. But it is impossible to determine

---

[8] Henry Beston, *The Outermost House* (New York: Ballantine, 1929), 20; cited by Val Plumwood, in *Feminism and the Mastery of Nature*, 164.

what we owe to animals that are not moral agents, without examining the relationships between our species and theirs, and between their species and the ecosystems of which it is part. Together, the Interspecific principle and the Transitivity of Respect principle imply that we have special moral obligations towards animal members of our social communities. Needlessly harming these animals violates unspoken 'contracts' between our kind and theirs, and often causes grief to human beings who care about them.

Killing any highly sentient animal is best avoided, other things being equal. But the more we come to understand the workings of biological communities, the more we come to see that the preservation of healthy and biologically diverse ecosystems is a necessity that must sometimes override concern for the lives of individual animals. Yet in other cases, the preservation of ecologically important species requires that individual animals be given a great deal of care and attention.

Theories of moral status that are based only upon intrinsic properties imply that we must condemn as irrational all such differences between the treatment of animals that belong to different species, but that appear to be comparable in their mental and behavioural capacities. On the multi-criterial account, such differences often make good moral sense. There remains an uncomfortable tension between the Anti-Cruelty principle, which bids us hesitate before harming any sentient being, and the Ecological principle, which permits us to recognize overriding obligations to members of endangered plant and animal species, to the species themselves, and to the earth's ecosystems. But tensions of this sort are common in moral and legal systems. The tension between what we owe to individual persons and other living things, and what we owe to our social and biological communities, is a ubiquitous part of our moral reality; to seek to resolve it by eliminating one of these principles in favour of the other is a mistake.

# 11

## *Conclusion*

Adopting a multi-criterial theory of moral status does not make it easy to solve all of the moral problems that arise from uncertainties about what we owe to other entities. However, it gives us a more adequate set of tools than any of the uni-criterial theories. On the multi-criterial account there are many types of moral status, and many of these come in varying degrees of strength. Moral agents, sentient human beings who are not moral agents, sentient non-human animals, non-sentient living things, and such other elements of the natural world as species and ecosystems—all have legitimate claims to moral consideration. Of all the entities with which we interact, only moral agents have full moral status based solely upon their mental and behavioural capacities. The rest have moral status that is partially determined by their social and other relationships (if any) to moral agents, and—in the case of entities that are not sentient human beings—by their roles within terrestrial ecosystems.

Accepting a plurality of fundamental principles of moral status precludes the generation of solutions to difficult moral problems through the mechanical application of a simple formula to the empirical data. But this is an unrealistic objective. The problems that Schweitzer encounters in claiming equal moral status for all living things, that Singer encounters in claiming equal status for all sentient beings, that Regan encounters in claiming equal status for all subjects-of-a-life, and that Kant encounters in claiming status only for moral agents, jointly demonstrate the futility of the search for a single intrinsic property, or set of intrinsic properties, to serve as the sole criterion of moral status. At the same time, the problems that Callicott encounters in seeking to base moral status entirely upon membership in social and biological communities, and those that Noddings encounters in seeking to base it solely upon the relationship of caring, jointly demonstrate that we cannot ignore intrinsic properties in favour of relational ones. The multi-criterial account permits us to take account of a wider range of both intrinsic and relational properties. One desirable result of this ethical eclecticism is that we will often find moral theory moving closer to moral common sense.

The web of common-sense judgements about moral status includes strong strands of widely shared beliefs, many of which can be supported by good reasons. I have tried to express some of these elements of moral common sense in the seven principles. There are weak strands in our common moral reasoning too, which will not stand up to critical scrutiny. Some of these can be repaired by more careful delineation of the stronger strands, as I have tried to do in the cases discussed here. Others require further critical and creative work. But I hope to have shown the possibility of a substantial degree of clarification of the primary principles of moral status that are relevant to current and future disputes. This should be of some value in moral discussion and education, and in moving towards a more widely shared and better supported consensus about many contentious moral issues.

# Bibliography

Anderson, Ian, 'Alien Predators Devastate Australian Wildlife', *New Scientist* (12 Sept. 1992), 9.
—— 'Rabbit Virus to be Let Loose?', *New Scientist* (25 Sept. 1993), 5.
Aquinas, Thomas, *Summa Theologica* (New York: Benzinger Brothers, 1947).
Aristotle, *Generation of Animals*, trans. A. L. Peck (Cambridge, Mass.: Harvard University Press, 1948).
—— *Politics* (London: Heinemann, 1932).
Arras, John, 'Toward an Ethic of Ambiguity', in John Arras and Nancy Rhoden (eds.), *Ethical Issues in Modern Medicine* (Mountain View, Calif.: Mayfield, 1989), 231–40.
Augustine, *Of the Work of Monks* (Grand Rapids, Mich.: Eerdmans, 1956).
Baier, Annette, *Moral Prejudices: Essays on Ethics* (Cambridge, Mass.: Harvard University Press, 1994).
—— *Postures of the Mind: Essays on Mind and Morals* (Minneapolis, Minn.: University of Minnesota Press, 1985).
Barber, Theodore Xenophon, *The Human Nature of Birds* (New York: Penguin Books, 1993).
Benjamin, Martin, 'Ethics and Animal Consciousness', in Thomas A. Mappes and Jane S. Zembaty (eds.), *Social Ethics: Morality and Social Policy* (New York: McGraw-Hill, 1987), 476–83.
Bentham, Jeremy, *An Introduction to the Principles of Morals and Legislation*, ed. J. H. Burns and H. L. A. Hart (London: University of London Press, 1970).
Beston, Henry, *The Outermost House* (New York: Ballantine, 1929).
Bigelow, Jim, and Pargetter, Robert, 'Morality, Potential Persons and Abortion', *American Philosophical Quarterly*, 25, No. 4 (Dec. 1987), 815–30.
Birch, Charles, and Cobb, John B., Jr., *The Liberation of Life* (Denton, Tex.: Environmental Ethics Books, 1990).
Birch, Thomas H., 'Moral Considerability and Universal Consideration', *Environmental Ethics*, 15, No. 4 ((Winter 1993), 313–32.
Blum, Deborah, *The Monkey Wars* (New York: Oxford University Press, 1994).
Brandt, R. B., 'The Morality and Rationality of Suicide', in Thomas A. Mappes and Jane S. Zembaty (eds.), *Biomedical Ethics* (New York: McGraw-Hill, 1991), 319–25.
Brody, Baruch, *Abortion and the Sanctity of Human Life* (Cambridge, Mass.: MIT Press, 1975).

Brown, Lester R., and Kane, Hal, *Full House: Reassessing the Earth's Population Carrying Capacity* (New York: Norton, 1994).

Burgess, J. A., and Tawia, S. A., 'When Did You First Begin to Feel It?— Locating the Beginnings of Human Consciousness', *Bioethics*, 10, No. 2 (Jan. 1996), 1–26.

Burton, Keith, 'A Chronicle: Dax's Case As It Happened', in John D. Arras and Bonnie Steinbock (eds.), *Ethical Issues in Modern Medicine* (Mountain View, Calif.: Mayfield, 1989), 195–9.

Callicott, J. Baird, 'Animal Liberation: A Triangular Affair', *In Defense of the Land Ethic: Essays in Environmental Philosophy* (Albany, NY: State University of New York Press, 1989).

—— 'The Case Against Moral Pluralism', *Environmental Ethics*, 12, No. 2 (Summer 1990), 99–124.

—— *Earth's Insights: A Survey of Ecological Ethics from the Mediterranean Basin to the Australian Outback* (Berkeley and Los Angeles: University of California Press, 1994).

—— *In Defense of the Land Ethic: Essays in Environmental Philosophy* (Albany, NY: State University of New York Press, 1989).

—— 'On the Intrinsic Value of Nonhuman Species', in Bryan G. Norton (ed.), *The Preservation of Species* (Princeton, NJ: Princeton University Press, 1988), 138–72.

—— 'Traditional American Indian and Western European Attitudes Towards Nature: An Overview', *Environmental Ethics*, 4 (1982), 293–318.

Carnap, Rudolf, 'Psychology in Physical Language', in A. J. Ayer (ed.), *Logical Positivism* (New York: Free Press, 1969).

Carruthers, Peter, *The Animals Issue: Moral Theory in Practice* (Cambridge: Cambridge University Press, 1992).

Cavalieri, Paola, and Singer, Peter (eds.), *The Great Ape Project: Beyond Human Equality* (New York: St. Martin's Press, 1993).

Chasoff, Ira J., 'The Prevalence of Illicit Drug Use during Pregnancy and Discrepancies in Reporting in Pinellas County, Florida', *New England Journal of Medicine*, 344 (1990), 1202.

Cheney, Jim, 'Callicott's "Metaphysics of Morals"', *Environmental Ethics*, 13, No. 4 (Winter 1991), 311–26.

Churchland, Paul M., 'Folk Psychology and the Explanation of Human Behavior', in John D. Greenwood (ed.), *The Future of Folk Psychology* (Cambridge: Cambridge University Press, 1991), 51–69.

Culver, Charles M., and Gert, Bernard, 'The Definition and Criterion of Death', in Thomas A. Mappes and Jane S. Zembaty (eds.), *Biomedical Ethics* (New York: McGraw-Hill, 1991), 389–96.

Darwin, Charles, *The Formation of Vegetable Mould, Through the Action of Worms* (London: John Murray, 1881).

Descartes, René, 'Animals Are Machines', in Tom Regan and Peter Singer (eds.), *Animal Rights and Human Obligations* (Englewood Cliffs, NJ: Prentice-Hall, 1976), 60–6.

—— *Discourse on Method and the Meditations* (New York: Penguin Books, 1968).

Dixon, Bernard, *Power Unseen: How Microbes Rule the World* (New York: W. H. Freeman, 1994).

Dworkin, Ronald, *Taking Rights Seriously* (Cambridge, Mass.: Harvard University Press, 1978).

Ehrlich, Paul R., and Ehrlich, Anne, *The Population Explosion* (New York: Simon & Schuster, 1990).

Eisler, Riane Tennehaus, *The Chalice and the Blade: Our History, Our Future* (San Francisco, Calif.: Harper & Row, 1987).

English, Jane, 'Abortion and the Concept of a Person', in Joel Feinberg (ed.), *The Problem of Abortion* (Belmont, Calif.: Wadsworth, 1984), 151–60.

Feinberg, Joel (ed.), *The Problem of Abortion* (Belmont, Calif.: Wadsworth, 1984).

Fenigsen, Richard, 'A Case Against Dutch Euthanasia', in Tom L. Beauchamp and LeRoy Walters (eds.), *Contemporary Issues in Bioethics* (Belmont, Calif.: Wadsworth, 1994), 500–6.

Ford, Norman M., *When Did I Begin? Conception of the Human Individual in History, Philosophy and Science* (Cambridge: Cambridge University Press, 1988).

Frey, R. G., *Interests and Rights: The Case Against Animals* (Oxford: Oxford University Press, 1980).

Gaard, Greta, 'Living Interconnections with Animals and Nature', in Greta Gaard (ed.), *Ecofeminism: Women, Animals, Nature* (Philadelphia, Pa.: Temple University Press, 1993), 1–12.

George, Kathryn Paxton, 'Should Feminists be Vegetarians?', *Signs: Journal of Women in Culture and Society*, 19, No. 2 (Winter 1994), 405–34.

Gewirth, Alan, *Reason and Morality* (Chicago, Ill.: University of Chicago Press, 1978).

Gilligan, Carol, *In a Different Voice* (Cambridge, Mass.: Harvard University Press, 1982).

Goodall, Jane, *In the Shadow of Man* (Boston, Mass.: Houghton Mifflin, 1971).

Gordon, Mary, *Good Boys and Dead Girls, and Other Essays* (New York: Penguin Books, 1991).

Grant, Michael, 'The Trembling Giant', *Discover* (Oct. 1993), 84–8.

Greenwood, John D., 'Reasons to Believe', in John D. Greenwood (ed.), *The Future of Folk Psychology* (Cambridge: Cambridge University Press, 1991), 70–92.

Grey, William, 'On Anthropomorphism and Deep Ecology', *Australasian Journal of Philosophy*, 71, No. 4 (Dec. 1993), 463–75.

Gribbon, John, 'Is the Universe Alive?', *New Scientist* (15 Jan. 1994), 38–40.
—— and Cherfas, Jeremy, *The Monkey Puzzle* (Buffalo, NY: Prometheus Books, 1982).
Griffin, Donald R., *Animal Thinking* (Cambridge, Mass.: Harvard University Press, 1984).
Gruen, Lori, 'Dismantling Oppression: An Analysis of the Connection Between Women and Animals', in Greta Gaard (ed.), *Ecofeminism: Women, Animals, Nature* (Philadelphia, Pa.: Temple University Press, 1993), 60–90.
Haezrahi, Pepita, 'The Concept of Man as an End-in-Himself', in Robert Paul Wolff (ed.), *Kant: A Collection of Essays* (Garden City, NY: Doubleday, 1967), 291–313.
Harrison, Beverly Wildung, *Our Right to Choose: Toward a New Ethic of Abortion* (Boston, Mass.: Beacon Press, 1983).
Hart, H. L. A., 'Death and Utility', *New York Review of Books*, 27, No. 8 (15 Nov. 1980).
Hartmann, Betsy, *Reproductive Rights and Wrongs: The Global Politics of Population Control and Contraceptive Choice* (New York: Harper & Row, 1987).
Harvard Medical School, Ad Hoc Committee to Examine the Definition of Brain Death, 'A Definition of Irreversible Coma', *Journal of the American Medical Association*, 205, No. 6 (6 Aug. 1968), 337–40.
Hegel, Georg Wilhelm Friedrich, *Philosophy of the Right* (Oxford: Oxford University Press, 1966).
Hill, Thomas E., Jr., 'Kantian Pluralism', *Ethics*, 10, No. 4 (July 1992), 743–62.
Hume, David, *An Enquiry Concerning the Principles of Morals*, in *Enquiries Concerning Human Understanding and Concerning the Principles of Morals*, ed. L. A. Selby-Bigge (Oxford: Oxford University Press, 1975).
—— *A Treatise of Human Nature*, ed. L. A. Selby-Bigge (Oxford: Oxford University Press, 1967).
—— *Essays, Moral, Political and Literary* (London: Longman, Green & Co., 1987).
Hunter, Nan D., 'Time Limits on Abortion', in Sherrill Cohen and Nadine Taub (eds.), *Reproductive Laws for the 1990s* (Clifton, NJ: Humana Press, 1989), 129–54.
*Hypatia: Special Issue on Ecological Feminism*, 6, No. 1 (Summer 1991).
Jaggar, Allison, *Feminist Politics and Human Nature* (Totowa, NJ: Rowman & Allanheld, 1983).
Jaini, Padmanab S., *The Jaina Path of Purification* (Berkeley, Calif.: University of California Press, 1979).
Jamieson, Dale, 'Killing Persons and Other Beings', in Harlan B. Miller and

William H. Williams (eds.), *Ethics and Animals* (Clifton, NJ: Humana Press, 1983), 135–46.

Jennings, H. S., *Behavior of Lower Organisms* (New York: Columbia University Press, 1906).

Jonas, Hans, 'Against the Stream: Comments on the Definition and Redefinition of Death', *Philosophical Essays—From Ancient Creed to Technological Man* (Englewood Cliffs, NJ: Prentice-Hall, 1974), 132–40.

—— *The Phenomenon of Life* (Chicago, Ill.: University of Chicago Press, 1966).

Kagan, Janet, *Hellspark* (New York: Tom Doherty, 1988).

Kahane, Howard, *Logic and Contemporary Rhetoric: The Use of Reason in Everyday Life* (Belmont, Calif.: Wadsworth, 1992).

Kamm, Frances, *Creation and Abortion: A Study in Moral and Legal Philosophy* (New York: Oxford University Press, 1992).

Kant, Immanuel, *Critique of Practical Reason*, trans. Lewis White Beck (Indianapolis, Ind.: Bobbs-Merrill, 1956).

—— *Dreams of a Spirit-Seer, Illustrated by Dreams of Metaphysics*, trans. Emanuel F. Goerwitz (London: Swan Sonnenschein, 1990).

—— *Lectures on Ethics*, trans. Louis Infield (New York: Harper & Row, 1963).

—— *Metaphysics of Morals*, trans. Mary Gregor (Cambridge: Cambridge University Press, 1991).

—— *The Moral Law: Kant's Groundwork of the Metaphysics of Morals*, trans. H. J. Paton (London: Hutchinson, 1948).

—— *Observations on the Feeling of the Beautiful and the Sublime*, trans. John T. Goldwaite (Berkeley and Los Angeles: University of California Press, 1960).

Kellert, Stephen R., 'The Biological Basis for Human Values of Nature', in Stephen R. Kellert and Edward O. Wilson (eds.), *The Biophilia Hypothesis* (Washington, DC: Island Press, 1993).

—— and Wilson, Edward O. (eds.), *The Biophilia Hypothesis* (Washington, DC: Island Press, 1993).

Kohlberg, Lawrence, 'Stages in Moral Development as a Basis for Moral Education', in C. M. Beck, B. S. Crittenden, and E. V. Sullivan (eds.), *Moral Education: Interdisciplinary Approaches* (Toronto, Ont.: Toronto University Press, 1971).

Kortlandt, Adriaan, 'Spirits Dressed in Furs?', in Paolo Cavalieri and Peter Singer (eds.), *The Great Ape Project: Equality Beyond Humanity* (New York: St. Martin's Press, 1993), 137–45.

Kuhse, Helga, *The Sanctity of Life Doctrine in Medicine: A Critique* (Oxford: Oxford University Press, 1987).

—— and Singer, Peter, *Should the Baby Live? The Problem of Handicapped Infants* (Oxford: Oxford University Press, 1981).

Leakey, Richard, and Lewin, Roger, *Origins Reconsidered: In Search of What Makes Us Human* (New York: Anchor Books, 1992).

Lee, Tannith, *The Silver Metal Lover* (New York: Doubleday, 1991).

Lem, Stanislaw, *His Master's Voice*, trans. Michael Kandel (New York: Harcourt Brace Jovanovich, 1968).

Leopold, Aldo, *A Sand County Almanac* (New York: Ballantine Books, 1970).

Locke, John, *An Essay Concerning Human Understanding*, ed. A. D. Woozley (Cleveland, Ohio: World, 1964).

Lomasky, Loren E., 'Being a Person—Does It Matter?', in Joel Feinberg (ed.), *The Problem of Abortion* (Belmont, Calif.: Wadsworth, 1984), 161–72.

Lorenz, Konrad, *On Aggression*, trans. Marjorie Kerr Wilson (New York: Harcourt, Brace, & World, 1962).

Lovelock, James, *The Ages of Gaia: A Biography of Our Living Earth* (New York: Bantam Books, 1990).

Luker, Kristen, *Abortion and the Politics of Motherhood* (Berkeley and Los Angeles: University of California Press, 1984).

Lynch, Joseph J., 'Is Animal Pain Conscious?', *Between the Species*, 10, Nos. 2 and 3 (Winter–Spring 1994), 1–9.

McCaffrey, Anne, *Decision at Doona* (New York: Ballantine, 1969).

McCloskey, H. J., 'Moral Rights and Animals', *Inquiry*, 22 (1979), 23–54.

—— 'Rights', *Philosophical Quarterly*, 16 (1965), 115–27.

—— 'The Right to Life', *Mind*, 84 (1975), 403–25.

MacIver, A. M., 'Ethics and the Beetle', *Analysis*, 8, No. 5 (Apr. 1948).

Macklin, Ruth, 'Consent, Coercion, and Conflicts of Rights', in Thomas A. Mappes and Jane S. Zembaty (eds.), *Biomedical Ethics* (New York: McGraw-Hill, 1991), 330–6.

Manning, Rita, *Speaking From the Heart: A Feminist Perspective on Ethics* (Lanham, Md.: Roman & Littlefield, 1992).

Maple, T. L., *Orang-Utan Behavior* (New York: Van Nostrand Reinhold, 1980).

Marcus, Ruth Barcan, 'Moral Dilemmas and Consistency', *Journal of Philosophy*, 77, No. 3 (Mar. 1980), 121–36.

Marquis, Don, 'Why Abortion is Immoral', *Journal of Philosophy*, 76, No. 4 (Apr. 1989), 183–202.

Martin, Michael W., 'A Critique of Moral Vegetarianism', *Reason Papers*, No. 3 (Fall 1976), 13–43.

—— 'Rethinking Reverence for Life', *Between the Species*, 9, No. 4 (Fall 1993).

Martin, P. S., 'The Discovery of America', *Science*, 179 (1973), 968–74.

Mayr, Ernst, *Toward a New Philosophy of Biology: Observations of an Evolutionist* (Cambridge, Mass.: Harvard University Press, 1988).

Midgley, Mary, *Animals and Why They Matter* (Athens, Ga.: University of Georgia Press, 1983).

—— 'Are You an Animal?', in Gill Langley (ed.), *Animal Experimentation: The Consensus Changes* (New York: Chapman & Hall, 1989), 1–18.

—— 'Duties Concerning Islands', in Peter Singer (ed.), *Ethics* (Oxford: Oxford University Press, 1994), 375–90.

Miles, H. Lyn White, 'Language and the Orang-Utan: The Old "Person" of the Forest', in Paolo Cavalieri and Peter Singer (eds.), *The Great Ape Project* (New York: St. Martin's Press, 1993), 42–57.

Mill, John Stuart, *Utilitarianism: With Critical Essays*, ed. Samuel Gorovitz (Indianapolis, Ind.: Bobbs-Merrill, 1971).

Mohr, James C., *Abortion in America: The Origins and Evolution of National Policy* (New York: Oxford University Press, 1978).

Nagel, Thomas, *The Possibility of Altruism* (Oxford: Oxford University Press), 1970.

—— 'What Is It Like to Be A Bat?', *Philosophical Review*, 83, No. 4 (Oct. 1974), 435–50.

Narveson, Jan, *Moral Matters* (Peterborough, Ont.: Broadview Press, 1993).

—— *Morality and Utility* (Baltimore, Md.: Johns Hopkins Press, 1967).

Nelson, Lawrence J., and Milliken, Nancy, 'Compelled Medical Treatment of Pregnant Women: Life, Liberty, and the Law in Court', in Thomas A. Mappes and Jane S. Zembaty (eds.), *Biomedical Ethics* (New York: McGraw-Hill, 1987), 742-8.

Nelson, Leonard, *System of Ethics*, trans. Norbert Guterman (New Haven, Conn.: Yale University Press, 1956).

Newland, Kathleen, *The Sisterhood of Man* (New York: Norton, 1984).

Nickel, James, *Making Sense of Human Rights: Philosophical Reflections on the Universal Declaration of Human Rights* (Berkeley and Los Angeles: University of California Press, 1987).

Nietzsche, Friedrich, *Beyond Good and Evil* (Chicago, Ill.: Henry Regnery, 1935).

Noddings, Nel, *Caring: A Feminine Approach to Ethics and Moral Education* (Berkeley and Los Angeles: University of California Press, 1984).

Noonan, John, 'An Almost Absolute Value in Human History', in Joel Feinberg (ed.), *The Problem of Abortion* (Belmont, Calif.: Wadsworth, 1984), 9–14.

Olson, Robert, 'Freedom, Selfhood, and Moral Responsibility', in A. K. Bierman and James A. Gould (eds.), *Philosophy for a New Generation* (New York: Macmillan, 1977), 534–48.

Patterson, Francine, and Gordon, Wendy, 'The Case for the Personhood of Gorillas', in Paolo Cavalieri and Peter Singer (eds.), *The Great Ape Project* (New York: St. Martin's Press, 1993), 58–79.

Petchesky, Rosalind Pollack, *Abortion and Woman's Choice: The State, Sexuality, and Reproductive Freedom* (New York: Longman, 1984).

Piers, Maria W., *Infanticide* (New York: Norton, 1978).

Piper, H. Beam, *Fuzzy Sapiens* (New York: Ace, 1983).

—— *Little Fuzzy* (New York: Ace, 1976).

Plumwood, Val, *Feminism and the Mastery of Nature* (London: Routledge, 1993).

President's Commission for the Study of Ethical Problems in Medicine and Biomedical and Behavioral Research, *Defining Death: Medical, Legal and Ethical Issues in the Determination of Death* (Washington, DC: US Government Printing Office, 1981).

Quammen, David, *The Song of the Dodo: Island Biogeography in an Age of Extinction* (New York: Scribner, 1996).

Rachels, James, 'Active and Passive Euthanasia', in Thomas A. Mappes and Jane S. Zembaty (eds.), *Biomedical Ethics* (New York: McGraw-Hill, 1991), 374–81.

—— *Created from Animals: The Moral Implications of Darwinism* (New York: Oxford University Press, 1991).

Radner, Denise and Michael, *Animal Consciousness* (Buffalo, NY: Prometheus Books, 1989).

Radhakrishnan, S., *Indian Philosophy*, vol. i (New York: Macmillan, 1929).

Rawls, John, *A Theory of Justice* (Cambridge, Mass.: Harvard University Press, 1971).

Reed, A. W., *Aboriginal Legends: Animal Tales* (French's Forest, NSW: Reed Books, 1978).

Regan, Tom, *All that Dwell Within: Essays on Animal Liberation and Environmental Ethics* (Berkeley and Los Angeles: University of California Press, 1982).

—— *The Case for Animal Rights* (Berkeley and Los Angeles: University of California Press, 1983).

Rhoden, Nancy, 'Cesareans and Samaritans', in Tom L. Beauchamp and LeRoy Walters (eds.), *Contemporary Issues in Bioethics* (Belmont, Calif.: Wadsworth, 1994), 337–42.

—— 'Treating Baby Doe: The Ethics of Uncertainty', in Tom L. Beauchamp and LeRoy Walters (eds.), *Contemporary Issues in Bioethics* (Belmont, Calif.: Wadsworth, 1994), 419–30.

—— 'Trimesters and Technology: Revamping *Roe v. Wade*', in John D. Arras and Nancy Rhoden (eds.), *Ethical Issues in Modern Medicine* (Mountain View, Calif.: Mayfield, 1989), 303–11.

Ritchie, D. G., 'Why Animals Do Not Have Rights', in Tom Regan and Peter Singer (eds.), *Animal Rights and Human Obligations* (Englewood Cliffs, NJ: Prentice-Hall, 1976), 181–4.

Robertson, John, *Children of Choice: Freedom and the New Reproductive Technologies* (Princeton, NJ: Princeton University Press, 1994).
—— 'Involuntary Euthanasia of Defective Newborns', in John D. Arras and Nancy Rhoden (eds.), *Ethical Issues in Modern Medicine* (Mountain View, Calif.: Mayfield, 1989), 220–30.
—— 'The Right to Procreate and In Utero Fetal Therapy', in John D. Arras and Nancy Rhoden (eds.), *Ethical Issues in Modern Medicine* (Mountain View, Calif.: Mayfield, 1989), 321–8.
Rodd, Rosemary, *Biology, Ethics, and Animals* (Oxford: Oxford University Press, 1990).
Rodman, John, 'Four Forms of Ecological Consciousness Reconsidered', in Donald Scherer and Thomas Attig (eds.), *Ethics and the Environment* (Englewood Cliffs, NJ: Prentice-Hall, 1983), 82–92.
—— 'The Liberation of Nature?', *Inquiry*, 20 (1979), 83–145.
Rollin, Bernard E., *Animal Rights and Human Morality* (Buffalo, NY: Prometheus Books, 1981).
Rolston, Holmes III, *Environmental Ethics: Duties to and Value in the Natural World* (Philadelphia, Pa.: Temple University Press, 1988).
—— 'Environmental Ethics: Values in and Duties to the Natural World', in Earl R. Winkler and Jerrold R. Coombs (eds.), *Applied Ethics: A Reader* (Oxford: Blackwell, 1993), 271–92.
Rorty, Richard, 'Mind–Body Identity, Privacy, and Categories', in John O'Connor (ed.), *Modern Materialism: Readings on Mind–Body Identity* (New York: Harcourt, Brace, 1969), 145–74.
Ruse, Michael, *The Philosophy of Biology* (London: Hutchinson, 1973).
Sandel, Michael J., *Liberalism and the Limits of Justice* (Cambridge: Cambridge University Press, 1982).
Sapontzis, S. F., 'A Critique of Personhood', *Ethics*, 91 (July 1981), 607–18.
—— *Morals, Reason, and Animals* (Philadelphia, Pa.: Temple University Press, 1987).
Schopenhauer, Arthur, *Studies in Pessimism: A Series of Essays* (St. Clair Shores, Mich.: Scholarly Press, 1970).
—— *The World as Will and Representation*, trans. E. F. J. Payne (New York: Dover, 1966).
Schweitzer, Albert, *Civilization and Ethics: The Philosophy of Civilization Part II* (London: A. & C. Black, 1929).
—— *Out of My Life and Time: An Autobiography* (New York: Holt, Rinehart & Winston, 1933).
—— *The Philosophy of Civilization* (Buffalo, NY: Prometheus Books, 1987).
—— *The Teaching of Reverence for Life*, trans. Richard and Clara Winston (New York: Holt, Rinehart & Winston, 1965).

Schweitzer, Albert, *The Words of Albert Schweitzer*, ed. Norman Cousins (New York: Newmarket Press, 1984).

Sherwin, Susan, *No Longer Patient* (Philadelphia, Pa.: Temple University Press, 1992).

Sidgwick, Henry, *The Methods of Ethics* (New York: Dover, 1966).

Singer, Beth J., *Operative Rights* (Albany, NY: State University of New York Press, 1993).

Singer, Peter, *Animal Liberation: A New Ethic for Our Treatment of Animals* (New York: Avon Books, 1975).

—— *Practical Ethics* (Cambridge: Cambridge University Press, 1979).

—— 'The Fable of the Fox and the Unliberated Animals', *Ethics*, 88, No. 2 (Jan. 1978), 119–26.

—— *The Expanding Circle: Ethics and Sociobiology* (New York: Farrar, Straus, 1981).

—— 'Not for Humans Only: The Place of Nonhumans in Environmental Ethics', in K. E. Goodpaster and K. M. Sayre (eds.), *Ethics and the Problems of the 21st Century* (Notre Dame, Ind.: University of Notre Dame Press, 1979), 191–206.

Skinner, B. F., *Beyond Freedom and Dignity* (New York: Bantam Books, 1971).

Steinbock, Bonnie, *Life Before Birth: The Moral and Legal Status of Embryos and Fetuses* (New York: Oxford University Press, 1992).

—— 'Speciesism and the Idea of Equality', *Philosophy*, 53 (1978), 247–56.

Stich, S. P., *From Folk Psychology to Cognitive Science: The Case Against Belief* (Cambridge, Mass.: MIT Press, 1983).

Stone, Christopher D., *Earth and Other Ethics: The Case for Moral Pluralism* (New York: Harper & Row, 1987).

Stone, Jim, 'Why Potentiality Matters', *Canadian Journal of Philosophy*, 17, No. 4 (Dec. 1987), 815–30.

Sumner, L. W., *Abortion and Moral Theory* (Princeton, NJ: Princeton University Press, 1981).

Sylvan, Richard, and Plumwood, Val, 'Human Chauvinism and Environmental Ethics', in D. Mannison, M. McRobbie, and R. Routley (eds.), *Environmental Philosophy* (Canberra, ACT: Department of Philosophy, Australian National University, 1980), 96–189.

Taylor, Paul, *Respect for Nature: A Theory of Environmental Ethics* (Princeton, NJ: Princeton University Press, 1986).

ten Have, Henk A. M. J., and Welie, Jos V. M., 'Euthanasia: Normal Medical Practice?', *Hastings Center Report*, 22, No. 2 (Mar.–Apr. 1992).

Thompson, Janna, 'A Refutation of Environmental Ethics', *Environmental Ethics*, 12, No. 2 (Summer 1990), 152–3.

Tooley, Michael, 'Abortion and Infanticide', *Philosophy and Public Affairs*, 2, No. 1 (Fall 1972), 37–56.

—— *Abortion and Infanticide* (Oxford: Oxford University Press, 1993).

—— 'In Defense of Abortion and Infanticide', in Joel Feinberg (ed.), *The Problem of Abortion* (Belmont, Calif.: Wadsworth, 1984), 120–34.

Veach, Robert, 'Whole Brain, Neocortical, and Higher Brain Related Concepts of Death', in John D. Arras and Bonnie Steinbock (eds.), *Ethical Issues in Modern Medicine* (Mountain View, Calif.: Mayfield, 1989) 148–56.

Warren, Mary Anne, *Gendercide: The Implications of Sex Selection* (Totowa, NJ: Rowman & Allanheld, 1995).

—— 'On the Moral and Legal Status of Abortion', *The Monist*, 57, No. 1 (Jan. 1973), 43–61.

—— *The Nature of Woman* (Inverness, Calif.: Edgepress, 1980).

Weir, Robert F., *Selective Nontreatment of Handicapped Newborns* (New York: Oxford University Press, 1984).

Wellman, Carl, 'Doing Justice to Rights', *Hypatia*, 3, No. 3 (Winter 1989), 153–60.

Wenz, Peter, *Environmental Justice* (Albany, NY: State University of New York Press, 1988).

Wilson, Edward O., 'Biophilia and the Conservation Ethic', in Stephen R. Kellert and Edward O. Wilson (eds.), *The Biophilia Hypothesis* (Washington, DC: Island Press, 1993).

—— *The Diversity of Life* (Cambridge, Mass.: Harvard University Press, 1992).

Wilson, Meredith, 'Rights, Interests, and Moral Equality', *Environmental Ethics*, 2, No. 2 (Summer 1980).

Wittgenstein, Ludwig, *Philosophical Investigations*, trans. G. E. M. Anscombe (New York: Macmillan, 1959).

Wolgast, Elizabeth, *The Grammar of Justice* (Ithaca, NY: Cornell University Press, 1987).

World Health Organization, Division of Family Health, *Health and the Status of Women* (Geneva: WHO, 1984).

—— *Reproductive Health: A Key to a Brighter Future* (Geneva: WHO, 1992).

Wright, Larry, *Teleological Explanations* (Berkeley and Los Angeles: University of California Press, 1976).

Ziff, Paul, 'The Simplicity of Other Minds', in Thomas O. Buford (ed.), *Essays on Other Minds* (Urbana, Ill.: University of Illinois Press, 1970).

Zimmer, Carl, 'Carriers of Extinction', *Discover*, 16, No. 7 (July 1995), 28–34.

# Index